Annual Editions: Dying, Death, and Bereavement, 15/e
George E. Dickinson and Michael R. Leming

http://create.mheducation.com

ISBN-10: 1259826848   ISBN-13: 9781259826849

Contents

Detailed Table of Contents

alternative funeral arrangements. The functions of funerals relative to the sociological, psychological, and theological needs of adults and children are also discussed.

Unit 6: Bereavement

The Grieving Process, Michael R. Leming and George E. Dickinson, *Understanding Dying, Death, and Bereavement*, Wadsworth-Cengage, 2016
This article discusses the seven basic coping strategies related to the bereavement process (shock and denial, disorganization, volatile emotions, guilt, loss and loneliness, relief, and reestablishment) and the four tasks of bereavement (accepting the reality of the loss, experiencing the pain of grief, adjusting to an environment in which the deceased is missing, and the withdrawing of emotional energy and reinvesting it in other relationships).

Disenfranchised Grief, Kenneth J. Doka, *Disenfranchised Grief: Recognizing Hidden Sorrow*, Lexington Books, 1989
Doka discusses the unique situation of bereaved survivors whose loss is not, or cannot be, openly acknowledged, publicly mourned, or socially supported.

Challenging the Paradigm: New Understanding of Grief, Kenneth J. Doka, Centre for Grief Education, 2007
Kenneth Doka discusses five significant ways in which earlier understandings of or paradigms of grief have been challenged. He also discusses three current challenges to the field of thanatology and two others that are likely to occur in the not-too-distant future.

Educators Tend to Overlook Student Grief, Experts Say, Evie Blad, *Education Week*, 2015
The article covers studies by the Coalition to Support Grieving Students, a group of education organizations, which suggest that many schools fail to provide sufficient support to grieving students. Information is provided on the coalition's website, grievingstudents.org, which offers resources such as professional development models, lesson plans, and suggestions on teacher collaboration.

Children at the Grave, Melissa Florer-Bixler, *Christian Century*, 2016
The article discusses the role of funerals in children's experience of death. Topics include the communal role of funerals in Christian life, the role of grief in the psychology of children, and the impacts of the death of family members on children. The author's experiences as a minister conducting funerals and attending a school career day are noted.

Programs Help Chaplains Handle Their Grief, Adelle M. Banks, *Christian Century*, 2014
The article reports the various programs launched in the U.S. as of March 2014 to help chaplains who comforted grieving military families in handling their grief. It cites as example the memorial ceremony held by the National Association of Evangelicals Chaplains Commission in January 2014 to allow chaplains a chance to grieve themselves. The opinion of Association of Professional Chaplains president Valerie Storms on the developments is also cited.

Memorial Hashtags and Selfies at Funerals: How We Mourn in the Digital Age, Laurie Penny, *New Statesman*, 2014
The article looks at social aspects of death, grief, and mourning as of 2014, focusing on the use of Internet and social media. The author expresses disagreement with those who have criticized the use of social media to express condolences or otherwise respond to a death, saying that it is death that is outrageous, not how anyone reacts to it, and that the most important thing is merely to be kind to those in mourning. The death of journalist and socialite Peaches Geldof is cited.

Parting Is Such Tweet Sorrow, Sabrina Bachai and Elijah Wolfson, *Newsweek*, 2014
The article focuses on the mourning carried out publicly through online resources, particularly social media, and the author's suggestion that it can be a positive part of the coping and healing process. Subjects discussed include the controversy such practice has aroused as of January 2014, use of social media profiles like Facebook pages as memorials, and analysis from psychiatry professor Tamara McClintock Greenberg.

Preface

Dying, death, and bereavement have been around for as long as humankind, yet as topics of discussion they have been "offstage" for decades in contemporary American public discourse. In the United States, dying currently takes place away from the arena of familiar surroundings of kin and friends, with approximately 80 percent of deaths occurring in institutional settings such as hospitals, free-standing hospices, and nursing homes. Americans have developed a paradoxical relationship with death: We know more about the causes and conditions surrounding death but have not equipped ourselves emotionally to cope with dying, death, and bereavement. The purpose of this anthology is to provide an understanding of dying, death, and bereavement that will assist in better coping with and understanding our own deaths and the deaths of others.

Articles in this volume are taken from professional/semiprofessional journals and from popular publications written for both special populations and a general readership. The selections are carefully reviewed for their currency and accuracy. Many of the articles have been changed from the previous edition through updating and responding to comments of reviewers. Most of the articles refer to situations in the United States, yet other cultures are represented. We strive to have current articles, though a few may be earlier, due to readers' requests to maintain them in this updated issue.

The reader will note the tremendous range of approaches and styles of the writers from personal, first-hand accounts to more scientific and philosophical writings. Some articles are more practical and applied, while others are more technical and research-oriented. If "variety is the very spice of life," this volume should be a spicy venture for the reader. Methodologies used in the more research-oriented articles range from quantitative (e.g., surveys/questionnaires) to qualitative (e.g., interviews/observation). Such a mix should especially be of interest to the student majoring or minoring in the social sciences. If a particular article seems too technical for your background, do not bog yourself down with the statistical analysis; rather look ahead to the discussion and conclusions.

These articles are drawn from many different periodicals, thus exposing the reader to a variety of publications in the library. With interest stimulated by a particular article, the student is encouraged to pursue other related articles in that particular journal. Learning outcomes, Internet references, and critical thinking questions are included with each article.

This anthology is organized into six units to cover many of the important aspects of dying, death, and bereavement. Though the units are arranged in a way that has some logical order, one can determine from the brief summaries in the table of contents whether another arrangement would best fit a particular teaching situation. Units cover issues in dying and death, life-cycle approach, and looks at the developmental aspects of dying and death at different age levels, the process of dying, and funerals and bereavement.

Annual Editions: Dying, Death and Bereavement, 15/e is intended for use as a supplement to augment selected areas or chapters of textbooks on dying and death. The articles in this volume can also serve as a basis for class discussion about various issues in dying, death, and bereavement.

Editors
George E. Dickinson

George E. Dickinson, Professor of Sociology at the College of Charleston (SC, USA), received his Ph.D. in sociology from LSU in Baton Rouge and his M.A. in sociology and B.A. in biology from Baylor University. He came to the College of Charleston in 1985, having previously taught in Pennsylvania, Minnesota, and Kentucky. Dickinson has been the author/co-author of over 90 articles in peer-reviewed journals, primarily on end-of-life issues and co-authored/co-edited 24 books/anthologies with Michael R. Leming, most recently *Understanding Dying, Death, and Bereavement*, Cengage Publishers, 2016. His research and teaching interest in end-of-life issues goes back to 1974 when he taught his first course in death and dying and in 1975 when he began end-of-life research. Over the years he has written about thanatology in medical, dental, nursing, child life, social work, pharmacy, and veterinary schools. He is on the editorial boards of *Mortality* (UK) and the *American Journal of Hospice & Palliative Medicine* (US). Twenty-first Century awards include the 2002 Distinguished Teacher/Scholar Award and the 2008 Distinguished Research Award at the College of Charleston, South Carolina Governor's Distinguished Professor Awards in 2003 and 2008, and the Association for Death Education and Counseling's

Death Educator Award in 2009. In 1999 he was a Visiting Research Fellow in palliative medicine at the University of Sheffield's School of Medicine (UK), in 2006 at Lancaster University's Institute for Health Research in the International Observatory on End-of-Life Issues (UK), and in 2013 at the University of Bristol's School of Veterinary Science (UK). Earlier, Dickinson did postdoctoral studies at Pennsylvania State University (gerontology), at the University of Connecticut (medical sociology), and at the University of Kentucky's School of Medicine (thanatology).

Michael R. Leming

Michael R. Leming is professor emeritus of sociology and anthropology at St. Olaf College in Minnesota and co-director, Spring Semester in Thailand. He holds degrees from Westmont College (B.A.), Marquette University (M.A.), and the University of Utah (Ph.D.), and he has done additional graduate study at the University of California at Santa Barbara.

He is co-editor (with George E. Dickinson) of *Understanding Dying, Death, and Bereavement; The Sociological Perspective* (8 Editions 2016): *Annual Editions: Dying, Death and Bereavement,* 16th ed. (McGraw-Hill, 1993, 1994, 1995, 1997, 2000, 2002, 2004, 2005, 2007, 2008, 2010, 2011, 2012, 2014, 2016) and co-author of *Understanding Families: Diversity, Continuity, and Change* (Allyn & Bacon, 1990, and Harcourt Brace, 1995). He is also co-editor (with Raymond DeVries and Brendan Furnish) of *The Sociological Perspective: A Value-Committed Introduction* (Zondervan, 1989, and Wipf & Stock Publishers, 2009). In 1995, he produced a documentary film entitled *The Karen of Musikhee: Rabbits in the Mouth of the Crocodile.* His most recent film project is a documentary film on the Karen produced by the BBC, for which he was the chief research consultant.

Dr. Leming was the founder and former director of the St. Olaf College Social Research Center, former member of the board of directors of the Minnesota Coalition on Terminal Care and the Northfield AIDS Response, and has served as a hospice educator, volunteer, and grief counselor. He has been teaching courses on death and dying for over 40 years. For the past 15 years, he directed The Spring Semester in Thailand program, which is affiliated with Chiang Mai University, and he lives in Thailand during Minnesota's coldest months.

Academic Advisory Board

Members of the Academic Advisory Board are instrumental in the final selection of articles for the Annual Editions series. Their review of the articles for content, level, and appropriateness provides critical direction to the editor(s) and staff. We think that you will find their careful consideration reflected in this book.

Fay Martin
Wayne State University

Richard M. Martin
Gustavus Adolphus College

Willis McAleese
Idaho State University

Frank McLaughlin
SUNY at Potsdam

Ottis L. Murray
University of North Carolina, Pembroke

Mark D. Reed
Georgia State University

Donna L. Reittinger
College of Saint Rose

Sharon Marie Rice
South Texas College

Octavio Roca
Miami Dade College

Terry M. Salem
Lake Land College

Aimee Sanchez-Zadak
Nova Southeastern University

Barry Schecter
SUNY Cortland

Shanta Sharma
Henderson State University

Stanley Snegroff
Adelphi University

David L. Sutton
Auburn University

Vidette Todaro-Franceschi
Hunter College, City University of New York

Craig Vivian
Monmouth College

Catherine Wright
Mitchell College

Unit 1

UNIT

Prepared by: George E. Dickinson, *College of Charleston*
Michael R. Leming, *St. Olaf College*

Issues in Dying and Death

Death, like sex, is a rather taboo topic. British anthropologist Geoffrey Gorer's writing about the pornography of death in the mid-20th century seemed to open the door for publications on the subject of death. Gorer argued that death had replaced sex as contemporary society's major taboo topic. Because death was less common in the community, with individuals actually seeing fewer corpses and being with individuals less at the time of death, a relatively realistic view of death had been replaced by a voyeuristic, adolescent preoccupation with it. Our modern way of life has not prepared us to cope any better with dying and death. Sex and death have "come out of the closet" in recent decades, however, and now issues are discussed and presented in formal educational settings. In the 21st century, the idea of Death Cafes and Death Dinners are evolving in the United States and the United Kingdom with the idea of coming to a particular restaurant or being invited to a private home on a certain day to only talk about death (not for therapy purposes but simply to talk about the topic). Baby Boomers are reaching retirement age and are changing the ways we handle death. End-of-life issues are frequently discussed in the popular media, as evidenced by documentaries and other drama programs about hospitals and emergency rooms and CSI series. Though we have come a long way toward educating the public about these historically taboo topics, we still have a long journey yet ahead of us.

We are beginning to recognize the importance of educating youth on the topic of dying and death. Like sex education, death education (thanatology, literally "the study of death") is an approved topic for presentation in elementary and secondary school curricula in many states, but especially the topic of death is optional, thus it rarely receives a high priority for funding. With terrorist attacks around the world, with natural disasters, and with mass shootings in schools, colleges, entertainment centers, places of work, and simply random shootings without any particular target, an increased interest in dying and death in the curricula of schools and colleges could have a positive impact on helping to cope with these various mega death-related situations.

In this section of the book, we will present particular topics which address issues related to dying and death. Many individuals show fear/anxiety regarding dying and death. Such fear tends to be especially prominent with middle-aged persons, particularly males. Just what constitutes a "good death" varies with individuals within the United States as well as around the world. For many in the United States, to die at home in one's sleep, without pain, in control of the situation, and having had a good day the day before is **the way** to die. How dead human remains are disposed of varies geographically around the world, but in the United States final disposition is largely via early burial, though cremation is rapidly catching up and soon will likely surpass early burial. There are numerous ways to dispose of cremated remains, though cremation itself is a final form of disposition, thus nothing by law would have to be done with the cremains.

The question of euthanizing a companion animal/pet is typically a stressful time for families. Having an experience with a pet death, whether euthanized or dying naturally, can be a learning experience for a child as the dead animal will be motionless, not needing to eat or drink, and soon will reveal changes in body composition. We often feel awkward in talking to a child about death because small children cannot grasp the abstract concept of death, thus it is frustrating to try and get across to them that granddad is dead and therefore can no longer "play ball" with his grandchild. Viewing the dead body may be traumatic to a small child, but the viewing is recommended by psychologists as it shows the reality of death. Grandad is really dead. Being honest and open with a child about death is the recommended way to handle this situation. The child may not understand what has happened to granddad, but being resilient as children are, she/he will most likely soon adjust to the death and her/his grieving will subside. No two individuals tend to grieve exactly alike, and grieving in the 21st century tends to be becoming more public. We see such a public display of grief through Facebook, roadside memorials, and automobile memorial stickers/writings. The idea is to let others know that you are hurting and you wish to share this with others. Grief shared is grief relieved.

Suicide is not a primary cause of death around the world, but it is a leading cause of death among adolescents and college-age individuals. Heart disease and cancer are the leading causes of death overall in the United States, but suicide is in the top three causes of death among this younger age group, with accidents (particularly auto accidents being #1) being the leading cause of death. The method of suicide for young people today leans toward hanging.

End-of-life issues are discussed much more today. An Advance Directive is now legal in each of the 50 states and given support from Medicare as of January 2016 for a person to visit her/his physician with the idea of discussing an Advance Directive (a Living Will and naming a durable power of attorney for health care). Hospitals will now ask when a patient is going in for a procedure if the patient has an Advance Directive, something unheard of prior to the 1970s. Religion plays a major role in coping with dying and death for many individuals, and religious beliefs also impact upon one's views about an Advance Directive. The issue of near death experiences (NDEs) is of interest to many individuals. Those persons who have had an NDE tend to come out of it with a positive outlook on life and an absence of fear about dying.

Prepared by: George E. Dickinson, *College of Charleston*
Michael R. Leming, *St. Olaf College*

Article

'Going to Switzerland' for Assisted Suicide Is Getting So Popular It's Become a Euphemism

"Suicide tourism" in Switzerland doubled between 2009 and 2012—a rise that may affect legislation in other countries.

Laura Bliss

Learning Outcomes

After reading this article, you will be able to:

- Provide information for anyone seeking to know more about assisted suicide.

- Share knowledge about countries represented in Dignitas in recent years.

For a fee, anyone with an terminal or unendurable illness can utilize the services of Dignitas, a Swiss organization that's helped more than 1,100 people from across the planet commit suicide.

The only catch: Those patients had to get to Switzerland, which has virtually no definitive regulations on assisted suicide (AS). It is unique in the world in that way; all other countries have bans or clear restrictions.

This legislative particularity has enabled a phenomenon known as "suicide tourism," the startling growth of which is the subject of a new study in the *Journal of Medicine and Ethics*.

Researchers at Zurich's Institute of Legal Medicine found that between 2008 and 2012, 611 people from outside Switzerland had been helped to die there. All but four went to Dignitas. Those numbers reflect a sharp, then steady rise in the number of AS cases, which doubled between 2009 and 2012.

"I have always been convinced that the right to die is, in fact, the very last human right," Ludwig Minelli, founder of Dignitas, told Bruce Falconer of *The Atlantic* in 2010. "Why should I be able to tell a Swiss lady suffering from breast cancer with metastases that Dignitas will help her, but tell a French lady with the same condition just on the other side of the border that we will not?"

Bordering countries, however, aren't the only places Switzerland's influx of AS-seekers are coming from. According to the study, residents from 31 countries, with a range of underlying diseases, sought AS in Switzerland. Most of these cases were from Germany (268) and the UK (126). Other top origins included France, Italy, the U.S., Austria, Canada, Spain, and Israel.

The researchers hypothesize that some of these countries have actually amended their own AS legislation in response to suicide tourism's rise. "Looking at the legislation in the top three countries," they write, "political debate is to be found in all three."

That's in part reference to a 2012 draft law in Germany that would make commercial assisted suicide punishable, and a 2010 clarification about the extent of punishment for assisting suicide in the U.K. There, the researchers write, "'going to Switzerland' has become a euphemism for AS."

For their part, Swiss legislators and voters have routinely rejected propositions that would limit the country's liberal AS policy and crack down on suicide tourism. Which is a little curious, since many Swiss are suspect of Dignitas' profit margins and its founder's zeal for death. In 2008, Minelli, who is in his eighties, filmed a "demonstration" of assisted suicides that used helium gas, rather than the standard lethal narcotic, on the patients. The video was met with outrage and disgust. Falconer writes of how a Swiss doctor and a Swiss lawyer described Dignitas' future prospects:

> "If Dignitas is not careful and tries to do crazy things, it might happen that foreigners can no longer come to Switzerland, which I think would be too bad," the doctor said. "Minelli is narrow-minded. It's very difficult to talk to him about what is reasonable and what is not . . . He is fighting against everything and everybody." She seemed unsure that Dignitas will survive him. "I can't imagine that he will give it over to anybody, unless he becomes ill or gets too old," she said. "But I hope he stops working soon."
>
> So does Brunner, the public prosecutor. Several years ago, citing Minelli's age, he joked to friends that his problem with Dignitas would ultimately be solved biologically.

If Dignitas shut its doors, there would be, as of now, no clear replacement; no other AS organization is currently willing to serve such an international clientele. And that, for certain people already suffering, would be another painful blow.

Critical Thinking

1. What are some of the negatives about assisted suicide with Dignitas in Switzerland?
2. Why might an individual choose to go to an assisted suicide "help facility" like Dignitas rather than simply killing themselves without help?
3. How would going to Dignitas to seek help with suicide differ from that in U.S. states where PAS is legal (e.g., Oregon, Washington, California, Montana, and Vermont)?

Internet References

A Brief History of Assisted Suicide
http://content.time.com/time/nation/article/0,8599,1882684,00.html
Assisted Suicide
www.nytimes.com/topic/subject/assisted suicide
Assisted Suicide Laws by State
www.euthanasia.com/bystate.html

LAURA BLISS is a staff writer at CityLab. She writes about the environment, infrastructure, and cartography, among other topics.

Prepared by: George E. Dickinson, *College of Charleston*
Michael R. Leming, *St. Olaf College*

Article

Offering a Choice to the Terminally Ill

THE EDITORIAL BOARD

Learning Outcomes

After reading this article, you will be able to:

- Share knowledge regarding the legal status of physician-assisted suicide in the United States.

- Discuss the pros and cons of euthanasia.

Last year, the radio host Diane Rehm watched in agony as her husband, John, starved to death over the course of 10 days.

Severely crippled by Parkinson's disease, his only option for ending the suffering was to stop eating and drinking. Physicians in most states, including Maryland, where he lived, are barred from helping terminally ill patients who want to die in a dignified way.

"He was a brilliant man, just brilliant," Ms. Rehm said in an interview. "For him to go out that way, not being able to do anything for himself, was an insufferable indignity."

Ms. Rehm, whose current affairs talk show at WAMU is distributed by NPR, the public radio network, has brought a strong and poignant voice to a debate gaining attention in state legislatures around the country.

Currently, only Oregon, Washington, Vermont, New Mexico, and Montana allow health care providers, under strict guidelines, to hasten the death of terminally ill patients who wish to spare themselves and their loved ones from the final, crippling stages of deteriorating health. Lawmakers in 15 other states and the District of Columbia have introduced the so-called aid in dying bills in recent months to make such a humane option available to millions of Americans at a time when the nation's population of older adults is growing.

The impetus for many of the bills was the widely publicized story of Brittany Maynard, a 29-year-old woman from California who moved to Oregon, after learning in the spring of 2014 that she had incurable brain cancer, so she could die on her own terms. The nonprofit organization Compassion & Choices, which has worked closely with Ms. Maynard's relatives and with Ms. Rehm, has played a leading role in getting state lawmakers to introduce bills.

The right-to-die movement has strong opponents, including the Catholic Church, which opposes any form of suicide. Meanwhile, some medical professionals argue that the practice is at odds with their mission as healers and worry that it could be abused. Unfortunately, many Americans associate the issue with Dr. Jack Kevorkian, a notorious advocate of assisted suicide who was convicted in 1999 of murder and who aided dozens of patients, many of whom were not terminally ill, in ending their lives.

As local lawmakers around the country debate the bills, they should consider how successfully and responsibly the law has been carried out in Oregon. The state's Death With Dignity Act, which went into effect in 1997, gives doctors the right to prescribe a lethal dose of medication to patients who are terminally ill and who have been advised of their alternatives, such as hospice care. The law provides layers of safeguards to ensure proper diagnosis of the disease, determine a patient's competency to make the decision, and protect against coercion. Last year, 105 patients in Oregon, a record high, died after receiving a lethal dose of medication.

Health care providers in states where assisted suicide is illegal face wrenching choices when dying patients ask them for help. In one case, prosecutors in Pennsylvania perversely charged Barbara Mancini, a nurse, with assisting a suicide for handing a bottle of morphine in February 2013 to her 93-year-old father, who was in hospice care. A judge dismissed the case the following year.

Some doctors caught in these painful situations end up handing patients lethal doses of painkillers with a wink and a nod, right-to-die activists say. But these unregulated practices put patients and doctors on dangerous terrain. "Making a secret process transparent makes it safer," Barbara Coombs Lee, the president of Compassion & Choices, said in an interview. Ms. Rehm said she and her husband had long agreed they would help each other die if either was in growing distress from a terminal illness. Her inability to help him die humanely is a situation no spouse should have to face.

"There was no question but that I would support him and honor whatever choice he would make," she said. "As painful as it was, it was his wish."

Critical Thinking

1. What are some of the arguments for and against euthanasia?

2. Why have views on euthanasia changed in recent years in the United States as some 67% of the population favors such?

3. How does Compassion & Choices work with the euthanasia movement?

Internet References

Euthanasia.com
www.euthanasia.com/

Euthanasia and Assisted Suicide
www.medicalnewstoday.com/articles/182951.php

Should Euthanasia or Physician-Assisted Suicide Be Legal?
http://euthanasia.procon.org/

Prepared by: George E. Dickinson, *College of Charleston*
Michael R. Leming, *St. Olaf College*

Article

Grief in the Age of Facebook

ELIZABETH STONE

Learning Outcomes

After reading this article, you will be able to:

- Help others who are grieving by sharing their grief, as grief shared is grief relieved.

- Know that grief can be shared electronically, if such is convenient and if this form of communication is more comfortable for you than a more personal means such as face-to-face or a hand-written note.

On July 17 last year, one of my most promising students died. Her name was Casey Feldman, and she was crossing a street in a New Jersey resort town on her way to work when a van went barreling through a stop sign. Her death was a terrible loss for everyone who knew her. Smart and dogged, whimsical and kind, Casey was the news editor of the *The Observer*, the campus paper I advise, and she was going places. She was a finalist for a national college reporting award and had just been chosen for a prestigious television internship for the fall, a fact she conveyed to me in a midnight text message, entirely consistent with her all-news-all-the-time mind-set. Two days later her life ended.

I found out about Casey's death the old-fashioned way: in a phone conversation with Kelsey, the layout editor and Casey's roommate. She'd left a neutral-sounding voice mail the night before, asking me to call when I got her message, adding, "It's OK if it's late." I didn't retrieve the message till midnight, so I called the next morning, realizing only later what an extraordinary effort she had made to keep her voice calm. But my students almost never make phone calls if they can help it, so Kelsey's message alone should have raised my antenna. She blogs, she tweets, she texts, and she pings. But voice mail? No.

Paradoxically it was Kelsey's understanding of the viral nature of her generation's communication preferences that sent her rushing to the phone, and not just to call boomers like me. She didn't want anyone to learn of Casey's death through Facebook. It was summer, and their friends were scattered, but Kelsey knew that if even one of Casey's 801 Facebook friends posted the news, it would immediately spread.

So as Kelsey and her roommates made calls through the night, they monitored Facebook. Within an hour of Casey's death, the first mourner posted her respects on Casey's Facebook wall, a post that any of Casey's friends could have seen. By the next morning, Kelsey, in New Jersey, had reached *The Observer*'s editor in chief in Virginia, and by that evening, the two had reached fellow editors in California, Missouri, Massachusetts, Texas, and elsewhere—and somehow none of them already knew.

In the months that followed, I've seen how markedly technology has influenced the conventions of grieving among my students, offering them solace but also uncertainty. The day after Casey's death, several editorial-board members changed their individual Facebook profile pictures. Where there had been photos of Brent, of Kelsey, of Kate, now there were photos of Casey and Brent, Casey and Kelsey, Casey and Kate.

Now that Casey was gone, she was virtually everywhere. I asked one of my students why she'd changed her profile photo. "It was spontaneous," she said. "Once one person did it, we all joined in." Another student, who had friends at Virginia Tech when, in 2007, a gunman killed 32 people, said that's when she first saw the practice of posting Facebook profile photos of oneself with the person being mourned.

Within several days of Casey's death, a Facebook group was created called "In Loving Memory of Casey Feldman," which ran parallel to the wake and funeral planned by Casey's family. Dozens wrote on that group's wall, but Casey's own wall was the more natural gathering place, where the comments were more colloquial and addressed to her: "casey im speechless for words right now," wrote one friend. "i cant believe that just yest i txted you and now your gone . . . i miss you soo much. rest in peace."

Though we all live atomized lives, memorial services let us know the dead with more dimension than we may have known them during their lifetimes. In the responses of her friends, I was struck by how much I hadn't known about Casey—her equestrian skill, her love of animals, her interest in photography, her acting talent, her penchant for creating her own slang ("Don't be a cow"), and her curiosity—so intense that her friends affectionately called her a "stalker."

This new, uncharted form of grieving raises new questions. Traditional mourning is governed by conventions. But in the age of Facebook, with selfhood publicly represented via comments and uploaded photos, was it OK for her friends to display joy or exuberance online? Some weren't sure. Six weeks after Casey's death, one student who had posted a shot of herself with Casey wondered aloud when it was all right to post a different photo. Was there a right time? There were no conventions to help her. And would she be judged if she removed her mourning photo before most others did?

As it turns out, Facebook has a "memorializing" policy in regard to the pages of those who have died. That policy came into being in 2005, when a good friend and co-worker of Max Kelly, a Facebook employee, was killed in a bicycle accident. As Kelly wrote in a Facebook blog post last October, "The question soon came up: What do we do about his Facebook profile? We had never really thought about this before in such a personal way. How do you deal with an interaction with someone who is no longer able to log on? When someone leaves us, they don't leave our memories or our social network. To reflect that reality, we created the idea of 'memorialized' profiles as a place where people can save and share their memories of those who've passed."

Casey's Facebook page is now memorialized. Her own postings and lists of interests have been removed, and the page is visible only to her Facebook friends. (I thank Kelsey Butler for making it possible for me to gain access to it.) Eight months after her death, her friends are still posting on her wall, not to "share their memories" but to write to her, acknowledging her absence but maintaining their ties to her—exactly the stance that contemporary grief theorists recommend. To me, that seems preferable to Freud's prescription, in "Mourning and Melancholia," that we should detach from the dead. Quite a few of Casey's friends wished her a Merry Christmas, and on the 17th of every month so far, the postings spike. Some share dreams they've had about her, or post a detail of interest. "I had juice box wine recently," wrote one. "I thought of you the whole time: (Miss you girl!" From another: "i miss you. the new lady gaga cd came out, and if i had one wish in the world it would be that you could be singing (more like screaming) along with me in my passenger seat like old times."

It was against the natural order for Casey to die at 21, and her death still reverberates among her roommates and fellow editors. I was privileged to know Casey, and though I knew her deeply in certain ways, I wonder—I'm not sure, but I wonder—if I should have known her better. I do know, however, that she would have done a terrific trend piece on "Grief in the Age of Facebook."

Critical Thinking

1. How can Facebook serve as a therapeutic device for grieving individuals?
2. Facebook makes the grief process more public. How is this helpful and how might it not be therapeutic?
3. How does grief via Facebook differ from traditional ways of grieving?

Internet References

Coping with Loss and Grief
    http://www.coping-with-loss-and-grief.com/
Grieving on Facebook
    http://modernloss.com/grieving-facebook/

Elizabeth Stone is a professor of English, communication, and media studies at Fordham University. She is the author of the memoir *A Boy I Once Knew: What a Teacher Learned From Her Student* (Algonquin, 2002).

Prepared by: George E. Dickinson, *College of Charleston*
Michael R. Leming, *St. Olaf College*

Article

Household Pet Euthanasia and Companion Animal Last Rites

GEORGE DICKINSON

Learning Outcomes

After reading this article, you will be able to:

- Understand why some individuals so revere their pets and wish to honor them, though sometimes in what may seem to you to be "unusual" ways.

- Share information regarding options for honoring companion animals.

- Know more about the dilemma for veterinarians when euthanasia is an option.

Statistics about pet ownership, illness, and death vary widely, but the onus to honor the beloved creatures upon their demise proves constant. Take literature. In ancient Greek poet Homer's *The Odyssey*, Argos the dog waited 20 years for wandering Odysseus to return, only to die upon recognizing its teary-eyed master. And Charles Dickens so adored Bob the cat that when it expired, the distraught Victorian writer had a paw stuffed, affixed to the top of an ivory blade, and transformed into a letter opener engraved to the kitty. No wonder Hallmark introduced pet sympathy cards in 1984 because, as the corporate website explains, "there has been a growing consumer demand for cards offering condolences for the loss of a pet, reflecting the fact that Americans often view pets as members of the family."

Estimates in recent years of companion animals owned in the U.S.: 69.9 million to 83.3 million dogs, 74 million to 95.6 million cats, 8.3 million to 20.6 million birds, and 4.85 million to 8.3 million horses, plus many speciality and exotic animals such as fish, reptiles, livestock, and rodents, according to the American Veterinary Medical Association, the U.S. Census Bureau, the U.S. Humane Society, the American Pet Products Association, and the American Society for the Prevention of Cruelty to Animals. The objects of affection populate significant portions of U.S. homes. Up to 56.7 million American households, or 47 percent, own dogs; up to 45.3 million, or 46 percent, own cats; up to 6.9 million, or 3.9 percent, own birds; and up to 2.8 million, or 1.8 percent, own horses. The more, the merrier: the average number of pets per household of those with animals: 1.6 or 1.7 dogs, 2.1 or 2.2 cats, 2.3 or 2.5 birds, and 2.7 or 3.5 horses, compile the American Veterinary Medical Association and the U.S. Census Bureau, respectively. For comparison, U.K. households totalled 8.5 million dogs and 8.5 million cats in 2013, with dogs in 25 percent of homes and cats in 19 percent, and with most people owning one pet.

It follows that equally large numbers of pets become fatally sick and otherwise perish each year. But no consensus emerges. "It is impossible to say how many companion animals die each year in the United States since no one keeps a registry, as we do for human deaths," stipulates bioethicist Jessica Pierce in her 2012 book, *The Last Walk*. "No data are available [either] for the numbers of dogs and cats euthanized each year in veterinary offices and homes." Inversely, a 2004 article in the *Journal of Applied Animal Welfare Science* puts more than 9 million owned dogs and cats dying in the U.S. in 1996, 7.9 per 100 dogs and 8.3 per 100 cats. No matter how discrepant the figures, and no matter how the calamity occurs, that's a lot of ailment to confront and grieving to process, research documents. And my recent survey of Phi Kappa Phi members who euthanized a household pet reinforces these findings.

Profound Connections

The bond between pets and humans, a special status that began in the early 1800s when people first kept them for enjoyment and not just utility, continues to strengthen. Dogs and cats in U.S. homes from the 1970s to 2012 skyrocketed from 67 million to 164 million cumulatively, tallies the Humane Society. The American Pet Products Association reports that in 2013–14, 68 percent of U.S. households own a pet, a substantial increase from an already majority of 56 percent in 1988 in the first year of its survey, and pet industry expenditures in 2013 were $55.72 billion versus $17 billion in 1994.

Demographics help explain the spike in pets and the anguish owners face when their animal suffers a terminal condition, compelling them to decide whether or not to put it down. John Homans, executive editor of *New York* magazine, writes in his 2012 book *What's a Dog For?* about the breakdown of social networks; people lead more isolated lives, have fewer children, and do not stay married long. University of California, Berkeley anthropologist Stanley Brandes, in a paper analyzing American pet cemetery gravestones, points to the rise of single-family households, childless couples, delayed first marriages, extended life expectancies, and, thus, more widows and widowers. People want to feel needed, Brandes adds, and pets require nurturing. So pets fill human emptiness, and when they hurt, owners by extension do too.

Indeed, people turn their companion animals into "fictive kin"—an anthropologic term meaning not related by blood, marriage or adoption, but like kin, such as a godparent. The owner considers the pet a treasured member of the family, therefore deserving honor. As Cindy Wilson, professor of family medicine at Uniformed Services University of the Health Sciences, and colleagues observe in an analysis of obituaries, "fictive kin can be applied to those human–animal relationships . . . [and] perceived to be as valuable as if the pets are actual family members." In about 85 percent of cases, the pet is a "fully accepted family member, social partner or sibling," experts assess in another study. Similarly, the American Veterinary Medical Association in 2011 found that 63.2 percent of pet owners claimed their companion animals as family members. An extreme example: billionaire hotel magnate Leona Helmsley, who left $12 million to Trouble, her cherished white Maltese, upon dying in 2007 at age 87. She disinherited her closest relatives in a decision to be overturned in court. Helmsley also requested that Trouble, when no longer, be buried with her and her husband in their mausoleum. This wish could not be granted, either (Trouble died a few years later at age 12 and was cremated, with the ashes privately retained); New York state law prohibits animal burials in human cemeteries.

It's human nature to take appreciative stock of someone dying or recently departed; so, too, an owner's esteem for a pet magnifies as its life ends. Tending to the companion animal during this difficult juncture and then mourning it are in some ways more complicated than doing so for people because the definition of a pet is debatable: honorary human or animal chattel? Some non-pet owners consider such concern and grief inappropriate. Pet owners, of course, disagree. This article, focusing on the euthanasia of household pets and the resulting lamentation, suggests that companion animals are honorary humans, not animal chattel. Who doesn't cry at the conclusion of *Old Yeller*, the 1956 children's novel by Fred Gipson or the 1957 film adaptation directed by Robert Stevenson? The titular dog, having protected a post-Civil War Texas family farm from danger several times, becomes infected with rabies after battling a wolf and must be shot.

Shared Burdens

When a household pet develops a late-stage chronic illness, untreatable pain, or other dire incapacity, the dilemma for the owner may not be if but when to terminate life. The owner relies on the veterinarian to advise the "right time" to euthanize—not too early, not too far-gone. A veterinarian euthanizes an animal about eight times per month in the U.S., according to studies from 1995 and 2011, and five times per month in the U.K., according to my research there last year.

Some pet owners struggle with ambivalence about euthanasia; others do not. One study indicated that "around 50 percent" feel guilty about settling on it. After all, no matter the logical, even humane basis, the result is an intimate "killed." What an awful thing to do to one so dear, the thinking goes. Those who make peace with the procedure apply the exact inverse logic. Pet owners who do get torn up over euthanasia often feel frustrated and inadequate and must realize that they have done everything within their means and that each decision derived from love. Euthanasia compels pet owners to come to grips with what sociologists call the "caring-killing paradox," writes bioethicist Pierce in *The Last Walk*. Giving themselves permission to aid in a pet's death process allows owners to progress from culpability to courage, taking on the role of "empowered, enlightened and positive facilitator" of a comfortable, if ultimate, alternative to pain and suffering.

The strain on veterinarians entails more than making the proper clinical recommendation. The veterinarian also has the "privilege" of helping decide life or death, remark veterinarians Moises H. Frid and Alberto T. Perea in a 2007 article in the *Journal of Veterinary Behavior*; veterinarians must educate and sensitize owners about this delicate time. In such situations, comment veterinarians William Folger and Margie Scherk in a 2010 edition of the *Journal of Feline Medicine and Surgery*, "Veterinarians are in a prime position to acknowledge and honor the human-animal bond." Veterinarian Mary S. Stewart, in her 1999 book *Companion Animal Death*, urges peers to reassure owners about providing a wonderful life and considerate death. Veterinarians, by sharing in the responsibility of euthanasia, assuage the pet owner's conscience. As Elisa Mazzaferro, who concentrates in emergency veterinary medicine at Cornell University Veterinary Specialists, puts it, "Euthanasia is a gift that you give an animal so he is no longer suffering, the gift of not getting worse. It's a selfless gift, often wrought with guilt, but I hope some people find peace knowing their animal is in a better place." These end-of-life discussions with owners perforce encompass another topic requiring tact: disposal of the remains (see below).

Owners stay in the room during pet euthanasia much more often than not: 67 percent in the U.S., according to a study of 349 veterinarians, and 86 percent in the U.K., in my 2013 study of 174 veterinarians. Why? One explanation is to honor the pet. Humans gather around dying people out of love, caretaking, and respect; obituaries often mention that the decedent was "surrounded by family" at the moment of death. In fact, some obituaries list pets among the survivors, in a growing trend. To show comfort, mercy, and veneration, pet owners also bear witness to the passing. They have veterinarians put household animals to sleep in language akin to the eternal repose of humans. For pet owners who wait outside during the procedure, seeing the animal die might be more than they can endure. There's another reason owners don't want to be in the room: to avoid upsetting the pet by revealing distress. Or perhaps not to "lie" to the animal that everything will be OK. Absence for the final breath thus signals courtesy and mindfulness. No matter where pet owners choose to be during euthanasia, their motivation seems honorable.

Farewell Figures

Cremation is most often the form of final disposition for companion animals left with veterinary clinics after euthanasia: 63 percent in the U.S. and 88 percent in the U.K., my studies indicate. These owners gave me several reasons. They don't have space to bury the pet themselves or it's illegal to do so. Cremation allows transport of ashes upon moving elsewhere, thus preventing leaving Fido or Whiskers behind in the yard. And, as will be discussed below, cremation costs less than burial in a pet cemetery.

Of the 33 percent of U.S. pet owners who wait outside during euthanasia or leave the premises entirely, they're more likely to bury their companion animals in pet cemeteries. This ritual dates to the late Paleolithic period; evidence unearths humans and dogs buried together. Pet cemeteries emerged in the U.S. in 1896 and in Great Britain in 1880. As of 2009, there are more than 600 pet cemeteries operating in the U.S. and, as of 2007, 25 in England and Wales. To compare just one category of humans, the U.S. Department of Veteran Affairs National Cemetery Administration maintains 131 national cemeteries.

Price Ranges

Just as data about pet ownership, illness, and death vary widely, so do the fees for pet euthanasia, cremation, and burial. Euthanasia costs $50 to $100 in a veterinary office and $295 to $400 at home. Euthanasia plus aftercare (i.e., transportation of the body to a crematory and the ashes scattered or returned in an urn) costs $400 to $800, depending on size of the pet and region of the country. The SPCA Serving Erie County, N.Y., for example, charges $40 for euthanasia and general cremation and $135 for euthanasia and a private cremation with a cedar urn for cats and dogs up to 20 pounds, $50 and $180 for dogs 21 pounds to 50 pounds, $60 and $210 for dogs 51 pounds to 90 pounds, and $70 and $265 for dogs 91 pounds to 120 pounds, respectively. Another source summarizes cremation outlays as $55 to $100 for puppies, kittens and small animals like birds, rabbits and ferrets, $100 to $150 for cats and dogs up to 50 pounds, and $150 to $350 for dogs between 50 pounds and 120 pounds, with extra costs for urns, pickup, even watching the cremation.

Caskets cost $90 to $145 and burial at a pet cemetery costs $500 to $730, generally speaking, with burials of small animals of less than 20 pounds at the lower end and large animals of more than 100 pounds at the upper end. The 10-acre Los Angeles Pet Memorial Park, in Calabasas, California, opened in 1928 "as the final resting place for animals of stars and the starring animals themselves, including MGM's lion and the dog from *Little Rascals*" and Charlie Chaplin's cat and Humphrey Bogart's dog. The site has interred at least 40,000 and maybe 45,000 companion animals. "There's a crematory, some offices and a shop selling urns, headstones, and coffins. The small staff connects grievers to florists, priests, and rabbis. Depending on the size of the plot and the quality of the casket, burial can cost $600 to $2,000." Another source, explicating that lots are sold by size, not location, states that a lot for a 5- to 6-pound cat costs $60 and a basic casket made of carbon fiber $66, while burial of a 70-pound dog costs $984, more if in an upscale casket. Amenities such as burial service and continuous maintenance are included. Granite headstones start at $310.

How do these allocations fit into a pet owner's budget? Yearly expenditures on food, supplies, medical care, and training average between $580 and $875 for dogs and $670 for cats and up to $200 for birds. The American Pet Products Association estimates for 2013–14 $621 for a veterinarian surgery and $231 for a routine visit for a household dog and $382 and $193, respectively, for a household cat. Household dogs receive 2.6 veterinary visits each year, cats 1.6, birds 0.3, and horses 1.9, at a cost of $227 per dog, $90 per cat, $14 per bird, and

$133 per horse, records the American Veterinary Medical Association, referencing 2012 (mean) data.

A typical human funeral in the U.S. costs $8,000 to $10,000. A human cremation costs much less, even with corollary components.

Far-reaching Implications

Although few companion animals end up in pet cemeteries, the very existence of these graveyards speaks volumes about attachment and honor. Adrian Franklin, a sociology professor at University of Tasmania, notes in his 1999 book *Animals and Modern Cultures* that such interment not only demonstrates devotion to the pets but also gives them a degree of sacredness not allotted to other beasts.

Initial epitaphs in U.S. pet cemeteries were impersonal, e.g., "My pet." By the early 1900s, the name was included, sometimes with the age or year of birth and death. After World War II, inscriptions etched in species and human familyties, and memorial photographs appeared. Since the 1980s, dog, cats, and even birds have been bestowed with the surnames of their owners on gravestones, symbolically converting the animals into blood relatives.

Some pet owners bury companion animals in the yard, though I cannot find data on how many. Legality fluctuates from locale to locale. In general, regulations mandate that graves be deep enough to protect humans and animals from disease. But these rules are often vague and enforcement is usually lax. Personally burying one's pet honors the companion animal, proponents argue, because intimates, rather than strangers, prepare the body for the last journey and because often it stays close to home in perpetuity: the yard. John Grogan, author of the 2005 besteslling memoir *Marley and Me*, after kneeling in front of the 13-year-old titular Labrador retriever when the verterinarian performed euthanasia, buried the family dog in the backyard. Grogan then ex-humed and reburied the remains after moving.

Society Poll

Some Phi Kappa Phi members, plus staff and friends, who consented to pet euthanasia confirm much of the above. Last June, the Society's Monthly Mentions email included a hyperlink to a germane survey that I created with Editor Peter Szatmary. There were 569 completed responses; 57 started but didn't finish. Eighty-four percent of respondents were female, at an average age of 33.96 years (median age = 37.1; range = 19–77 years).

The main reasons cited for pet euthanasia were cancer, renal failure, stroke, crippling arthritis combined with other frailties, and general debilitation. "He was suffering from kidney disease, intestinal disease, [was] deaf, dehydrated, [had] arthritis, a bone spur on his hip. We decided his quality of life was beginning to suffer too much," One respondent explained, for regular intravenous fluids to keep him alive. Another pet owner called euthanasia "the toughest decision I have ever had to make in my life, and I constantly think there was something [else] I could have or should have done," buttressing the earlier reference to ambivalence about the procedure.

Eighty-two percent of respondents asked their veterinarian whether euthanasia was the right thing to do, and 98 percent agreed that the veterinarian made the proper recommendation, which was euthanasia 80 percent of the time. Euthanasia occurred at the clinic 90 percent of the time; 61 percent of those patients were dogs, 36 percent cats, and 3 percent other such as guinea pigs, rabbits, and ferrets. Seventy-four percent of owners stayed with their pet during euthanasia, and their comments were positive, all things considered. One respondent said, "Pyper finally seemed to relax, as if all her pain, cares, and worries disappeared." Another wrote, "Her whole face took on the most peaceful appearance, as if she was healthy again. She looked beautiful again."

Yet the very idea of euthanasia polarized respondents. One pet owner pronounced, "Putting your pet to sleep is quite a euphemism. A better description is paralyze your pet and then stop their heart/breathing." Another declared, "Before he was brought in for me to hold, I was crying so hard and asking God 'Why?' and suddenly the door of the room opened slowly and gently, which made me think I can't be selfish."

No prevailing wisdom arose about what to do with the euthanized body. Fifty-eight percent of owners chose cremation: 29 percent storing the cremains in an urn at home, 5 percent scattering them in a favorite place, 1 percent putting them in a box, and 23 percent asking the veterinarian to dispose of them. Thirty-six percent buried their euthanized pet: 32 percent in sundry places such as the home garden or family farm and 4 percent in a pet cemetery. One percent donated the cadaver to a veterinary school. Five percent checked "other" but did not specify.

Besides homages via urns and gravestones, commemorations took numerous forms. The more frequent answers included photos on walls or in family albums, paw imprints, and monetary donations to animal shelters. Others said getting tribute tattoos, planting a tree/bush, displaying the animal's collar, posting on Facebook or other online memorials or making their own pet homepages, and making "a yearly toast to Flicker's life on his birthday including all family members via Skype or speakerphone." Fifty-eight percent obtained another pet, typically the same type of animal, over a vast range of time: one day to 25 years.

More than 90 percent agreed that the veterinarian did an overall excellent job and exhibited compassion and care toward the animal and the owner. Eighty-nine percent agreed that the veterinarian possessed good communication skills. Twenty percent of the time the veterinarian suggested palliative care instead of euthanasia, and 76 percent of those clients heeded the advice. Only 21 percent of veterinarians offered grief support, whether individual or group, face-to-face, by phone, or online. Twenty-five percent of owners took advantage of this outreach. The scant bereavement counseling warrants further investigation to determine if there is an industrywide problem the field ought to address.

Moral Compass

The interpretation, function, and rank of household pets have elevated since the 1800s. Today, when a companion animal dies or is euthanized, owners respond with customs comparable to those for dead humans. "Our pets are members of our family and deserve to be treated with dignity and respect," asserts an American funeral home that also cremates pets. What's more, owners now mourn and honor their companion animal by commissioning a portrait, buying a stone accent for the yard, or having jewelry crafted in the pet's image or from its ashes—by adapting conventions historically applied to human counterparts. Only time will tell if such patterns will persist.

Critical Thinking

1. Discuss the options available for honoring one's companion animal.
2. Is the role of the veterinarian regarding the question of euthanasia to respond to the client's wishes without questioning him/her or should he/she not act so quickly?
3. What are the advantages/disadvantages of earth burial versus cremation of a companion animal?

Internet References

American Humane Association
http://www.americanhumane.org/animals/adoption-pet-care/caring-for-your-pet/

Association for Pet Loss and Bereavement
aplb.org/support/euthanasia/pet_euthanasia.php

pet MD
www.petmd.com

GEORGE DICKINSON, Professor of Sociology at College of Charleston, his Phi Kappa Phi chapter, spent spring 2013 at University of Bristol (U.K.) School of Veterinary Sciences researching pet end-of-life issues. He has authored or coauthored 24 books, including *Understanding Dying, Death, and Bereavement*, now in its eighth edition (Wadsworth/Cengage), and more than 90 scholarly articles primarily on end-of-life topics in humans and pets. Dickinson has been a research fellow in palliative medicine at University of Sheffield Medical School and Lancaster University School of Health and Medicine.

Article

Prepared by: George E. Dickinson, *College of Charleston*
Michael R. Leming, *St. Olaf College*

Diversity in Death: Body Disposition and Memorialization

GEORGE E. DICKINSON

Learning Outcomes

After reading this article, you will be able to:

- Discuss numerous options regarding final disposition of dead human remains.

- Know the various current trends in disposing of a dead human body.

- Present information regarding the economic factors related to human body disposition.

I didn't attend the funeral, but I sent a nice letter saying I approved.

Mark Twain

A Harris poll, commissioned by the National Funeral Directors Association (Carpenter, 2005), found that 62% of Americans want some kind of personalized funeral, from cowboy-themed caskets to elaborately produced video eulogies to graveside butterfly releases. Robert Fulton and Greg Owen (1988) described the post-World War II Baby Boomers (born between 1946 and 1964) as primarily experiencing death at a distance. Unlike earlier generations, they were probably born in hospitals and are no longer likely to die from infectious diseases. Unlike their parents and grandparents, this generation experienced the maximum benefits of an urbanized and technologically advanced society. Fulton and Owen note that as the commercial meat processing industry removed the slaughtering of animals from the home, so did modern healthcare institutions shield this group from general exposure to illness and death. Death became

invisible and abstract. This generation was the first in which a person could reach adulthood with only a 5% chance that an immediate family member would die.

With an estimated 77 million Baby Boomers reaching the age of 50 between 1996 and 2015, funeral homes are learning to give customers the same thing they want in their cars—options (Irwin, 2005). It is likely that death will become a major topic, perhaps an obsession, with many people of this generation, predicted Hali Weiss (1995). Weiss went on to predict that they will demand more meaningful deaths and burials in the 21st century, just as they took control of the childbirth experience. With cremation rates rising from 10% in the 1970s to over 30% in 2010 (Leming & Dickinson, 2011), a gradual rejection of traditional burial practices is on the horizon. And this trend is expected to continue, as the Cremation Association of North America estimates that by 2025 more than half of dead human remains will be disposed of via cremation (Funeral Operations Industry, 2010). Indeed, theologian Douglas Davies (2002) and sociologist Tony Walter (1994) note a shift from an institutional to an individual notion of death, leaving its mark on ritual activity, memorials, and places of ritual.

This article will explore options available today in the United States to dispose of dead human remains and ways of memorializing the dead. Additionally, an explanation will be sought as to why these changes from traditional ways are occurring. Data analysis will be from media sources and the Internet.

Recent Personalized Death Trends

The $15-billion-a-year funeral-cemetery industry (Hoovers, 2010) is obviously thriving, yet funeral homes are willing to recognize the need to change their image in order to keep up with the changing times. The focus is not death but the learning of new skills to dramatically improve celebration of life experiences. In a way, funeral directors are becoming event planners, and funeral homes are becoming one-stop shops by expanding their service offerings—some equipped with dining halls and multipurpose rooms for after-service receptions (Spors, 2005). Many options for body disposition and memorialization exist today, whether or not a funeral home is involved. Let's take a look at some of these personalized options.

Cremation Options

Cremation is a final form of disposition therefore, nothing has to be done with the cremains. Some recent personalized death trends, however, involve cremation. With cremation, the dead are mobile and can be divided up among significant others. There has been a dramatic increase in placing cremains in what was a special place(s) for that person. Such behavior reflects how we collectively appreciate past lives (Jenkins, 2006). Place the cremains in the deceased person's favorite fishing lake or scatter them over a field where she enjoyed walking.

Recent options for cremains, other than burial, placement in an urn on the mantel, or scattering on a favorite spot, include the following:

1. One can put the cremains in paint for a painting, then have it framed to put on the wall.
2. Cremains can be placed into orbit at a cost ranging from $2,500 to $12,000 depending on the weight (1 gram to 7 grams) and length of time in orbit (10 years to 240 years), with a 10% discount for veterans (Memorial Spaceflights, 2011).
3. Cremains can be inserted in an Eternal Reef, a concrete artificial reef (like a large wiffle ball), in the ocean at a cost ranging from $4,000, if in the reef with others' cremains, to $7,000, if in a reef "alone" (Saslow, 2011). The reefs vary in weight from 650 to 4,000 pounds.
4. Perhaps by 2025, more Americans will follow the lead of Hunter S. Thompson, as his cremains were packed inside a firework and blasted from a cannon to a height of 500 feet above his home in Colorado in 2005 (Honigsbaum, 2005).
5. Or an individual may opt to place the cremains in a birdbath, wind chimes, sundial, or in an urn that disintegrates when dropped in water or in a necklace or bracelet to be worn.

Not only are there options for dispersing cremains, but there is an opportunity to watch the cremation process itself. For example, at Neil Bardal's crematorium in Winnipeg, Ontario, not only can the body be viewed before cremation,

but an individual can also watch the main event, not unlike watching your car go through a car wash, through a window. The owner of the crematorium encourages people to witness the cremation, though most families prefer not to watch (Jokinen, 2010).

Varied Casket Choices

If earth burial is to be the final form of disposition of dead human remains, caskets which make a statement are available. Screen painting on metal caskets is available. Caskets can be customized to fit the personality of the deceased. Such paintings may include gardening, hunting and fishing, music, military, or cooking themes. These full-color designs reflect the decedent's special interests. Additionally, embroidered pictures of the deceased person's favorite hobby or pets or alma mater can be put on the head panel of the casket.

One can be frugal and buy a casket that also serves as a planter, a bookcase, a sofa, or an entertainment center, until needed for burial. For the convenience of the consumer, a casket can be purchased online from your discount retailer at Costco, since 2004, and now at Walmart, as of 2009 (Watson, 2009). Walmart offers 15 casket choices and over 130 urns and cremains containers. The caskets priced between $895 and $2,899 can be delivered within 48 hours. The urns vary in design from the pinstriped "Executive Privilege" model for the "buttoned-down businessman" to the metallic lavender "Lovely in All Ways" vessel offered for a more feminine style, with some urns being made of organic materials.

The Lien Foundation in Singapore ("Happy Coffins" Make Funerals Less Grim, 2010) has introduced "happy coffins" which are intended to take the fear out of death. Traditional negative associations with coffins have been transformed to a celebratory symbol of courage, life, and beauty, as advertised by the Lien Foundation. Examples of recent interests expressed in their casket designs include whimsical floating angels and an embroidery motif with "thankful" stitched into the side. Also, craftsmen in the African nation of Ghana have gained international acclaim for their flashy, custom-built coffins which are individually designed to resemble an object with special meaning to the deceased individual (e.g., shaped like a fish, a corvette, Nike sneakers, or Coca-Cola bottles).

Theme Funerals and Other Options

Theme funerals are popular with some individuals. Bodies are no longer always clothed in suits and Sunday dresses but may be dressed in attire according to their sport (golf, for example, or football) or of a favorite pastime such as a beach-combing or motor-cycling, thus dressed in their Harley-Davidson outfit— attendance in absentia. Music at the funeral may be that of the Beatles, rather than traditional selections from a hymn book. Other funeral options include a butterfly or dove release at the funeral, a videotape of the funeral, or photos of the deceased in the casket. Families have incorporated slide shows, short documentaries about the deceased, and home videos into services. Visitation at the funeral may include conversation stimulants such as memory boards (photos and other memorabilia). Thus, the role of funeral directors as event planners is obvious in the 21st century.

In addition to being more diversified in funeral options today, funeral homes are expanding their services to use their facilities for weddings and meeting spaces for organized community groups. With more competition from home funerals and discount retail casket and urn competitors such as Costco and Walmart, it behooves them to be more diversified. They will provide a caterer for a reception following the funeral, if desired by the family. Some funeral homes are even expanding their businesses to include pet services/cremations in order to give an edge over competitors in later luring in family members for funeral services following a successful encounter with the deceased pet (McQueen, 2011).

Environmentally Correct Options

For environmentally concerned individuals, a green funeral is an option— no embalming, no toxic chemicals, a biodegradable coffin made from willow, wicker, or bamboo, and no vaults, just whole bodies or ashes. Woodland burial sites are used. Thus, land preserved for the dead can protect the land from urban sprawl and allow the dead to make a statement from their graves (Chawkins, 2003). Memorial trees are often planted, in lieu of a headstone. For a non-green funeral, yet for one with environmental concerns, an Ecopad (casket made by hand of recycled newspaper with cost around $500–$700) can be used for burial (Purcell, 2009). Death is part of the cycle of life: green funerals honor the idea of "dust to dust" (Basler, 2004).

A green funeral in itself is not only for saving the planet and for one's conscience, it typically is overall less expensive than a traditional funeral. The whole package for a green funeral ranges between $2,500 and $4,000 (Purcell, 2009; Tweit, 2010). As green funeral advocates note, the green funeral helps the living know that the deceased person is at peace in the natural cycle of life.

Composting the dead may become a trend in the near future, one that also would be favorable for environmentalists. The body is frozen, then immersed in liquid nitrogen which causes it to crumble into dust (Frank, 2001). Placed in a biodegradable container, it disintegrates within 6 months and makes good potting soil.

Yet another option is dissolving bodies in lye and flushing the brownish, syrupy residue down the drain (Love, 2008). The process is called "alkaline hydrolysis" and was developed to dispose of animal carcasses. It is similar to a large pressure cooker and uses lye, 300-degree heat, and 60 pounds of pressure per square inch. Currently, two U.S. medical centers use it on human bodies but only on cadavers donated for research. A Glasgow-based company installed the first alkaline hydrolysis unit in August 2011, at a St. Petersburg, Florida funeral home (Bowdler, 2011). Some in the funeral industry suggest that this procedure could someday rival burial and cremation, due to its environmental advantages. Alkaline hydrolysis does not take up much space in cemeteries and eases concerns about crematorium emissions (carbon dioxide and mercury from dental fillings). A drawback of bio-cremation is that the machines range in cost from $200,000 to $400,000, a hefty sum for funeral establishments to absorb. Yet for the consumer, the average price for alkaline hydrolysis is around $2,500, only slightly more than cremation by fire (Funeral Homes Seek . . ., 2010).

Another environmentally correct option, if cremated, is the earlier mentioned artificial reef (Eternal Reef). This reef provides homes for the fish, thus is environmentally a good alternative. In order to visit this final resting place, an individual would have to be proficient in scuba diving. A shortcoming of cremation, however, is that it requires a significant amount of non-renewable energy and emits toxins, such as mercury, into the atmosphere (Purcell, 2009).

Roadside Memorials

Roadside memorials, marking the site of motor vehicle accidents, are becoming popular ways to memorialize a deceased individual. Such memorials are more prevalent today and supposedly have their origins in the Southwest, reflecting Hispanic customs and the influence of Catholicism after the arrival of Spanish conquistadors in the 16th century (Petersson, 2009). The religious symbols of a cross mark the sites as sacred, or micro sacred sites, as Jennifer Weisser noted (2004). Indeed, religious memorials are more common (73%) than secular memorials (Dickinson & Hoffmann, 2010). The cross typically has a plaque with names, dates, and sometimes messages.

Twenty-three states (46%) have adopted a policy regarding the placement of roadside memorials along state highways (Dickinson & Hoffmann, 2010). Some states have adopted "green memorials" where, instead of erecting metal or concrete memorials, trees, bushes, and/or gardens are planted to memorialize the cite of the deceased.

Various decorations accompany the markers and changes occur with anniversaries and holidays. It is not unusual to see a Teddy bear or toys beside the cross of a child or photographs or a football jersey on the marker of a young person.

Such behavior of giving to the deceased individual reflects a care that continues from life (Petersson, 2009). Especially if the deceased individual was a child, the parent(s) may feel a need to continue the care—even after death. This act of placing personal items on the marker may be viewed as a symbolical and ritual tool that facilitates a tangible connection between the living and the dead.

Automobile Memorials

In recent years, there has been a tendency in the United States for drivers to identify themselves as bereaved by memorializing the deceased person on the back windshield of their car: "We love you _____ (1988–2010). You will always be in our hearts." Or the sticker on car rear windows may read "In Loving Memory of _____" (along with birth and death dates). These are sometimes called "In Loving Memory Decals" and can be ordered from different companies on the Internet. The majority of these memorials are for young males, yet various ages and relationships are represented, according to Pamela Roberts and colleagues' analysis of some 200 memorials in California (2009). Sometimes, these memorial stickers are distributed at funerals, though some are more crudely handwritten on the rear windshield. If one does not so wish to share the grief with the public but instead wants (needs?) a personal reminder of the memory of the deceased individual, car memorial magnets for the inside of the car can be obtained via the Internet for a deceased adult person or an infant.

As one website says regarding their In Loving Memory Decals, "We specialize in custom loving memory window decals and memorial car window stickers. All of our products make great gifts" (In Memory Decal, 2009). With the death of a baby, one can even purchase pregnancy and infant loss car magnets, pregnancy and infant loss car magnet remembrance ribbons, and "in memory of" car magnets (Remembering Our Babies, 2010).

Other Keepsakes and Options to Place in the Grave

For keepsakes of the deceased, stuffed Teddy bears can be given to young survivors, with another bear placed in the casket, thus providing a "connection" with the dead person. Or Thumbies, fingerprint impression keepsakes, can serve as a reminder of the dead person (Thumbies, 2005). Thumbies are fashioned from the print of the thumb or forefinger of the deceased in solid 14k gold or sterling silver via a three-dimensional wax model. Thumbies are purchased as a charm to be worn on a chain as a necklace or in the form of a bracelet.

If a survivor prefers diamonds, a diamond can be made from carbon from the body of the deceased by a Chicago company called "LifeGem." The process takes about 16 weeks. The cost of a quarter-carat diamond, not including cremation or setting, is $1,195, whereas a three-quarter-carat diamond costs $9,995 (Copeland, 2003). The diamonds are blue, due to the presence of boron, but LifeGem plans to offer red, yellow, and white diamonds in the future. One of the more famous recent deaths to soon have a diamond made from his hair is that of Michael Jackson. Carbon from Michael Jackson's hair is being converted into a LifeGem diamond (LifeGem, 2009). If gold is desired, a ring can be made from the gold in the deceased individual's teeth—a diamond can then be inserted into the gold ring.

A keepsake to be placed in the grave is optional with some casket manufacturers today but may be meaningful for survivors. To give things to the deceased individual reflects a care that continues even after death, the need to care being therapeutic for the survivor, especially if the deceased is a child (Petersson, 2009). Personal items such as a letter or a picture or other momentos can be placed in the casket in a small drawer that opens out of the lid just in front of the deceased individual's face. In addition, other items can be placed within the casket, outside of the drawer.

Some individuals prefer to take their cell phone with them into the grave, especially the tech-savvy and the young (Mapes, 2008). A few individuals have been known to even leave their cell phones on "to call their loved one later." Some funeral gravesite attendees call the deceased just as the casket is lowered into the ground. As a faint ring can be heard, perhaps this is the new version of "Taps" for those who were on the phone much of the time. Though more popular in the United Kingdom, Australia, and South Africa, this idea of taking the phone into the grave is catching on in the United States. Some individuals have been buried with their iPod, but it is the cell phone which seems to be the burial gadget of choice. Individuals like to surround themselves with those things they love: family photos, a fishing rod, a piece of treasured jewelry, or for some a cell phone.

Cemetery Gravestone Options

More choices for gravestone changes are occurring in the 21st century. Vidstone LLC of Miami sells its Vidstone Serenity Panel, a 7-inch solar-powered LD monitor that can be inserted into a standing gravestone or mausoleum (Spors, 2005). With the push of a button, visitors can use headphones and watch a 7- to 10-minute video that shows photos of the deceased, along with a soundtrack, all from a small memory chip inside a device that opens like the front cover of a book. The panels sell for a suggested retail price of $1,999.

Photos of the deceased individual (sealed to prevent water damage) can be inserted into the gravestone. These typically oval-shaped displays are atavistic to early 18th-century gravestone carvings of a portrait of a deceased individual. Along with the photo, a gravestone can be programmed to be motion-sensitive so that when an individual approaches the gravesite, a voice can be heard welcoming the visitor and giving a profile of the deceased person's life (the voice can be pre-recorded by the deceased herself or it can be the voice of someone else).

Another option for the gravestone is the attachment of an electronic device the size of an iPod with biographical information on the deceased individual and various family memories (Krangel, 2007). The device is called "Cemetery 2.0" and is an Internet-enabled gravestone.

Obituaries

Today's newspaper obituaries are often more personalized than some in the past have been, giving particular traits of the decedent and making the reader feel more like she really knew the person after reading the obituary. Outstanding exceptions to this "newness" are the *New York Times* and the *Times* (London), which have traditionally had beautifully written, detailed personalized obituaries, especially of individuals of note. Professional obituary writers are available today to highlight the decedent to the public. Typically, however, the funeral home gathers statistical data of the deceased person and writes the obituary.

Obituaries today also give e-mail addresses through which an individual might express sympathy to the grieving family members. Some funeral homes provide a website as a place where individuals can read online obituaries.

Internet Options

It is not surprising in the 21st century that the deaths of celebrities such as Michael Jackson or political figures such as U.S. diplomat Richard Holbrook or the memorial service for the six individuals killed in Tucson, Arizona on January 8, 2011 are promoted as international web events (Holson, 2011). Several software companies have created easy-to-use programs to help funeral homes cater to bereaved families.

MyDeathSpace has a link on MySpace where the details of deceased individuals' lives can be examined. On some of the postings, they poke fun at the dead, while others reveal a life filled with compassion and empathy (Maxwell, 2006). For guests who cannot attend a funeral, some funeral homes offer family photos and home movie footage for showing over the web or the funeral can be viewed "live" over the Internet (Markowitz, 2005). Participating online can be a healthy alternative when attending in person is not possible, as such participation may actually comfort surviving relatives to know those unable to attend are taking part, though remotely (Vallis & Rook, 2007).

A recent option for those grieving over the death of a significant other is Facebook. Facebook has a memorializing policy in regard to the pages of those who have died (Stone, 2010). Such is a place where individuals can save and share their memories of those who have died. Individuals all over the world can post messages, photos, and videos. A person's Facebook page can remain active in perpetuity, unless family members request that it be taken down. Months or years after the death, therefore, friends can continue to post on the deceased person's wall, not to share their memories but to write to the deceased (Miller, 2010a). With Facebook, individuals all over the world can post messages and photos and videos. Specialized sites offer interactive forums in which the bereft can chat with therapists and with each other.

A rather unique option on the Internet is an e-mail service called "my-last- e-mail.com" which, on the day of the death of an individual, will e-mail pre-arranged messages to individuals from the deceased individual. Thus, if you wanted to say something positive (or negative!) to someone, but could not do it to her face, this mail service would do that for you—after your death with no chance for reprisal, if a negative e-mail!

Cryonics and Mummification: Rare and Expensive

The very expensive alternative of cryonics (body freezing in liquid nitrogen) has been around for a number of years. A healthy sum of $150,000 is needed for body preservation or for neuropreservation (head only), a lesser amount of "only" $80,000 (Alcor Extension Foundation, 2009). Though not the choice of most individuals, of the three main U.S. cryonics organizations (Alcor in Arizona, Cryonics Institute in Michigan, and the American Cryonics Society in California), Alcor had 88 frozen bodies and 903 members waiting in September 2009 (Alcor Extension Foundation, 2009). Cryonics was recently highlighted by the media with the flap over whether former American baseball great Ted Williams' body should be cremated or placed in a cryonic state.

Cryonics is based on the idea that someday a cure will be found for the decedent and, after thawing out, he will come alive again. Such a practice fits the United States, notes Kerry Howley (2010), as the United States is not necessarily an easy place to take up the banner of letting go, thus cryonics is an act of not "letting go." The heads and bodies stored in steel tanks are pointedly referred to not as remains or cadavers but as "patients." A stopped heart is no good reason to stop fighting for your life, notes Howley.

Another expensive option is mummification, processed in Salt Lake City, Utah, at a cost of $35,000-plus ($61,000 if encased in bronze). Mummification involves dehydration of the body and is a permanent condition where the body may be placed on display. Though available, these two options are not popular and are infrequently utilized. Different, for sure, yet cryonics and mummification do not seem to fit most individuals' idea of final disposition of a dead body.

Why These Changes?

Just what sense can we make of these changes? High-tech savvy young people are into technological items while Baby Boomers are coming of age and beginning to reach their retirement years. With high-tech gadgets to aid in grieving and with peers of Baby Boomers beginning to die, an interest in dying, death, and disposal comes into focus.

Individualization

For thousands of years, death has been acknowledged by rituals and community grieving. With modernization, however, as families split up and relocate to distant places, society has become more individualized, and many of the rituals and rites have been lost along with a sense of togetherness (Katims, 2010). Young people and Baby Boomers tend to express their individuality regarding the final disposition of human remains and seek more personalized funerals. Likewise, gravestones are becoming more individualized. Alternatives to tradition are being sought. Individuals today are following the advice of Frank Sinatra's "my way." Individuals today want to take control of their lives—and their deaths. As British sociologist Tony Walter and British theologian Douglas Davies noted earlier, a shift is occurring from an institutional to an individual notion of death.

Legalization of physician-assisted suicide in Oregon in 1997 and Washington in 2008, for example, shows the self-autonomy of today. Individuals want to control not only how they die but when. Federal district court rulings have upheld this desire under the due process clause of the Fourteenth Amendment to the Constitution: Individuals have a right to determine how and when they will die. After death, many are choosing ways to be memorialized that their parents and grandparents would not even have considered.

For many individuals today, preplanned and prepaid funerals are their choices. With the funeral "paid in full" prior to the individual's death, he does not have to fret over who will pay for the funeral. The decedent will have paid in advance, thus would have had a feeling of control over final affairs. The details of the funeral are ironed out, and the deceased family member would then have had it "my way." Knowing that one's house is in order makes individuals feel secure and gives a feeling of self-autonomy.

As part of the process of combating the tendency to deny death, the modern funeral eschews euphemisms and allows mourners to personalize funeral rituals and work with professional funeral directors to create meaningful rituals that both reflect and celebrate the unique life of the decedent. The process of personalization allows family members to deliver their eulogies and create memorial tables as attempts to combat depersonalization and over professionalization that had characterized funerals of an earlier era. In the 1960s and 1970s, social and cultural changes occurred in the United States. Mainstream religious affiliations were declining; thus, a more secular view of the world was emerging, making traditional religious rituals such as funerals and earth burials less attractive. A more heterogeneous population was evolving, with continued migration into the United States and with more internal migration from the farm to the city. With more mobility in today's society, there may no longer be the feeling of attachment to a particular locale by survivors, thus less of a need to bury a body to continually visit. And for many individuals today, the idea of visiting a gravesite is appalling.

With cremation, the cremains are mobile and can be taken along as one moves from one locality to another, if an individual so wishes. Morever, cremains can be divided up and shared with various members of the family, unlike a dead body. Additionally, cremains take up less land space than bodies in caskets.

The Cost of Dying

Americans are beginning to rewrite the way in which the final chapter of life is handled, thus are becoming a major influence on the funeral industry. Since 1984, the Federal Trade Commission has required funeral homes to produce itemized pricing; therefore, the consumer knows what is being purchased. Traditionally, the method used was unit pricing which did not delineate the various services and products for which the consumer was paying (Leming & Dickinson, 2011).

Cost is likely a reason for the increased frequency of cremation over earth burials since the 1970s (price differences of $1500-plus for cremation compared to $6,200-plus for earth burials, not including grave expenses). In addition, cremation is quick, efficient, relatively clean, does not waste land and is less intrusive on the environment. With the Federal Trade Commission now requiring a laundry list of all costs, consumers are in a better position to do comparative shopping, thus getting a better bang for their buck.

The Resurrection of Death

As social historians note (Leming & Dickinson, 2011), we are now in the "resurrection of death" phase of death and bereavement (1945–present). The periods called "living death" (1600–1830) and the "dying of death" (1830–1945) are behind us. The dropping of the atomic bomb on the Japanese city of Hiroshima on August 6, 1945, ushered in a new era in death and dying. "For the first time in six centuries, a generation has been born and raised in a thanatological context, concerned with the imminent possibility of death of the person, the death of humanity, the death of the universe, and, by necessary extension, the death of God," wrote Edwin Shneidman (1973, p. 189). The threat of "megadeath" was a constant reminder of the fragility of life and uncertainty of existence—ideas that the Puritans could surely appreciate. The sheer fact that atomic weapons are available to numerous countries places massive destruction of entire societies in the limelight. The terrorist attacks on New York City, Madrid, and London reinforce these anxieties. Earthquakes, volcano eruptions, hurricanes, and the threat of more terrorist attacks make 21st-century Americans only too aware that death surrounds and shapes our very existence. With mass media coverage, we are instantly exposed visually to these horrible events and follow 24/7 the recovery efforts. To die a peaceful death may seem a rare gift in this world of violence and uncertainty.

The modern thanatology movement, influenced by Jessica Mitford's *The American Way of Death* (1963) and Elisabeth Kübler-Ross' *On Death and Dying* (1969), resurrected death in the consciousness of American life and thus transformed the contemporary American funeral (Leming & Dickinson, 2011). Mourners were encouraged to feel and experience the reality of death.

Death seems more upfront today as evidenced by roadside memorials which are places where the presence of the deceased can be felt; the absent person, according to some survivors, is still present (Petersson, 2005). It "marks the spot," the place where death occurred. Personal items placed by a roadside memorial could be an enabling of a connection between the deceased's personal life and the impersonal site, reinforcing it as a memorial space (Petersson, 2005). Yet for some, these memorials are seen as private expressions of grief located in public places. Roadside memorials can provide solace to grieving families and also serve as a reminder of the potential consequences of inattention at the wheel. Likewise, such a display as an automobile memorial can telegraph to others a loss and continuing bonds with the dead. Such a car memorial display is a personalized demonstration of affection performed in the broader public that is available to all, note Roberts and colleagues (2009).

Within the borders of a cemetery, death is kept "in order" (Petersson, 2005). Outside the cemetery, where people live, a marker by the roadside could serve as a reminder of that person as friends and family drive by each day—"outside" the cemetery in the world of the living. Death may not seem so orderly on the roadsides, as markers are placed at the point of death, not within the confines of the grid of a cemetery. Cultural geographers Kate Hartig and Kevin Dunn (1998) propose that roadside memorials may be filling a gap in the trend toward gardens of remembrance and plaque-gardens, leaving the survivors with no personalized space to visit. On the other hand, as Anna Petersson notes, the roadside memorial may be seen as an additional way of expressing the deceased's identity and social person rather than as a replacement for the grave lot in the cemetery.

Additionally, the roadside memorial may be negative in that it may remind some of the premature death of a friend or family member from an auto accident. These memorials may be viewed as distractions and environmentally incorrect. Within the home, however, where remembrances of the deceased individual may be kept (photographs and other personal objects, for example), such an environment is an overly positive place, suggests Petersson (2005). The "presence" of the deceased individual can be felt in the home, or perhaps at the roadside memorial, but not at the cemetery, since this is not where that individual had lived—or died. There is no "connection" to the place of cemetery.

Perhaps the Internet, via Facebook for example, is helping people to become more open about grieving. Such a non-face-to-face encounter might make it easier to relate. If individuals publicize their lives online, they are not afraid to show vulnerability and share their feelings, perhaps setting the stage for a new model of grieving (Katims, 2010), as the average Facebook user has aged to 33 years old (Miller, 2010a). Rather than detaching from the dead as Freud prescribed, survivors are "staying in touch" (Leticia, 2007). Cyber solace is a way for individuals to grieve in private and yet to share grief as well. The web has put grievers in touch with all sorts of individuals who can help support them through their pain, notes Lauren Katims (2010). Grief shared is grief relieved.

Deinstitutionalization

Beginning in the 1960s, death and sex were no longer taboo subjects. Indeed, somewhat of a deinstitutionalization in several areas has begun. Natural childbirth has been reinvented, with less emphasis on hospitalized-controlled births, as home births are occurring. Baby Boomers are the generation that demanded public breast feeding and home-schooling for their kids. Midwives are often preferred over medical doctors. Self-written marriage vows are more acceptable today. Working out of one's home became more popular in the 1980s than in previous years. Individualized care is challenging institutional care. Dying at home, away from the institutionalized settings of hospitals and nursing homes, via homebound hospice programs, emerged in the 1970s. Cookie-cutter, prefabricated funeral home offerings are being replaced by customized burials and memorial services (Rybarski, 2004). Younger generations are incorporating technological innovations into their way of viewing dying, death, and bereavement and sharing their grief publically while at the same time having the option of privacy (through the Internet via Facebook, for example). Face-to-face encounters can be avoided, yet personal thoughts can be shared. Home funerals are resurfacing, as 45 of the 50 states do not require a funeral home to be involved in earth burials.

Increased interest in cremation could also be suggesting that the body is not the sacred object that it once was thought to be. Many individuals today have grown indifferent to the habits of organized religion, notes Lisa Miller (2010a). A majority of Americans believe in an afterlife, yet only 26% think that they will have bodies in heaven and 30% believe in reincarnation (Miller, 2010b). Cremation was once believed to be the ultimate desecration of the human body, as evidenced by the Roman Catholic Church's stand until fairly late in the 20th century. Stephen Prothero in *God Is Not One* (2010) believes that the rise in cremation is related to a growing disregard for the doctrine of resurrection.

Having memorials away from the institutionalized cemetery is fitting for today's consumers. Thus, roadside memorials allow the survivors to be more personal, without the restrictions of cemetery rulings. The construction of roadside memorials is a specific expression of a bigger phenomenon, a disregarding of institutional forms such as formal church rituals and the custom of burial in a church cemetery. Formal religion may no longer satisfy needs in a secular society.

An institutionalized death is being transformed into a meaningful end-of-life experience. Baby Boomers grew up under post-World War II child-centered philosophies which gave them a clear sense of their own importance and perhaps contributed to their natural feeling of world changers, notes Rosabeth Moss Kanter (2006). They are in a situation where the child has become the man/woman and is now in the driver's seat, no longer in the backseat. They are in control. They can feel better about the dying stage of life, if they planned for it and were a part of the process. Traditional, institutionalized rituals are history. No longer are their parents running the show. And a different show it now is.

Conclusion

A shift from traditional earth burials to cremation with its numerous options and the individualized preference for memorialization is certainly on the U.S. horizon early in the 21st century.

The omega of one's life has come a long way from the mid-20th century with wakes at home followed by burial in the ground. A more secular orientation in a very mobile society with more environmental concerns lends credence to less of a sacredness to the dead body and importance of preservation of dead human remains. Monetary concerns of final disposition are also a factor in these changes, with cremation being significantly less expensive than earth or above-ground burials. Though a fourth of the U.S. population believes that they will have bodies in heaven, the majority do not believe this, thus a more comfortable setting for cremation.

One could argue that death has been resurrected as evidenced through roadside and automobile memorials, Facebook, and "talking" gravestones in cemeteries. One's privacy in grief is being shared with the public, thus "therapy" for one's loss. Traditional mourning is governed by conventions, but in the age of Facebook, selfhood is publically represented (Stone, 2010). Cremains of the dead person can be carried out in public via a necklace or bracelet or diamond made from the carbon in the dead person's body. What was a most institutionalized death is now being transformed into a meaningful end-of-life experience, an experience catering to the whims of those involved, not that done merely out of tradition. As Bob Dylan wailed back in the 1960s, "The times they are a'changin.'" Indeed, the times are changing regarding body disposition and memorialization trends.

References

Alcor Extension Foundation. (2009). *Cryonics at Alcor.* Retrieved July 13, 2010 from www.alcor.org

Basler, B. (2004, July/August). Green graveyards—A natural way to go. *AARP Bulletin,* p. 3.

Bowdler, N. (2011, August 30). New body "liquefaction" unit unveiled in Florida funeral home. *BBC News Science and Environment.* Retrieved August 30, 2011 from www.bbc.co.uk/news/science-environment-1411555

Carpenter, M. (2005, January 11). Baby boomers find solace in customized, multimedia funerals. *Pittsburgh Post-Gazette,* p. B1.

Chawkins, S. (2003, December 12). Environmentally friendly burials growing in the United States. *Los Angeles Times.* Retrieved from losangelestimes.com

Copeland, L. (2003, January 5). Diamond made of dearly departed seen as creative tribute or tasteless. *The Washington Post,* p. 6G.

Davies, D. J. (2002). *Death, ritual and belief: The rhetoric of funerary rites* (2nd ed.). London/New York: Continuum.

Dickinson, G. E., & Hoffmann, H. C. (2010). Roadside memorial policies in the United States. *Mortality, 15*(2), 152–165.

Frank, L. (2001, June 13). Composting the dead? Retrieved November 11, 2005 from www.bric.postech.ac.uk.kr

Fulton, R., & Owen, G. (1988). Death and society in twentieth century America. *Omega, 18,* 379–394.

Funeral homes seek to legalize "bio-cremation" as a green alternative. (2010). Retrieved from LATimes.com

Funeral Operations Industry. (2010). Retrieved April 28, 2010 from www.hoovers.com/funeral-operations

Happy coffins make funerals less grim. (2010). Retrieved November 2, 2010 from www.aolnews.com/weird-news/article /happy-coffins-make-funerals-less-grim/19656424

Hartig, K. V., & Dunn, K. M. (1998, March). Roadside memorials: Interpreting new deathscapes in Newcastle, New South Wales. *Australian Geographical Studies, 36*(1), 5–20.

Holson, L. M. (2011, January 24). For funerals too far, mourners gather on the Web. *The New York Times,* p. A1.

Honigsbaum, M. (2005, September 16). Coffins are so last century for Britons seeking life after death. *The Guardian,* p. 10.

Hoovers. (2010). *Funeral operations: Industry overview.* Retrieved May 1, 2010 from www.hoovers.com/funeral-operations

Howley, K. (2010, July 5). Until cryonics do us part. *The New York Times.* p. MM48.

In Memory Decal. (2009). Retrieved April 23, 2010 from www. inmemorydecal.com

Irwin, S. Preplanned right into their graves. Cox News Services. Retrieved May 29, 2005 from www.coxnetspecialedition.com /se/content/lifestyle06/19funera

Jenkins, T. (2006, January 16). Dying to be on the box. *Spiked Culture.* Retrieved February 15, 2007 from www.spiked-online.com

Jokinen, T. (2010, May 7). Backstage at the crematorium. *The Week,* 44–45.

Kanter, R. M. (2006, July & August). Back to college: Ending a career will soon mark the start of a new life. *AARP The Magazine.* Retrieved August 22, 2007 from www.aarpmagazine .org/lifestyle/back_tocollege.html

Katims, L. (2010, January 5). Grieving on Facebook: How the site helps people. *Time/CNN.*

Krangel, E. (2007, January 7). Tombstones go high tech. *The Berkshire Eagle.* Great Barrington, MA, p. E1.

Kübler-Ross, E. (1969). *On death and dying.* New York: Macmillan.

Leming, M. R., & Dickinson, G. E. (2011). *Understanding dying, death, and bereavement* (7th ed.). Belmont, CA: Wadsworth/ Cengage Learning.

Leticia, F. (Ed.). (2007). *Contemporary freud: Turning points and critical issues.* Geneva: International Publishers Association.

LifeGem. (2009, July 14). *Michael Jackson's hair from fateful Pepsi commercial soon to become LifeGem diamond.* Retrieved April 29, 2010 from http://www.lifegem.com/secondary /MichaelJacksonLifeGem.aspx

Love, N. (2008, May 9). New option for funeral homes. Associated Press, *The Post and Courier,* p. 6A.

Mapes, D. (2008, December 16). Bury me with my cell phone. MSNBC. Retrieved from msnbc.com

Markowitz, J. (2005, April 17). Funerals have come a long way, baby. *Pittsburgh Tribune-Review.* Pittsburgh, PA.

Maxwell, T. (2006, November 8). In grief, young people turn to the web for cyber solace. *Chicago Tribune.* Chicago.

McQueen, B. (2011, Winter). Pet death care: New community service, new marketing, new revenue source. *The Independent,* pp. 10–14.

Memorial Spaceflights. (2011). *Earth orbit service.* Retrieved June 30, 2011 from http:// www.celestis.com/services_orbital.asp

Miller, L. (2010a, March 1). R.I.P. on Facebook: The uses and abuses of virtual grief. *Newsweek.*

Miller, L. (2010b, April 5). Body and soul: Far from heaven, *Newsweek,* pp. 56–57.

Mitford, J. (1963). *The American Way of Death.* New York: Simon & Schuster.

Petersson, A. (2005, September 15–18). *The production of a proper place of death.* Unpublished paper presented at the Conference on Social Context of Death, Dying and Disposal, Bath, England.

Petersson, A. (2009). Swedish Offerkast and recent memorials. *Folklore, 120*(1), 75–91.

Prothero, S. (2010). *God is not one.* New York: HarperCollins.

Purcell, T. (2009, November 1). *Leaving a natural legacy.* Retrieved June 30, 2011 from http://www.doitgreen.org/article/health /LeavingaNaturalLegacy

Remembering Our Babies. (2010). Retrieved April 23, 2010 from www.rememberingourbabies.net

Roberts, P., Villao, T., Romero, H., & Ceballos, R. (2009, September 9–12). *Traveling tributes: Car memorials in Southern California.* Unpublished paper presented at the Conference on the Social Context of Dying, Death and Disposal, Durham, England.

Rybarski, M. (2004, June 1). Boomers after all is said and done. *American Demographics, 26*(5), pp. 32–34.

Saslow, R. (2011, June 12). Green burials return dead to the earth. *The Washington Post.*

Shneidman, E. (1973). Megadeath: Children of the nuclear family. In *Deaths of Man.* Baltimore: Penguin Books.

Spors, K. K. (2005, October 16). Funeral Homes Try New Twists. *Wall Street Journal,* p. 3.

Stone, E. (2010, March 5). Grief in the age of Facebook. *The Chronicle Review,* p. B20.

Thumbies: Fingerprint Impression Keepsakes. (2005). Brochure produced by Meadow Hill Company, Fox River Grove, IL.

Tweit, S. J. (2010, September–October). Dying to be green. *Audubon,* pp. 80–44.

Vallis, M., & Rook, K. (2007, March 29). Grieving goes digital as funeral webcasts debut. *National Post.* Retrieved March 31, 2007 from canada.com

Walter, T. (1994). *The Revival of Death.* London/New York: Routledge.

Watson, B. (2009, November 1). Save money, die better: Walmart now selling discount coffins, urns online. *Company News, Economy, Wal-Mart Stores.*

Weiss, H. (1995, September–October). Dust to dust: Transforming the American cemetery. *Tikkun Magazine,* pp. 2–25.

Weisser, J. A. (2004). *Micro sacred sites: The spatial pattern of roadside memorials in Warren County, Ohio.* Unpublished master's thesis, University of Cincinnati, Cincinnati, OH.

Critical Thinking

1. What sense can be made of today's personalized death trends?

2. What are the cultural and social changes contributing to these dying and death shifts toward individualization of death rituals?

3. Why is final body disposition being deinstitutionalized, if indeed you feel it is?

Internet References

Disposition of Remains: Statutes by State
   http://legalsupportservicesllc.org/wp-content/uploads/2014/06/Disposition-of-Remains-Statues-by-State2.pdf

US Funerals On-line
   www.us-funerals.com

George E. Dickinson is Professor of Sociology at the College of Charleston, SC (USA). His research interests include end-of-life issues for healthcare professionals and end-of-life offerings in healthcare professional schools. He is the co-author of *Understanding Dying, Death and Bereavement* (7th Edition) (2011) and *Annual Editions: Dying, Death and Bereavement* (13th Edition) (2012).

Prepared by: George E. Dickinson, *College of Charleston*
Michael R. Leming, *St. Olaf College*

Article

Bring Back the Autopsy

SANDEEP JAUHAR

Learning Outcomes

After reading this article, you will be able to:

- Present some of the pros and cons of an autopsy.

- List some of the reasons for the decline of the autopsy.

I recently attended an autopsy at the hospital where I work, in a room in the basement adjoining the morgue. The corpse, a newborn baby, was lying peacefully, as if napping, on a steel table with rusted wheels. He had succumbed to hypoxia, low oxygen levels in the blood, a few minutes after a full-term delivery. Did he have a heart defect? Had the umbilical cord been compressed? Had he breathed meconium, the first stool, into his lungs? The purpose of the autopsy was to find out.

I'd come that afternoon to witness what has become a rarity: the non-forensic medical autopsy. "Autopsy" means to see for oneself, and that is exactly what doctors once did. Fifty years ago we performed autopsies on roughly half of patients who died in hospitals. Today, the number of autopsies has dwindled to less than 10 percent, with next to none in nonacademic hospitals.

The reasons for the decline are many. In 1971, the Joint Commission on Accreditation of Hospitals stopped requiring hospitals to perform autopsies. In 1986, Medicare, presumably skeptical of the usefulness of autopsies, stopped directly paying for them. Since then, private insurers have followed Medicare's lead.

Perhaps the biggest reason for the autopsy's demise is that doctors no longer seem to view the procedure as essential. We used to use autopsies as an educational tool, to learn what we'd gotten right and what we'd missed. Today, many doctors believe that medical tests will reveal all they need to know about how and why a patient died.

Nothing could be further from the truth. Despite technological improvements in medicine, diagnostic errors remain rampant. According to a recent Institute of Medicine report, misdiagnoses contribute to some 10 percent of patient deaths and account for 6 percent to 17 percent of patient harm in this country. Most Americans will be affected by at least one diagnostic error in their lifetime.

Strangely, diagnostic accuracy is rarely raised as a safety issue. Compared with treatment errors, such as medication overdoses or wrong-limb amputations, diagnostic errors receive little attention. Of course, they are harder to identify. Many doctors never find out about them because they never learn the outcomes of their cases.

This is where autopsies can be very useful. Even though modern testing can give us a lot of information, 10 percent to 30 percent of autopsies still reveal undiagnosed medical problems. Studies have found that patients at hospitals that perform more autopsies suffer fewer major diagnostic mistakes.

Still, it isn't easy to ask a family for an autopsy. When I was a resident I took care of an elderly man in whom a mysterious fever had taken up residence like a malevolent squatter. His temperature was 102 degrees or higher for weeks. He lost a third of his body weight. All tests—bacterial, viral, oncologic, and rheumatologic—were normal. They remained that way until he died. An autopsy would probably have been useful. It could have shown us what we had missed. But none of us wanted to ask his grieving wife for permission.

Feedback and reflection are critical in any human enterprise, but especially so in medicine, where the stakes are so high. We don't always see the correct diagnosis when our patients are alive. However, it can be pretty obvious in the splayed-out tissues of an autopsy.

The autopsy I attended took two hours. The pathologist cut into the baby's plum-size heart. It was normal. So, too, were the intestines, the liver and the kidneys.

After the initial examination, the pathologist placed the baby's chest and abdominal organs on a neighboring table for closer inspection. It was there that we noticed the tiny lungs had yellowish spots on their surface. The pathologist didn't know what to make of this, but when he sliced the lungs open, yellowish-green meconium was present in all the major breathing tubes out to the furthest branches. He said it was the worst case of meconium aspiration he had ever seen.

It occurred to me that the baby's parents could perhaps now have some closure—as well as some potentially useful information. The diagnosis was not, say, a hereditary abnormality that could affect other children they might choose to have.

My hospital, I learned, is a regional autopsy center. It receives bodies from a dozen affiliated health care sites. (The baby in fact had been transferred from another hospital.) I was told that the hospital had increased the number of stored bodies, almost doubling the number of storage lockers. Yet the autopsy rate has not budged.

Reviving the autopsy would be a good thing, giving doctors a sorely needed tool to improve diagnosis. At the very least, Medicare and private insurers should start paying for autopsies again, so that financial considerations do not limit their use. Electronic hospital records should give doctors reminders to ask for them. Despite the emphasis on metrics and data in medicine today, we ignore perhaps the most important information of all: what we can see for ourselves.

Critical Thinking

1. If a hospital desired to conduct an autopsy on your father to help determine the cause of his death, would you be willing to grant permission?

2. As some view the human body as sacred, how would you argue with them in favor of an autopsy, if it was thought that such a procedure could help medical science prevent deaths in the future?

3. Why do some medical doctors today think that an autopsy is no longer useful?

Internet References

Autopsy
www.forensicpathologyonline.com/e-book/autopsy

Autopsy (Post Mortem Examination, Necropsy)
www.medicinenet.com/autopsy/article.htm

How Autopsies Work
http://science.howstuffworks.com/autopsy.htm

SANDEEP JAUHAR, a cardiologist and a contributing opinion writer, is the author, most recently, of "Doctored: The Disillusionment of an American Physician."

Prepared by: George E. Dickinson, *College of Charleston*
Michael R. Leming, *St. Olaf College*

Article

When Dying Alone in Prison Is Too Harsh a Sentence

RACHAEL BEDARD

Learning Outcomes

After reading this article, you will be able to:

- Discuss "compassionate release."

- Argue about the pros and cons of medical parole.

- Understand better the whole issue of allowing seriously ill or elderly prisoners to be considered for release.

My patient, a man in his 60s, whispered "Gracias, God bless" over and over as I moved his legs during an exam. Our palliative care team had been called in to help manage his pain after his liver cancer recurred. The cancer had already metastasized to his spine, creating pressure on his spinal cord that left him nearly paralyzed from the waist down. He seemed like a felled tree. We found him tearful and scared. But he wasn't alone.

At his side were the corrections officers who had accompanied him from the prison where he was incarcerated on a conspiracy charge related to a drug arrest. They guarded his door day and night and screened all his visitors. As the doctors told him that his life would soon be over, his officers watched television, ate snacks, and read the newspaper. One day on my way out of his room, I asked an officer whether the patient would be told that he was being moved to a different prison once he left the hospital. He wasn't entitled to know, said the officer flatly, because he was "property of the state."

In our prison system, there are various programs called "compassionate release" or sometimes "medical parole," whereby elderly or seriously ill prisoners may be released to the community before the end of their sentence. Since 1992, 371 people have been released through the medical parole program in New York State. (For the sake of comparison, about 100 inmates die from natural causes every year in the New York prison system.) Only 30 inmates filed applications for medical release in 2014, of whom 17 were released and six died before their review. In the federal prison system, the numbers are even more dismal; 101 federal inmates were approved for compassionate release in 2014 out of a total federal prison population of 214,000 people.

My patient's sentence was short and he would have been eligible for parole within a year. He had a loving family desperate to have him home, where they could care for him. I called the prison to follow up and asked the doctor there if he intended to file a petition for medical parole. He told me he had but warned that the process was cumbersome. Still, he was hopeful.

There are medical reasons, not just compassionate ones, for early release. Providing care to a patient with an illness this serious is complex and prone to error in the best of circumstances. He needed palliative care teams to do what they do well: develop advanced care plans, identify the patient's goals of care, aggressively manage pain and other symptoms, and facilitate communication among different specialists.

While my patient was in the hospital, we could not provide him with any information about when he was leaving or when he would follow up with his doctors. After being discharged, he was sent to a different prison and was housed in its medical facility. Scared and alone, he began to decline quickly. Initially, his wife wasn't allowed to visit. When she finally got permission, she was alarmed to find him so ill and she struggled with being apart from him.

Within a few weeks, he became acutely sick with an infection and was admitted to a hospital near the prison. His wife traveled two hours each way to see him. His children had to get special permission to visit, and his daughters initially had trouble getting approved because they did not share his last name. His wife told me she sat at his bedside and sang him their private love song, over and over.

When his time came, she was in a car making the long drive home for the night, and a corrections officer was at his side. A date to review his application for release had been set for four weeks after the night that he died. His wife later lost her job for having spent so much time with him.

Our aging, ill prisoner population is both a humanitarian crisis and an economic challenge that demands the collaborative attention of physicians, corrections officials, legislators, and advocates who can devise national guidelines for medical parole. Dr. Brie Williams, a palliative care physician at the University of California, San Francisco, who is an expert in correctional health, has called for a national commission to develop an evidence-based approach to address the compassionate release process, with an eye toward reducing the red tape that can tie up critical cases when every day matters.

It shouldn't be acceptable that my patient, who posed no danger to the community and who had a family who loved him, should have died incarcerated. He deserved the chance to make peace at the end of his life, to be with family. If we value sparing other people this kind of death, we need a fairer, more functional and quicker system that makes compassionate release a real possibility.

Critical Thinking

1. Why should we even consider allowing an inmate with a serious illness or one who is very elderly to be released from prison rather than stay and finish out his/her sentence?

2. Should prisons with hospice programs be allowed to have outsiders come into the hospice unit to minister to those who are dying or should such be restricted to inmates?

3. Would you be willing to visit an inmate(s) who is terminally ill in a prison? If no, why not?

Internet References

Dying in Chains: Why Do We Treat Such Prisoners Like This?
http://www.theguardian.com/society/2013/nov/09/sick-prisoners-handcuffing-terminally-ill

Dying in Prison for Love of Family
http://www.cato.org/publications/commentary/dying-prison-love-family

Terminally Ill Inmates Dying in Prison When They Don't Have to
http://www.care2.com/causes/terminally-ill-inmates-dying-in-prison-when-they-dont-have-to.html

RACHAEL BEDARD is a fellow in geriatrics and palliative medicine at the Icahn School of Medicine at Mount Sinai Hospital in New York.

Unit 2

Prepared by: George E. Dickinson, *College of Charleston*
Michael R. Leming, *St. Olaf College*

UNIT

Dying and Death across the Life Cycle

Death is something that we must accept, though no one really understands it. We can talk about death, learn from each other, and help each other. By better understanding death conceptualization at various stages and in different relationships within the life cycle, we can help each other. It is not our intent to suggest that age should be viewed as the sole determinant of one's death concept. Many other factors influence this cognitive development such as level of intelligence, physical and mental well-being, previous emotional reactions to various life experiences, religious background, other social and cultural forces, personal identity and self-worth appraisals, and exposure to or threats of death. Indeed, a child in a hospital for children with serious illnesses is likely to have a more sophisticated understanding regarding death, as she/he may be aware of dying and death, more so than an adult who has not had such experiences. Nonetheless, we discuss dying and death at various stages from the cradle to the grave or, as some say, the womb to the tomb.

The death of a child and that of a spouse are both toward the top of a list of 100 stresses that an individual has in life. The death of a child is so illogical, as the child has not lived through the life cycle. One can anticipate attending the funeral of a grandparent and then a parent. We do not, however, anticipate attending the funeral of a child, as the adult is expected to die before the child. Such is the rational sequence of the life cycle.

Research on very young children's conceptions of death does not reveal an adequate understanding of their responses, yet young children are often more alert regarding death than we give them credit for. Adults often recall vivid details about their first childhood death experiences, whether a pet or a person, and for many it was a traumatic event filled with fear, anger, and frustration. When talking to a child about dying and death, it is advisable to be honest and answer the questions as they arise. Do not give more information than needed to a small child, as she/he will ask follow-up questions if not satisfied with the initial response. The average age of a first death experience is around 8 years. Without prior experience on how to react to a death, children look up to adults and tend to mimic adult behavior, not otherwise knowing how to respond. Regarding a child diagnosed with a terminal illness, if adults have good rapport with children and if the adults are "big enough" to listen, the child will "do the telling." The key here is open communication.

As noted above, a child's first experience with death may be that of a pet/companion animal. Whether the first death experience or not, oftentimes such a death is even more traumatic than that of a grandparent. The child may have been the primary caregiver for the pet, feeding and taking care of it. The grandparent may have lived a great distance away, with the child only having seen him one or two times, thus the child may have felt closer to the pet than the grandparent.

Veterinarians have a difficult role in their profession in that they have the legal authority, unlike medical doctors, to euthanize an animal. Whether relating to a child or an adult at such a time requires special compassion and skills on the part of the veterinarian in relating to both the animal and the humans involved. The need for more education for both physicians and veterinarians in relating to clients/patients regarding dying and death is apparent from recent research studies. It is important that these professionals practice detached concern (concern for the individuals involved, yet not too involved), yet this is a difficult line to walk. Medical and veterinary schools are doing a better job today with the concern for important communication skills in doctor-patient interaction, yet more of an emphasis on this topic would be a win-win situation for both the professional and the client and family.

With palliative care coming onto the horizon in medical fields in the 1980s, more of a holistic emphasis is seen in medicine today. An emphasis on pain control via analgesics, especially morphine, and the significance of the psychological, spiritual, social, and physical well-being of a patient with a terminal illness is emphasized. Such end-of-life concerns and care is important to all individuals, whether young or old or somewhere in between. While to some extent death anxiety/fear exists throughout the life cycle, it is especially high with middle-aged individuals, particularly men, and relatively low with older adults. Medical personnel taking a holistic approach to all aspects of concerns of individuals with life-threatening conditions could enhance significantly their end-of-life issues.

Article

Prepared by: George E. Dickinson, *College of Charleston*
Michael R. Leming, *St. Olaf College*

Patients Must Initiate End-of-Life Conversations

Anne Elizabeth Denny

Learning Outcomes

After reading this article, you will be able to:

- Discuss advanced care planning and how Medicare will now cover such planning.

- Talk about the concern for medical doctors to be more informed regarding advanced care planning.

- Know about the confusion in the United States today regarding the confusion of different medical specialists confronting a patient regarding her/his prognosis.

Just because Medicare will pay for advance care planning doesn't mean healthcare providers are prepared to begin end-of-life planning conversations with patients.

At a November 5 presentation in the Twin Cities, Harvard physician Dr. Angelo Volandes borrowed from Charles Dickens when sharing his perspective that this may be the best of times to be sick in our country and the worst of times to die.

He noted that the advance of medical care and technology allows doctors to treat and even cure diseases and conditions in ways that were unthinkable even 20 years ago. Volandes, who writes extensively on the delivery of end-of-life care in the U.S., also reflected that sadly, the very force for good—the advances of medicine that can aggressively treat disease—is most often the enemy of a peaceful death.

In its "Facing Death" documentary, PBS' *Frontline* reported that 70 percent of Americans voice the desire to die at home, surrounded by loved ones, experiencing comfort instead of suffering. Yet 70 percent of adults die in hospitals and nursing homes.

In his book, *Being Mortal*, Dr. Atul Gawande, a peer of Volandes, writes that the average patient has 12 different doctors in his or her final year. Many if not most patients have a hospitalist and a litany of specialists—pulmonologist, cardiologist, nephrologist, hematologist, and other "ists." All of these doctors can add up to impersonal and confusing care.

For example, my friend Beth told me about her experience as her mom's healthcare decision maker after her mother suffered a tragic accident in August. Beth shared that multiple doctors approached her, all within about 30 minutes of one another. She felt overwhelmed and confused as each physician independently recommended a treatment plan and listed possible outcomes. Only one doctor spoke her mother's name. Beth told me she wished one person could have woven together the entire picture for her mother's care, including the support of palliative medicine.

When my time comes, I want to see the faces of loved ones, not nameless doctors. I want comfort, peace, and the warmth of familiar surroundings. How about you?

Advance care planning (ACP) will be a reimbursed service in 2016.

Late last month, Medicare announced that beginning in January it will pay healthcare providers for advance care planning—that is, conversations with patients about future and end-of-life healthcare preferences. This is a huge and hard-won victory after the 2008 "death panel" political skirmish that derailed reimbursement for end-of-life conversations between physicians and patients.

Are doctors prepared for advance care planning conversations? Realistically, no.

Most physicians are not trained to have conversations about end-of-life healthcare choices. Many believe that initiating advance care planning conversations signals surrender to the foe of death. Alternatively, suggesting additional treatment options aligns with a doctor's training to solve the problem. It just feels better to offer some sense of hope, even if treatment is likely futile.

How should we respond to the concept of Medicare reimbursing a doctor for a given "procedure" (the talk) for which the doctor had no training—or never practiced? That's a hard one to answer.

Patients can and should drive advance care planning.

Given the reality that most healthcare providers have little experience in the art of advance care planning and can be reluctant participants, each of us need to initiate these important conversations with our doctors. We have to own the responsibility of exploring and defining our own treatment preferences in a medical emergency if unable to speak for ourselves. Creating a healthcare directive is the first step. Expressing your treatment preferences in writing will prepare you for the conversation with your healthcare provider.

Why wait?

Waiting for the crisis, or waiting for your doctor to ask the questions . . . neither approach serves you nor protects your family from the painful conflict of arguing over the treatment choices presented by the medical team in the emergency room. You can be the hero of your family by proactively discussing your wishes before the emergency happens. And, your doctor will thank you.

Critical Thinking

1. What is the opposition to Medicare covering discussions with physicians regarding end-of-life care?
2. What are the advantages to having end-of-life discussions?
3. Why are some medical doctors hesitant to have end-of-life discussions with patients?

Internet References

AARP
www.aarp.org
The Conversation Project
http://theconversationproject.org/

Denny, Anne Elizabeth . "Patients Must Initiate End-of-Life Conversations", *Minneapolis Star-Tribune*, November 2015. Copyright © 2015 by Minneapolis Star Tribune. Used with permission.

Article   Prepared by: George E. Dickinson, *College of Charleston*
Michael R. Leming, *St. Olaf College*

Good Mourning

For more than three decades, George Dickinson has been exploring the ways Americans handle death and end-of-life issues. So, we asked the 2009 Death Education Award recipient and acclaimed scholar to talk about one of his latest research interests—the issues surrounding the passing of a pet.

GEORGE DICKINSON

Learning Outcomes

After reading this article, you will be able to:

- Discuss the advantage of having pets and how to deal with the situation when a pet is dying/dies.

- Describe some of the issues involved for veterinarians regarding euthanasia of a companion animal.

- Identify options for disposal of a pet after euthanasia.

For many of us, a pet is a significant member of the family. We talk to pets and care for them as if they were our children. We tend to have a very human bond with our companion animals. Pets often live with us as many years as our children live at home before leaving for college or emancipation. Pets can make us feel needed, can relieve loneliness, and can serve as friends and companions. Therefore, the death of a pet is a traumatic experience. As occurs with any other member of the family, that death leaves a huge void.

Our first childhood death experience typically is around the age of 8. And that first experience is often a pet. Recollections of this event are among our more vivid childhood memories. The death of a pet presents a good opportunity for a parent to explain death to a small child: The animal is immobile, not breathing, not eating or drinking because it is dead. This situation provides a setting for the parent to be a role model by being open with the child about what happened. If the parent cries, this lets the child know that crying is OK. It's helpful if the parent is involved in a burial, if earth burial is the chosen means of final body disposal.

Our children had guinea pigs. A guinea pig's lifespan is short, thus we had a lot of funerals for guinea pigs at our house. In our routine, I was the official grave digger; the children wrapped the animal in a cloth (shroud), placed it in the hole, covered it with dirt and then put a rock or something else over it to mark the spot in the backyard. As the ceremony progressed and the children related a memory of the pet, each of us felt tears rolling down our cheeks. Such parental participation showed my children that our companion animals had importance.

For adults, and especially the elderly, pets can be excellent companions. A dog, for example, typically wags its tail and genuinely seems happy to see its owner enter the house. The pet can help lessen a feeling of isolation and loneliness for a person living alone. The companion animal does not seem to get out of sorts about the stresses in life. A pet can be most relaxing for an individual stroking it and thus even contribute to better health for the individual. The loss of a beloved pet, therefore, can certainly be traumatic for the owner, who—no longer being needed by the companion animal—may feel a true sense of emptiness.

Unlike the person who loses a friend or relative and receives outpourings of sympathy and support, one who loses a pet is often ridiculed for overreacting or for being foolishly emotional. Such an unsympathetic response is called disenfranchised grief (grief not openly acknowledged, socially sanctioned or publicly shared). Today, however, the death of a pet is being recognized in many circles similarly to that of the death of a human—as evidenced by the recent development of Hallmark sympathy cards for owners of deceased pets. Grieving for a pet and for a human has many similarities: feeling preoccupied, experiencing guilt, and mistaking shadows and sounds as being from the dead companion.

The death of a pet is experienced uniquely by veterinarians—especially when they are performing euthanasia, granting "merciful relief" from irreversible pain or an incurable malady. Though the states of Oregon and Washington now allow physician-assisted suicide, medical doctors are not allowed to practice euthanasia; and, for them, their role ends when the patient dies, as the follow-up functions are handled by medical staff, then the mortuary. Veterinarians, however, are often asked to dispose of the animal's body. Additionally, veterinarians have the added pressure of a client asking for advice as to whether or not to "put the pet to sleep" (*sleep*, an interesting euphemism for *death*), and if so, when. The owner of the companion animal does not wish to euthanize too quickly, yet does not want to wait beyond the time when death perhaps should have occurred. Thus, veterinarians give advice, themselves not knowing when is "just right" for the death. Such stress is somewhat limited to the veterinary medicine profession.

From the veterinarian's perspective, the most legitimate reasons for euthanizing a companion animal revolve around the animal's quality of life. The final decision, however, rests with the human guardian. Following a decision to euthanize, the owner often has a feeling of regret for having given permission for euthanasia, no matter the severity of the illness or the animal's incapacity.

Together with Paul and Karin Roof, I recently conducted an end-of-life survey of 463 veterinarians in the Southeast and found that the average veterinarian practices euthanasia 7.53 times per month. The majority of companion animal owners opt to stay with the animal during the procedure, and two-thirds of owners leave the pet with the veterinary clinic for disposal. Those who leave the animal at the clinic more often choose cremation, while those who take the dead animal away typically bury the animal. It also found that veterinarians feel that more education on end-of-life issues is needed in veterinary school, though the more recent graduates feel more favorable toward their end-of-life education than earlier graduates. Currently, the 28 veterinary medicine schools in the United States average 15 hours on end-of-life issues within their curriculum. This is similar to U.S. baccalaureate nursing schools' 14 hours and U.S. medical schools' 12 hours on end-of-life issues.

Good, open communication by professionals is pivotal in any end-of-life discussion, be it involving a companion animal or a human. Whether the terminally ill family member is a human or a pet, the process of dying and the event of death are among the more stressful experiences humans have. We can be supportive of each other and remember that a death—pet or human—should not be reacted to as disenfranchised grief; rather, it should be socially sanctioned and publicly shared.

Much like those for humans, hospices for pets are evolving in the 21st century. Some of these hospice programs focus on teaching pet owners how to care for their terminally ill pets at home, yet others handle the pet at a free-standing hospice facility. If euthanasia isn't an option (the owner "simply cannot put Fido down"), hospice care might be the solution for a terminally ill companion animal. Palliative care within a hospice setting, where pain control is paramount, presents a peaceful way for an animal to die. And who wants to see anything/anyone die in pain when analgesics are a reasonable option? Is not quality of life better than quantity of life?

Pets—like family members—leave a tremendous void in our lives when they die. Life goes on, however, and we must cope with the loss. We should talk openly about our feelings. Grief shared is grief relieved. We don't "get over" the loss of a family member, pet or human, but we simply learn to live with the fact that member will no longer be literally present. Through memories, however, the human or companion animal "lives on." Gone but not forgotten.

Critical Thinking

1. How did your family handle the death of your pets when you were a child?
2. What is your experience with veterinarians regarding their role in the death of one of your pets?
3. Should we have hospice facilities for pets, as we now have for humans?

Internet References

Home Vet
www.homevet.com
The Humane Society of the United States
www.humanesociety.org

GEORGE DICKINSON is a professor of sociology.

Article   Prepared by: George E. Dickinson, *College of Charleston*
                                             Michael R. Leming, *St. Olaf College*

Drawing Portraits of Dying People in Hospice Taught This Artist about Living

TARA BAHRAMPOUR

Learning Outcomes

After reading this article, you will be able to:

- Discuss an artist's perspective on her role in drawing portraits of individuals who are dying.

- Share some of the artist's frustrations in painting portraits of dying individuals.

- Present how painting portraits of those who are dying is uplifting to the artist and how such gives her a greater appreciation for life.

Claudia Biçen seemed to be living the millennial dream. The tall, striking British American worked at a San Francisco start-up, surrounded by people eager for the next big shining thing.

But, living in that city she calls "the center of the future," Biçen felt disconnected. She had studied anthropology and cultural narratives of mental illness. After leaving her job, she began to poke into the city's hidden corners—specifically, into hospices. Armed with a tape recorder, a camera and a pencil, she began spending hours with some of the culture's most invisible people: those who would soon die.

This week, the project she started two years ago came to a head: her portrait of Jenny Miller, a 71-year-old barber sick with two kinds of cancer, took its place in the National Portrait Gallery. It will hang there until early next year along with other winners of the Outwin Boochever Portrait Competition at the National Portrait Gallery, a national award granted every three years to outstanding portrait artists.

Miller is one of nine hospice patients portrayed in *Thoughts In Passing*, Biçen's series of pencil and cut-out portraits accompanied by audio clips. All had been told that they had 6 months or less to live. And, in different ways, all found that the nearness of death sharpened their understanding of life.

Sitting in the museum's atrium the day before the show opened, Biçen, 29, said she embarked on the project believing the dying might have lessons to teach her.

"Birth and death—these two moments of life are really sacred, and everything in between is kind of the madness of life," she said. "I thought that lying there on your deathbed you're going to be confronting your life. What did it feel like to be dying? I think most people haven't had a conversation with someone who is dying. It's just pushed out of social consciousness and I think that's problematic."

She had volunteered before, with orphans in Africa and people who were struggling with addiction or suicidal thoughts. And she had studied Buddhism, whose philosophy is accepting of transience and impermanence.

Still, approaching the hospices was intimidating. Would they think it presumptuous, this young woman with so much ahead of her, barging in on those whose lives had been curtailed?

Of the 10 hospices she contacted, "Every single one said yes. Yes, we want to bring people who are dying into the public eye; yes, we want to create a legacy for people; and yes, we like your work."

Between March 2014 and November of last year she met between 4 and 7 times with each person, getting to know them, talking about their lives, and recording the conversations. It took another 40 to 50 hours to do each portrait, which she drew from photos she had taken.

Her criteria for choosing people: they couldn't have dementia, and they had to be willing to delve into the delicate, often painful, subject of their own mortality.

"Most people are not right for this project because most people are not going to be able to go there," she said. Some people in hospice are still in denial about what that means, and even those who accept it may not be ready to talk about it with a stranger or have their portrait done when they are so ill. "It was a big ask of people. I was very aware that it's a huge ask."

In the portraits, which are life-sized, the subjects' words are written literally on their sleeves—and all over their clothing—in Biçen's neat, even handwriting.

It is, she said, "a metaphor for how we carry our stories with us."

It is also, she hopes, a way to slow people down. "You see artwork and you take a snapshot and move on. I thought, 'how can I draw people in?' When you're up close to the piece you have kind of an intimate experience."

The recordings help. The subjects' voices can be wavering and raspy; weathered from the years and the sicknesses they are confronting. They are meant to evoke a conversation between viewer and subject.

"I wanted to create a feeling of compassion and empathy, of seeing yourself in that person," Biçen said. "We put the elderly and the dying away, we shut them away. We've kind of given up on them. They're no longer productive . . . Particularly in American culture, productivity is so much at the core of what we value in people."

Biçen's subjects were based in the San Francisco Bay Area, but they and their stories are as far as possible from the hyper-charged dot-com perspective. They are more universal. A truck driver looks back and wishes he'd spent less time on the road and more with his family. A Texas farm girl born in 1916 says she accepts the idea that she will soon go, "just like my mama did."

Finding a diverse range of people was a challenge. "Eighty-four percent of people in hospice are white," she said, adding that in African-American and Latino cultures there is more of a tendency to die at home.

Although the project is about death and dying, for Biçen it has been life-affirming. "Even though they were dying they were almost living more deeply than they had before. People talk about moving into the now. Having the future stripped away really pulls you into the now. They would sit and look at the beauty of a tree. One man, Harlan, would leave his window open 24 hours a day so he could see the sunrise because it meant he had made it to another day."

But it was not easy to become close to people with so little time left. Five died before their portraits were finished. That hit Biçen hard.

"It's this really empty feeling. I'd said, I'm going to go back, I'll do one more interview. It really woke me up to what I was doing, and I really realized I can't sit around and say, 'Oh, I'll go

next week.' I think it really showed me my own denial. I hadn't really come to terms with the fact that they were [dying]."

Biçen never studied art formally, but her submission made an impression on Dorothy Moss, associate curator of painting and sculpture at the museum, and the director of the competition. "We were really struck by her draftsmanship and the expression on her face," she said. "There's something really compelling about that gaze."

Miller, whose gaze it is, had a more matter-of-fact reaction.

"There's too many wrinkles," she joked, speaking by phone from a hospital in San Francisco that she was moved to recently. She has outlived the two months she'd been given when Biçen showed up at her door.

Miller, who spoke of being abused and neglected as a child, said she appreciated the interest Biçen took in her. The two would go to the park with Biçen's dogs and eat sandwiches, and Miller began to talk about what would happen when she died.

"Someday, I'm going to help grow a beautiful tree, and that doesn't seem so bad," she said. But until Biçen came, she said she'd never spoken with anyone about these things. "There hadn't been anyone to tell."

The family of Ena, a nurse who died last month at 97, contacted Biçen after her funeral. "They had the memorial and sent out the portrait and the audio. Several members of her family called me to say how much it helped them in their mourning process."

The daughter of Harlan, the truck driver, who died at 53, said she has listened to the interview around 100 times. "She says it feels like it almost brings him alive again."

At parties, when Biçen tells people what she does, their faces often go blank. Some say, why would you want to do that? But friends and family get it. And the subjects themselves had strong reactions to seeing the portraits. One couldn't talk for several minutes; he just cried.

Doing the project has also made Biçen slow down and look more closely at her own life. She has started making audio recordings and drawings of her grandmother. She speaks at high schools, assigning students to talk to older people in their community. "I think it's something kids want to talk about and we're not providing the space. Being a teenager is that time when you're thinking about these big existential questions."

As for the lessons she sought from the dying, the main one is simple.

"I went into this thinking that every person was going to provide me with some kind of wisdom," she said. "But people just die as themselves. We die as ourselves. There isn't going to necessarily be some kind of revelation or change—this is it."

But rather than think more about dying, she now thinks about it less. "This anxiety about my mortality, I feel like now it has gone away." She laughed. "I mean, I'm sure it'll come back. But hey, you know what? You have everything now, so just be with it. Tomorrow is not promised. When you hear that from people who are standing on the edge, you listen."

Critical Thinking

1. Assuming you could paint, how would you feel about asking an individual with a terminal illness if you could paint her/him?

2. How do you personally think that painting a portrait of one who is dying would be beneficial to you? Beneficial to her/him?

Internet References

Hospice Patients Embrace Life
http://www.wvh.org/documents/Hospicepatientsembracelife.statesmanarticle.pdf

Program Offers Lasting Connections with Hospice
http://www.gainesvilletimes.com/archives/109310/

Unit 3

Prepared by: George E. Dickinson, *College of Charleston*
Michael R. Leming, *St. Olaf College*

UNIT

The Dying Process

While death comes at various ages and in differing circumstances, for most of us there will be time to reflect on our lives, our relationships, our work, and what our expectations are for the ending of life. This is referred to as the dying process: death the event, dying the process. In recent decades, a broad range of concerns has arisen about that process and how aging, dying, and death can be confronted in ways that are enlightening, enriching, and supportive. Efforts have been made to delineate and define various stages in the process of dying so that comfort and acceptance of our inevitable death will be eased. The fear of dying may heighten significantly when actually given the prognosis of a terminal illness by one's physician. Awareness of approaching death allows us to come to grips with the profound emotional upheaval that will be experienced. Fears of the experience of dying are often more in the imagination than in reality. Yet, when the time comes and death is forecast for the very near future, it is reality, a situation that may be more fearful for some than others. We need to accept the fact that dying and death are normal within the life cycle. The normal pattern is to be born, then go through a maturation process, and eventually die.

Dying differs with cultures, with some more accepting than others. As British anthropologist Colin Turnbull once noted, Americans think that they will live forever, yet Africans know when it is time to die and are accepting of that fact. Some historians, however, suggest that the United States is in a stage called "Resurrection of Death." We went through the "Living Death" stage from 1600 to 1830 when death was most acceptable and not questioned to the "Dying of Death" stage from 1830 to 1945 when death was covered up and cemeteries were moved out from cities (out of sight, out of mind) and funeral homes were established in the late 1890s with pride on their beautifying the corpse to make it "look alive." Now with the "Resurrection of Death" stage from 1945 with the dropping of the atomic bombs on Japan and more recently the terrorist attacks on the United States and other countries, we are reminded that death can happen very quickly and take out hundreds, sometimes thousands, of lives in one sweep. Thus, today we are most cognizant of death, no longer out of sight and mind.

The introduction of the modern hospice movement began in the Western world in the late 1960s with Dame Cicely Saunders establishing Saint Christopher's Hospice in London. She then came over to the United States in the 1970s and helped set up a similar hospice program called the Connecticut Hospice. The world of dying, therefore, shifted somewhat as hospice is into palliative care, thus an effort to ease the dying process. Analgesics such as morphine can help to reduce one's pain in the dying process, thus enhancing the journey from life into death. The overwhelming majority of individuals who enter a hospice program, whether in home hospice care or within an institutional setting (freestanding hospice, nursing home, or hospital), die within the program within a few weeks or months. Occasionally, however, an individual will leave/be removed from a hospice program, creating some concern for those involved with the patient.

Religion can, and does, play a major role for many individuals in the dying process. For some individuals, religion can help reduce death anxiety/fear during their latter days of life. Their reward is in the afterlife, for some religions, thus consoling to those dying and their significant others. If an individual with a terminal illness has a quality of life philosophy she/he is likely to not wish for prolonged measures to keep her/him alive. On the other hand, one with a sanctity of life philosophy, often correlated with some religions' beliefs, would request being kept alive no matter the pain or whatever. For the sanctity of life way of thinking, it is often felt that the body is the temple which houses the soul, thus this God-given living body should not be terminated under any circumstances and a Do Not Resuscitate document (DNR) would not be appropriate.

A Near Death Experience (NDE) is a situation where the individual "dies," yet comes back and lives on. An NDE typically is very assuring to the dreamer about an afterlife and usually reduces her/his fears/anxieties about an afterlife. Research evidence from NDEs suggests that the experience reflects culture, such as one's religion, depending on whether the dreamer is Muslim, Christian, Buddhist or whatever. For example, during the NDE, if the dreamer sees someone from the past, the person has not changed at all, and if a religious figure is seen, it is typically from the religion of the dreamer (e.g., Jesus Christ, if the dreamer has a Christian background).

Prepared by: George E. Dickinson, *College of Charleston*
Michael R. Leming, *St. Olaf College*

Article

Good Vibrations

Music therapy makes medicine out of melodies.

RACHAEL CARNES

Learning Outcomes

After reading this article, you will be able to:

- Discuss the power of music in dealing with illnesses and other crises.

- Cite how music therapy integrates into the team approach in relating to individuals suffering from various medical issues.

- Identify professional organizations where music therapy is pivotal to their existence.

Have you ever listened to a song and, without even realizing it, started tapping your toes? Have you ever been brought to tears through music? Most of us can probably answer "yes."

There's a science, and a whole profession, built around the reason why.

I'm in the cheery downtown studio of Danielle Oar, a board-certified music therapist and owner of Refuge Music Therapy, LLC in Eugene.

"The core central to music therapy," Oar says, "is that, as an allied health profession, we use evidence-based intervention and research to utilize the neurological perception of music and its inherent aesthetic experience."

Music connects to the very essence of what makes us human, she says.

Oar notes how memorizing lyrics encourages development in the language centers of our brains and how hearing a song engages memory through the prefrontal cortex. Music's rhythmic patterns assist with cognitive processing and logic, and its emotional resonance touches our feeling center, the limbic system.

"Before we're even conscious of what's going on in the music, we're aware of it—across all regions of our brains," Oar says.

The Power of Music

Music therapists understand music theory, but they also delve into the psychology of music, Oar says.

Emily Jensen, also a board-certified music therapist, concurs. Jensen has worked with various populations, utilizing music therapy for 15 years.

"The opportunity to effectively facilitate change in a client's physiology, behavior, or emotional state through this powerful secondary agent is truly awe-inspiring," Jensen says.

"Music has an innate power to organize our thoughts, to socialize us, uniting us with one another," she says. "The mastery and practice of musical skill-building provides an individual with a sense of achievement that, in my experience, transfers into many other aspects of leading a healthy and happy life," Jensen adds.

A typical clinical music therapy session lasts about 55 minutes and is offered to a mix of individuals and groups. The work includes ongoing assessment and documentation to identify strengths and opportunities.

Some insurance carriers cover music therapy, and Oar says that, with new state licensure requirements in 2016, she hopes the number of insurance providers recognizing the profession will increase.

Emotion Unleashed

"When you have an emotional reaction to music," Oar asks, "where do you feel it? How do you know you feel it?"

These are questions people like Oar have been asking for a long time.

Some of the earliest references to music therapy are several hundred years old, with its earliest proponents looking to music as a means to treat disease in institutional settings.

But the work gained traction in the last century, notes Emily Ross, assistant professor and clinical coordinator of music therapy at Marylhurst University.

"In the 1940s, with the influx of soldiers returning from the war, musicians would go to veteran hospitals to play and found that music had a unique ability to help veterans open up, connect with others and begin to process their experience," Ross says.

"However," she continues, "the musicians were not equipped with the knowledge or training to contain all this emotion that the music unleashed. Hence, the concept of cross-training people in psychology and music was born."

Music therapy provides an alternative to more traditional talk therapy and can be adapted across the lifespan.

"My practice works with all ages and abilities," Oar says. "From the beginning of life to the end of life, from neonatal, to children with autism, early childhood, teens."

Oar works with people with mental health issues such as depression and schizophrenia, as well as clients living with Parkinson's, dementia, terminal illness, and pain.

But do we need to attend a music therapy session to reap the rewards of music?

A Vital Medium

Across town, music is used recreationally in a popular program offered through the city of Eugene's Adaptive Recreation program. In Melody Makers, says class founder and co-teacher David Helfand, "the goal is to make music accessible to everyone, regardless of skill level, where everyone is in the band."

Adds Helfand's co-teacher Zoe Demant: "I believe that music speaks a universal language, one that everyone can participate in on some level no matter their ability. It is a strengths-based class. We focus on what people can and want to do, rather than their challenges. The other powerful thing about music is the community that it creates."

Another local group, Strings of Compassion, is a musical and clinical service that uses harp and voice to serve the needs of people who are terminally ill, receiving comfort care or on hospice. Offered through PeaceHealth Sacred Heart Medical Center, Strings of Compassion provides trained, certified Music-Thanatology (the union of music and medicine in end of life care.)

Members of the Music-Thanatology Association International (MTAI) in vigils play in the hospital, patient homes, nursing homes and foster care homes, free of charge.

Whether it's playing in the middle-school band or attending the symphony, music is a vital medium, and many take great pleasure and even healing in listening to or playing music.

And for some, working with rhythm and melody with a supportive and caring guide like Oar or Jensen can be a lifeline.

Shared Rhythm

Back in her cozy studio, Oar takes me on a tour of some of the tools of her trade. Tucked away on shelves are shakers, drums, and bells. A guitar is propped against the wall. Tidy and unobtrusive, the instruments are available but not overwhelming.

"The room is set up for sensory sensitivities," Oar says.

Kneeling on the floor, Oar gently taps a drum, describing how she and a client might work together to establish a shared rhythm. She begins to sing. On the surface, it's a simple remedy to use rhythm and the human voice in a call-and-response pattern.

"I have been so moved by music, and I just know that there's more than what the brain perceives," Oar says. "That's where music is felt, and that's the space in which I work."

Critical Thinking

1. What role does music therapy play in comforting an individual dealing with end-of-life issues?
2. Give examples of how you think music therapy can be beneficial to one who is dying.
3. What experiences have you personally had with music therapy in relating to an individual with a terminal illness? If you have had no such experience, what is your reaction to this therapy as helpful to an ill person?

Internet References

American Music Therapy Association
   www.musictherapy.org
Banner Health
   www.bannerhealth.com
Music Therapy in Hospice Palliative Care
   www.virtualhospice.ca

RACHAEL CARNES has written for *The Stranger* in Seattle, as well as *Eugene Weekly*, since the mid-nineties. Rachael covers dance, theater, performance art, as well as human interest stories. As the founder of a local nonprofit, Sparkplug Dance, she teaches movement to kids in our community who juggle any number of risk factors.

Prepared by: George E. Dickinson, *College of Charleston*
Michael R. Leming, *St. Olaf College*

Article

Being Discharged from Hospice Alive: The Lived Experience of Patients and Families

REBEKA WATSON CAMPBELL

Learning Outcomes

After reading this article, you will be able to:

- List feelings of individuals who are discharged from hospice alive.

- Cite reasons why an individual might be released from a hospice program alive.

- Describe the feeling of individuals discharged from hospice as being in-between living and dying.

Introduction

The National Hospice and Palliative Care Organization (NHPCO) estimates that 1.86 million patients received end-of-life care from hospice organizations in the United States during 2010 and as many as 259,000 hospice patients were discharged alive.[1] Moreover, literature suggests that approximately 35% of discharged patients die within six months of discharge from hospice, suggesting that hospice benefits were in fact appropriate for this population.[2] As hospice enrollment continues to grow, the number of patient discharged alive is likely to keep pace.

Admission and discharge characteristics of hospice patients are well documented.[3] Over the last 30 years, hospice admission diagnoses have shifted from malignant diseases to nonmalignant chronic illnesses. Furthermore, patients with nonmalignant chronic illness have higher live discharge rates than those with malignant diseases.[2] Almost two-thirds (61.7%) of hospice patients have chronic terminal illnesses requiring symptom and pain management;[4] however, predicting death often proves difficult because of the disease processes involved.[5] Indeed, Lynn and Forlini reported that many chronically ill patients have a 50% chance of surviving for six months the day prior to their death.[6] The difficulty in accurately predicting a six-month demise for patients with nonmalignant diagnoses means that thousands of U.S. patients are discharged from hospice due to ineligibility or extended prognosis only to die shortly thereafter.[2,7,8] These patients are effectively denied the benefits of hospice and potentially suffer negative outcomes as a result; it is also possible that live discharge from hospice may have adverse effects on patients' quality of life and health status, resulting in increased patient suffering.[9]

Methods
Design

This transcendental phenomenological study seeks the universal meaning or *essence* of being discharged from hospice alive as shared by those experiencing it. Moustakas's transcendental phenomenological design that guided this study[10] is based on Edmond Husserl's philosophy of subjective openness.[11] As interpreted by Moustakas, transcendental "adheres to what can be discovered through reflection on subjective acts and their objective correlates;" and phenomenology "utilizes *only* the data available to consciousness—the *appearance* of objects."[10]

School of Nursing, University of Texas Medical Branch Galveston, Galveston, Texas. Accepted January 20, 2015.

Moustakas stresses that "intervening caring" means to "attend fully, to feel some responsibility for, to want to protect from further pain, . . . to watch over in a protective and supportive way, to feel compassion for. . . . Caring means to enter [the other's] world, to understand the views, feelings, and experiences."[12] His notion of "anticipatory caring as a concernful presence"[12] speaks to the essence of being-with another during a period of breakdown or suffering. Moustakas's notions guide understanding the essence of the phenomenon of being discharged alive and provide the philosophical underpinnings for this study.[10,11]

Collection

Understanding the phenomena from the perspective of those who have lived it was achieved through in-depth interviews with the intent to capture the meaning of the live hospice discharge experience in the participant's own words. Interviews were conducted using unstructured open-ended questions. The initial interview question was, "Tell me about being discharged from hospice." Probe questions including, "Tell me more about that" were used to gather additional information or clarify statements. Interviews lasted from 30 minutes to two hours. Each participant was interviewed twice to develop rapport through prolonged engagement. All interviews were audiorecorded and transcribed verbatim.

Participants completed a demographic form consisting of information on age, race, gender, diagnosis, and hospice discharge date. Field notes and journals were kept to record participant behaviors, including expressions and mannerisms or other data pertinent to the setting of the interview, to monitor personal assumptions and bias throughout the research process, and to establish a decision trail in order to inform future interviews or data analysis.

Analysis

In accordance with Moustakas's interpretive approach, each interview transcript was read several times to allow the researcher to become familiar with the data and identify statements relevant to the experience of live hospice discharge.[10] He refers to these statements as the invariant meaning units. These meaning units were then clustered into themes. A textural description of the experience was developed using the meaning units and themes.

These descriptions are highly detailed, giving the experience context and depth. After reflection on each textural description, a structural description of the experience was developed. As textural and structural descriptions were merged, the fundamental meaning or essence of each individual's experience was revealed. Finally, a composite description was synthesized by integrating all individual descriptions into a universal description.

Moustakas's approach enables researchers to maintain the uniqueness of each participant's lived experience, while allowing a description and understanding of the composite essence of the phenomenon.[10]

Sample

Purposive sampling design utilizing network snowball sampling was employed to recruit 12 volunteers. Recruitment was limited to volunteers who were 18 years of age or older, who had been discharged from hospice alive due to decertification or adult family members of individuals who had been discharged from hospice alive. Potential participants must have had the ability to speak and understand English and must have been willing to participate in interviews. No participants were excluded based on race, ethnicity, gender, religion, or socioeconomic status.

Recruitment was achieved with the assistance of several local area hospice organizations and began after institutional review board approval was granted. Participating hospice agencies identified potential volunteers and sent each a recruitment flyer detailing the study and the primary investigator's contact information. Persons who were interested in participating in the study then contacted the researcher. Participants were also asked to refer potential volunteers for recruitment.

Setting

Interview locations were determined by the individual participants. All data collection, including the enrollment process and interviews, occurred at a time and place of the participant's choosing, typically the participant's residence.

Results

The current study findings are reported along with the primary themes: suffering "AS" and the paradox of hospice discharge.

Suffering "AS"

Suffering is the act of feeling or enduring pain or distress; sustaining injury, disadvantage, or loss.[13] The "AS" in the theme suffering "AS" is a meaning-structure and refers to how a phenomenon is interpreted—the meaning of that phenomenon to an individual. The primary theme and subthemes demonstrate the how of suffering in this phenomenon. The eight subthemes that support the primary theme suffering "AS" are abandonment, unanswered questions, loss of security, loneliness, uncertainty, anger and frustration, physical decline, and bearing exhaustive witness.

Abandonment

Abandonment implies the withdrawal of help or support or the leaving behind of someone meant to be a personal responsibility.[14] Participants in this study convey feeling abandonment. Hospice simply stopped coming or left the families feeling lost or forsaken. Feelings of abandonment certainly added to the anxiety and desperation some participants shared as they described their experience.

I felt angry and frustrated and abandoned. . . . My husband cried. He thought nobody cared about him. He cried. It's like you are not worthy, you are not worth our time. –Bobbie

Unanswered questions

Participants reported having unanswered questions regarding their experience. Many of these questions were standard discharge planning topics. Others were more fundamental and related to the reason for discharge. These participants were unsure why they were discharged and reported having a great deal of difficulty immediately following the discharge securing the services and care required.

What do we do now? Where do we put him? What do you do afterwards? Where do you go? –Chelsea

Loss of security

Security is the feeling of being safe and protected; freedom from worry or loss.[15] The participants of this study state that the loss of security was a major concern after discharge. While on hospice service they felt confident everything would be taken care of in the event of an emergency. Now, off of hospice services, they are acutely aware of how alone they are. Surprisingly, this feeling is more pronounced in the transcripts of family members than the patients themselves.

I know that there'd be somebody there to check on me. –Adam

Loneliness

Similar to loss of security is the feeling of loneliness. Different from physically being alone, these participants are bearing the burden of their own, or their loved one's death in a way that they feel alone in the journey. For some, it is the close companionship of others that eases this burden. For others, even with family and friends around, they feel alone in the responsibility to care for their loved one. Hospice provided a respite from this loneliness through the presence of staff, the reduction of responsibility, or simply time away to tend to self. Discharge from hospice represents a return to that loneliness.

On hospice you knew that you were never, never alone. –Brooke

Uncertainty

Uncertainty ultimately relates to communication or lack thereof. These participants related their understanding of the discharge as nebulous, i.e., more potential than reality. As merely a potential, the discharge process did not take on the urgency or importance participants could understand until it was too late, leaving the patient and family without access to necessary equipment or care. This uncertainty associated with the pending discharge lends itself to fear of the unknown and ultimately the next theme, anger and frustration.

I remember the off and on. I remember the uncertainty . . . the conflict of information. There was a lot of that in the very beginning, because the nurse said, "We cannot continue to see you," and the social worker could not explain the reasoning behind the discharge at first. It seemed like she was trying in many ways to get the situation remedied so that he did not have to be discharged from hospice; this went on for a couple of months. –Bobbie

Anger and frustration

Participants clearly articulated their feelings of anger and frustration regarding the hospice discharge. This anger and frustration comes largely from a lack of effective communication between hospice staff and family members. These participants were angered not only by the loss of services that they had come to rely on and value but also the manner in which the services were removed.

When he was on hospice, it was the best our family ever had. That's why we are so angry: because we had the best and they took it from us and they took it away. He was more independent, he was happier, he was better than he had ever been and they took it from us. That's what we are angry about. –Casey

Physical decline

In the theme physical decline, the participants discuss the deterioration of health after hospice discharge. Although not all participants experienced this aspect of the phenomena, for those that did, it was extreme and powerful and usually preceded the patient's death.

It wasn't much life—just like a zombie sitting here. I'd go for days at a time without oxygen, because I'm trying to learn not to use oxygen, because I'm not going to have it. –Alfred

Bearing exhaustive witness

Bearing exhaustive witness refers to the pain and helplessness endured by the family member participants. These participants help us to understand that suffering is not only the physical pain experienced with disease, but it is also the anguish of helplessly watching those we love wrestle with illness and disability.

I feel like I was screaming and yelling, and I was pleading and pleading and pleading, "Please, help us! Please help us!" and nobody seemed concerned. "It's not my job. I'm sorry, it's not my problem. I have other things, I have my own life to deal with, I can't deal with yours. And it's not important to me if your husband dies." I just feel like I was just a failure. I was supposed to be taking care of him and I allowed them to just terminate him [crying]. I didn't want that, I didn't want him to be terminated. He didn't want to—he said, "I want to live." –Bobbie

Paradox of hospice discharge

A paradox is a tenet or proposition contrary to received opinion; an assertion or sentiment seemingly contradictory, or opposed to common sense; that which in appearance or terms is absurd, but yet may be true in fact.[16] The paradox of hospice discharge is exactly that—seemingly contradictory, opposed to common sense, yet true. Four subthemes shape the paradox of hospice discharge: having support & needing support, mixed feelings, not dying fast enough, and hospice equals life.

Having support and needing support

Having support and needing support is a subtheme that encompasses the time before, during, and after hospice discharge. Participants attribute great value to the support they received from their family and hospice team members. For some, the support received gave them the confidence to move forward after their discharge. For others, discharge represented a loss of support they could not find outside of hospice.

I felt like I had a pretty good caregiver, and I had a pretty good organization looking out after me. So then they come along, and said, "Well, you know, it's in remission, so nothing we can do right now." So that made me feel a lot better. –Adam

Mixed feelings

Several participants reported mixed feelings regarding their hospice discharge. There was relief at the notion of not being labeled as dying. However, the knowledge that the disease remained dampened the feeling. As most of the participants were enrolled into hospice primarily for chronic disease processes, they recognized the variable nature of the continual exacerbations and periods of improvement and realized the potential for relapse.

Well, it was mixed feelings. That's a pretty serious thing. I wasn't too excited to be in hospice. That's kind of a finalistic kind of thing. –Alec

Not dying fast enough

Not dying fast enough to qualify for services is a theme seen throughout the transcripts. The participants of this study understood the eligibility requirements established by the Centers for Medicare and Medicaid Services were created to protect the system from abuse. They also understood the disease processes that enabled their enrollment onto hospice in the first place, although terminal, were not producing a quick enough demise to remain on hospice. This knowledge caused some frustration and anger at somehow being blamed for failing to die according to some abstract schedule that is not congruent with their disease process.

You're not cooperating by dying when we thought you would, and you stabilized instead; so we're going to have to discharge you. –Andrew

Hospice equals life

Almost counterintuitive to our society's understanding of hospice, the participants in this study equate hospice with life, not death. Through the support, care, and equipment provided by hospice, these participants were able to remain out of hospital and stabilize. There was no intent to seek a cure by these participants—only a desire to live to the potential allowed by their disease. The loss of hospice represents a return to dying and suffering.

I figure if it wasn't for them, I'd have been dead a long time ago, because I was going to get to the point where I wasn't going back in the hospital anymore. . . . I mean, you go in a week, come home a week, go back the next week. That gets old. . . . I think hospice has kept me living. –Alfred

Discussion

Suffering is the feeling of being alone, alienated, estranged from the community one feels part of. This can be particularly distressing for the chronically ill.[17] Whether it is the understanding of the terminal status of the underlying disease process that preceded the hospice enrollment or the attachment developed while part of the hospice community, participants reported being distressed by the discharge. Discharge from hospice leaves the patient and families in a place that might be described as the in-between of living and dying. No longer are they a member of the hospice community, actively dying and eligible for the care and support they have become accustomed to. Still yoked to a disease that is terminal, they are no longer part of the living either.

Conclusion

The narratives in this study are fraught with paradoxes. Yet the true paradox of hospice discharge is we are surprised by its complexity. Findings of this study support the assumption that the challenges met by patients and families during transition *into* hospice might be the same challenges encountered during the transition *out of* hospice.

The Centers for Medicare and Medicaid Services has guidelines regarding hospice discharge:

> "The hospice notifies its Medicare administrative contractor and Survey administrator of the circumstances surrounding the impending discharge. The hospice should also consider referrals to other appropriate and/or relevant state/community agencies or health care facilities before discharge."[18]

This provision falls short regarding instructions as to how a hospice agency might provide services or to what extent services are required. A dilemma exists in the situation of live hospice discharge. Must we wait for instructions from a regulating body, or should we instead rely on our own ethical stance as health care professionals to do the right thing? Somehow we must provide support to patients and families in need and in doing so we can reduce suffering and improve care. However, we must also provide funding and resources for these services. Without a mandate from a payer source, hospice organizations will be unable and in some cases even barred from providing them.

Author Disclosure Statement—No competing financial interests exist.

References

1. National Hospice and Palliative Care Organization: *NHPCO Facts and Figures: Hospice Care in America, 2011 ed.* www.nhpco.org/files/public/statistics_research/2011_facts_figures.pdf. (Last accessed August 29, 2012.)
2. Kutner J, Meyer S, Beaty B, et al.: Outcomes and characteristics of patients discharged alive from hospice. *J Am Geriatr Soc* 1996;52:1337–1342.
3. Hospice Association of America: *Hospice Facts and Statistics, November 2010.* www.nahc.org/facts/HospiceStats10.pdf. (Last accessed September 6, 2012.)
4. National Hospice and Palliative Care Organization: *NHPCO Facts and Figures: Hospice Care in America, 2009 ed.* www.nhpco.org/files/public/Statistics_Research/NHPCO_facts_and_figures.pdf. (Last accessed September 5, 2012.)
5. Joshi K, Guthmann R, Kishman C: How do we decide when a patient with nonmalignant disease is eligible for hospice care? *J Fam Pract* 2006;55:525–529.
6. Lynn J, Forlini J: "Serious and complex illness" in quality improvement and policy reform for end-of-life care. *J Gen Intern Med* 2001;16:315–319.
7. Huskamp H, Beewkes Buntin M, et al.: Providing care at the end of life: Do Medicare rules impede good care? *Health Aff* (Millwood) 2001;20:204–211.
8. National Hospice and Palliative Care Organization: *NHPCO Facts and Figures: Hospice Care in America, 2007 ed.* www.nhpco.org/research. (Last accessed September 4, 2012.)
9. Kapo J, MacMoran H, Casarett D: "Lost to follow up:" Ethnic disparities in continuity of hospice care at the end of life. *J Palliat Med* 2005;8:603–608.
10. Moustakas C: *Phenomenological Research Methods.* Thousand Oaks, CA: Sage, 1994.
11. Husserl E, Findlay JN (trans): *Logical Investigations.* London: Routledge, 2008. (Original work published 1900.)
12. Moustakas C: *Being-in, Being-for, Being-with.* Northvale, NJ: Jason Aronson, 1995.
13. Dictionary.com. Suffering. (n.d.). dictionary.reference.com/browse/suffering. (Last accessed September 24, 2012.)
14. Thefreedictionary.com. Abandonment. (n.d.). www.thefreedictionary.com/Abandonment. (Last accessed September 24, 2012.)
15. Dictionary.com. Security. (n.d.). dictionary.reference.com/browse/security?s=t. (Last accessed September 24, 2012.)
16. Dictionary.com. Paradox. (n.d.). dictionary.reference.com/browse/paradox. (Last accessed September 24, 2012.)
17. Diekelmann N: *First Do No Harm: Power, Oppression, and Violence in Healthcare.* Madison, WI: University of Wisconsin, 2002.
18. Centers for Medicare and Medicaid Services: Chapter 2, The certification process. In: *State Operation Manual.* www.cms.gov/manuals/downloads/som107c02.pdf. (Last accessed September 6, 2012.)

Critical Thinking

1. Which of the feelings of those expressed after being discharged from hospice alive do you think you would display?
2. What are some of the reasons as to why an individual can be discharged from hospice alive? Do you think that such reasons are valid?
3. How does this research endeavor to utilize the phenomenological design?

Internet References

National Hospice and Palliative Care Organization
   http://www.nhpco.org/sites/default/files/public/newsline/2012/NL_September12.pdf

Today's Hospitalist
   http://www.todayshospitalist.com/index.php?b=articles_read&cnt=432

Article

Prepared by: George E. Dickinson, *College of Charleston*
Michael R. Leming, *St. Olaf College*

A New Vision for Dreams of the Dying

Jan Hoffman

Learning Outcomes

After reading this article, you will be able to:

- Know about dreams of individuals as they are beginning the journey into death.

- Describe characteristics of one in the latter stages of the dying process as viewed through dreams.

- Cite how dreams for a dying individual impact on her/his perception of the death she/he is facing.

One evening in the late fall, Lucien Majors, 84, sat at his kitchen table, his wife Jan by his side, as he described a recent dream.

Mr. Majors had end-stage bladder cancer and was in renal failure. As he spoke with a doctor from Hospice Buffalo, he was alert but faltering.

In the dream, he said, he was in his car with his great pal, Carmen. His three sons, teenagers, were in the back seat, joking around.

"We're driving down Clinton Street," said Mr. Majors, his watery, pale blue eyes widening with delight at the thought of the road trip.

"We were looking for the Grand Canyon." And then they saw it. "We talked about how amazing, because there it was—all this time, the Grand Canyon was just at the end of Clinton Street!"

Mr. Majors had not spoken with Carmen in more than 20 years. His sons are in their late 50s and early 60s.

"Why do you think your boys were in the car?" asked Dr. Christopher W. Kerr, a Hospice Buffalo palliative care physician who researches the therapeutic role of patients' end-of-life dreams and visions.

"My sons are the greatest accomplishment of my life," Mr. Majors said.

He died three weeks later.

For thousands of years, the dreams and visions of the dying have captivated cultures, which imbued them with sacred import. Anthropologists, theologians, and sociologists have studied these so-called deathbed phenomena. They appear in medieval writings and Renaissance paintings, in Shakespearean works and set pieces from 19th-century American and British novels, particularly by Dickens. One of the most famous moments in film is the mysterious deathbed murmur in "Citizen Kane": "Rosebud!"

Even the law reveres a dying person's final words, allowing them to be admitted as evidence in an unusual exception to hearsay rules.

In the modern medical world, such experiences have been noted by psychologists, social workers and nurses. But doctors tend to give them a wide berth because "we don't know what the hell they are," said Dr. Timothy E. Quill an expert on palliative care medicine at the University of Rochester Medical Center. Some researchers have surmised that patients and doctors avoid reporting these phenomena for fear of ridicule.

Now a team of clinicians and researchers led by Dr. Kerr at Hospice Buffalo, an internist who has a doctorate in neurobiology, are seeking to demystify these experiences and understand their role and importance in supporting "a good death"—for the patient and the bereaved.

These events are distinct from "near-death experiences," such as those recalled by people revived in intensive care units, said Pei C. Grant, the director of the research team. "These are people on a journey toward death, not people who just missed it."

Hospice Buffalo, in Cheektowaga, N.Y., cares for 5,000 patients a year, mostly with visits to private homes and nursing facilities. After doctors, nurses, social workers, or chaplains ask patients, "How have you been sleeping?" they often follow up with, "Can you recall any dreams?"

Mainly Comforting Visions

I was laying in bed and people were walking very slowly by me. The right-hand side I didn't know, but they were all very friendly and they touched my arm and my hand as they went by. But the other side were people that I knew—my mom and dad were there, my uncle. Everybody I knew that was dead was there. The only thing was, my husband wasn't there, nor was my dog, and I knew that I would be seeing them.—Jeanne Faber, 75, months before her death from ovarian cancer.

For their primary study, published in *The Journal of Palliative Medicine,* the researchers conducted multiple interviews with 59 terminally ill patients admitted to acute care at Hospice Buffalo, a facility furnished in warm woods, with windows that frame views of fountains, gazebos, and gardens. Nearly all the patients reported having had dreams or visions. They described the majority of their dreams as comforting. About one in every five was associated with distress, and the remainder felt neutral.

The dreams and visions loosely sorted into categories: opportunities to engage with the deceased; loved ones "waiting;" unfinished business. Themes of love, given or withheld, coursed through the dreams, as did the need for resolution and even forgiveness. In their dreams, patients were reassured that they had been good parents, children and workers. They packed boxes, preparing for journeys, and, like Mr. Majors, often traveled with dear companions as guides. Although many patients said that they rarely remembered their dreams, these they could not forget.

A 76-year-old patient said he dreamed of his mother, who died when he was a child. He could smell her perfume and hear her soothing voice saying, "I love you."

An older woman cradled an invisible infant as she lay in bed. (Her husband told researchers it was the couple's first child, who had been stillborn.)

Nine days before she died, a 54-year-old woman dreamed of a childhood friend who had caused her great pain decades earlier. The friend, who had since died, appeared as an old man and said, "Sorry, you're a good person," and "If you need help, just call my name."

This is certainly research in its infancy. The investigators, counselors and palliative care doctors, are trying to identify and describe the phenomena. Dr. Quill said that he believed the studies would help make these experiences more accessible to skeptical doctors.

"The huge challenge of this work is to help patients feel more normal and less alone during this unusual experience of dying," he said. "The more we can articulate that people do have vivid dreams and visions, the more we can be helpful."

Other research suggests that dreams seem to express emotions that have been building. Tore Nielsen, a dream neuroscience researcher and director of the Dream and Nightmare Laboratory, at the University of Montreal, surmised that at the end of life, such a need becomes more insistent. Troubled dreams erupt with excessive energy. But positive dreams can serve a similar purpose.

"The motivation and pressure for these dreams is coming from a place of fear and uncertainty," he said. "The dreamers are literally helping themselves out of a tough spot."

In the weeks and days before death, the dreams of the patients in the study tended to occur with greater frequency, populated with the dead rather than the living. The researchers suggest that such phenomena might even have prognostic value.

"I was an aggressive physician, always asking, 'Is there more we can do?' " said Dr. Kerr, who is also the chief medical officer for Hospice Buffalo. "There was a patient who I thought needed to be rehydrated, and we could buy him some time." But, he said, a nurse, familiar with the patient's dreams, cautioned: " 'You don't get it. He is seeing his dead mother.' He died two days later."

Certainly, many dying patients cannot communicate. Or they recount typical dream detritus: a dwarf lifting the refrigerator, neighbors bringing a chicken and a monkey into the patient's apartment. And some patients, to their disappointment, do not remember their dreams.

Dr. Kerr, who recently gave a talk at TEDxBuffalo about the research, said he was simply advocating that health care providers ask patients open-ended questions about dreams, without fear of recrimination from family and colleagues.

"Often when we sedate them, we are sterilizing them from their own dying process," he said. "I have done it, and it feels horrible. They'll say, 'You robbed me—I was with my wife.' "

Complexities of Delirium

While the patient was lying in bed, her mother by her side, she had a vision: She saw her mother's best friend, Mary, who died of leukemia years ago, in her mother's bedroom, playing with the curtains. Mary's hair was long again. "I had a feeling she was coming to say, 'You're going to be O.K.' I felt relief and happiness and I wasn't afraid of it at all."—Jessica Stone, 13, who had Ewing's sarcoma, a type of bone cancer, a few months before she died.

Many in hospice suffer from delirium, which can affect up to 85 percent of hospitalized patients at the end of life. In a delirious state, brought on by fever, brain metastases or end-stage changes in body chemistry, circadian rhythms are severely disordered, so the patient may not know whether he is awake or dreaming. Cognition is altered.

Those who care for the terminally ill are inclined to see end-of-life dreams as manifestations of delirium. But the Hospice Buffalo researchers say that while some study patients slipped in and out of delirium, their end-of-life dreams were not, by definition, the product of such a state. Delirious patients generally cannot engage with others or give a coherent, organized narrative. The hallucinations they are able to describe may be traumatizing, not comforting.

Yet the question remains of what to make of these patients' claims of "dreaming while awake," or having "visions"—and the not-uncommon phenomena of seeing deceased relatives or friends hovering on the ceiling or in corners.

Donna Brennan, a longtime nurse with Hospice Buffalo, recalled chatting on the couch with a 92-year-old patient with congestive heart failure. Suddenly, the patient looked over at the door and called out, "Just a minute, I'm speaking with the nurse."

Told that no one was there, the patient smiled, saying it was Aunt Janiece (her dead sister) and patted a couch cushion, showing "the visitor" where to sit. Then the patient cheerfully turned back to Mrs. Brennan and finished her conversation.

In her notes, Mrs. Brennan described the episode as a "hallucination," a red flag for delirium. When the episode was recounted to Dr. Kerr and Anne Banas, a Hospice Buffalo neurologist and palliative care physician, they preferred the term "vision."

"Is there meaning to the vision or is it disorganized?" Dr. Banas asked. "If there is meaning, does that need to be explored? Does it bring comfort or is it distressing? We have a responsibility to ask that next question. It can be cathartic, and patients often need to share. And if we don't ask, look what we may miss."

Dr. William Breitbart, chairman of the psychiatry department at Memorial Sloan Kettering Cancer Center, who has written about delirium and palliative care, said that a team's response must also consider bedside caregivers: "These dreams or visions can be interpreted by family members as comforting, linking them to the legacy of their ancestry.

"But if people don't believe that, they can be distressed. 'My mother is hallucinating and seeing dead people. Do something about it!'" Dr. Breitbart trains staff to respect the families' beliefs and help them understand the complexities of delirium.

Some dream episodes occur during what is known as "mixed-state sleep"—when the boundaries between wakefulness and sleep become fragmented, said Dr. Carlos H. Schenck, a psychiatrist and sleep expert at the University of Minnesota Medical School. Jessica Stone, the teenager with Ewing's sarcoma, spoke movingly about a dream of her dead dog, Shadow.

When she awoke, she said, she saw his long, dark shape alongside her bed.

Dr. Banas, the neurologist, favors the phrase end-of-life experiences. "I try to normalize it for the family, because how they perceive it can push them away from that bedside or bring them closer," she said.

Reliving Trauma

The patient had never really talked about the war. But in his final dreams, the stories emerged. In the first, the bloody dying were everywhere. On Omaha Beach, at Normandy. In the waves. He was a 17-year-old gunner on a rescue boat, trying frantically to bring them back to the U.S.S. Texas. "There is nothing but death and dead soldiers all around me," he said. In another, a dead soldier told him, "They are going to come get you next week." Finally, he dreamed of getting his discharge papers, which he described as "comforting." He died in his sleep two days later.—John, 88, who had lymphoma.

Not all end-of-life dreams soothe the dying. Researchers found that about 20 percent were upsetting. Often, those who had suffered trauma might revisit it in their dying dreams. Some can resolve those experiences. Some cannot.

When should doctors intervene with antipsychotic or anti-anxiety medication, to best allow the patient a peaceful death? For the Hospice Buffalo physicians, the decision is made with a team assessment that includes input from family members.

Dr. Kerr said: "Children will see their parents in an altered state and think they're suffering and fighting their dying. But if you say: 'She's talking about dead people, and that's normal. I'll bet you can learn a lot about her and your family,' you may see the relative calming down and taking notes."

Without receiving sufficient information from the family, a team may not know how to read the patient's agitation. One patient seemed tormented by nightmares. The Hospice Buffalo team interviewed family members, who reluctantly disclosed that the woman had been sexually abused as a girl. The family was horrified that she was reliving these memories in her dying days.

Armed with this information, the team chose to administer anti-anxiety medication, rather than just antipsychotics. The woman relaxed and was able to have a powerful exchange with a priest. She died during a quiet sleep, several days later.

This fall, Mrs. Brennan, the nurse, would check in on a patient with end-stage lung cancer who was a former police officer. He told her that he had "done bad stuff" on the job. He said he had cheated on his wife and was estranged from his children. His dreams are never peaceful, Mrs. Brennan said.

"He gets stabbed, shot or can't breathe. He apologizes to his wife, and she isn't responding, or she reminds him that he broke her heart. He's a tortured soul."

Some palliative care providers maintain that such dreams are the core of a spiritual experience and should not be tampered with. Dr. Quill, who calls people with such views "hospice romantics," disagreed.

"We should be opening the door with our questions, but not forcing patients through it," Dr. Quill said. "Our job is witnessing, exploring and lessening their loneliness. If it's benign and rich with content, let it go. But if it brings up serious old wounds, get real help—a psychologist, a chaplain—because in this area, we physicians don't know what we're doing. "

Solace for the Living

In the first dream, a black spider with small eyes came close to her face. Then it turned into a large black truck with a red flatbed, bearing down on her. Terrified, she forced herself awake. In another dream, she had to pass through her laundry room to get to the kitchen. She glanced down and saw about 50 black spiders crawling on the floor. She was so scared! But when she looked closer, she saw they were ladybugs. She felt so happy! "Ladybugs are nice and I knew they weren't going to hurt me," she recounted later. "So I made my way to the kitchen."—Rosemary Shaffer, 78, two months before she died of colon cancer.

The Hospice Buffalo researchers have found that these dreams offer comfort not only for the dying but also for their mourners.

Kathleen Hutton holds fast to the end-of-life dream journals fastidiously kept by her sister, Mrs. Shaffer, a former elementary schoolteacher and principal. Rosemary Shaffer wrote about spiders and trucks, and then the ladybugs. In one dream, she saw flowers at a funeral home, which reminded her of those her daughter painted on handmade scarves. She felt loved and joyful.

"I was glad she could talk about dreams with the hospice people," Ms. Hutton said. "She knew it was her subconscious working through what she was feeling. She was much more at peace."

Knowing that has made her own grief more manageable, said Ms. Hutton, who teared up as she clasped the journals during a visit at the hospice's family lounge.

Several months ago, Mrs. Brennan, the nurse, sat with a distraught husband, whose wife had pancreatic cancer that had spread to the liver. She had been reporting dreams about work, God and familiar people who had died. The patient thought that she would be welcomed in heaven, she said. That God told her she had been a good wife and mother.

"Her husband was angry at God," Mrs. Brennan said. "I said: 'But Ann is not. Her dreams aren't scary to her at all. They are all about validation.'

"He just put his head down and wept."

Critical Thinking

1. What did you learn about recent research on dreams individuals have prior to their death?

2. How do the dreams of those in the latter stages of dying differ from individuals having near death experiences?

3. What are some of the positive outcomes of dreams experienced by the dying?

Internet References

Next Avenue
   www.nextavenue.org/what-the-dreams-of-the-dying-teach
Psychic Library
   http://psychiclibrary.com/beyondBooks/death-and-dying-dreams/

Prepared by: George E. Dickinson, *College of Charleston*
Michael R. Leming, *St. Olaf College*

Article

The Impact of Faith Beliefs on Perceptions of End-of-Life Care and Decision Making among African American Church Members

JERRY JOHNSON ET AL.

Learning Outcomes

After reading this article, you will be able to:

- Discuss the relation between faith beliefs and end-of-life care in the African American community.

- Cite how faith beliefs of African Americans can support discussions about palliative care and hospice.

- Identify the challenges of communicating with African Americans about end-of-life care.

Introduction

Despite the documented desire among African American patients with life-limiting illnesses or of their family members to minimize pain and suffering, African Americans underuse palliative care and hospice services.[1,2] Although African Americans represent 13% of the U.S. population, in 2011 only 8.5% of hospice enrollees were African American.[3] In a 2010 study of a national sample of 220,000 Medicare patients, the non-white patients, most of whom were African American, were 20% less likely to enroll in hospice than their white counterparts.[4] For minorities who enrolled in hospice, the same study showed that non-white patients were more likely to have an intensive care unit stay (16.9% versus 13.3%) and to disenroll from hospice (11.6% versus 7.2%). Because of this disproportionately low rate of participation of African Americans in palliative care and hospice, many African Americans who are eligible for end-of-life (EOL) care are deprived of the benefits associated with palliative care and hospice services.[5–7]

Improved communication within families and between families and health professionals about EOL decisions and expectations of care is necessary for African Americans to make informed choices about palliative care and hospice.[8–11] A recent study of persons with metastatic lung and colorectal cancer who had chosen chemotherapy and who had discussed chemotherapy with a physician revealed African Americans were 2.93 times as likely as whites to have the inaccurate belief that chemotherapy was "very likely to lead to cure."[12] Spiritual and cultural beliefs, distrust of health systems and health professionals as an outgrowth of historical events and social patterns, and insufficient knowledge about palliative care and hospice resources contribute to ineffective communication about EOL care.[13–16] Therefore, efforts to improve communication must consider each of these factors.

African American churches present an opportunity to engage the African American population in a dialogue about palliative care and hospice services.[17–20] Compared with other racial and ethnic groups, African Americans are among the most religious.[21–24] These faith beliefs may contribute to statements that portray palliative care as the antithesis of having faith—"Only the Lord knows when I am going to die"—revealing the need to involve the church as a venue to educate African American patients and families about palliative care and hospice and ensure them that palliative care and hospice care can align with their religious beliefs.[25,26] Yet, few studies have involved the African American church in research designed to improve communication about EOL care and decision making.[27–29] The studies that have involved the African American church have not targeted the persons within traditional African American church structures who most often visit persons with life-limiting illnesses.

In a multiyear participatory research project, we have engaged the leadership and congregants of African American churches in Philadelphia with the goal of developing a comprehensive, church-based education and support program that will improve communication about palliative care and hospice among African American patients, their family members, and health professionals. We found that members of church ministries (e.g., deacons, health or bereavement ministries) commonly visit persons with life-limiting illnesses on behalf of the church. However, these persons often are unprepared to bridge the communication gaps about EOL care. For example, they are not prepared to help persons understand the distinction between goals of care and processes of care, distinctions critical to EOL decision making. Nor do they understand the meaning of interventions such as artificial feeding and cardiopulmonary resuscitation that are frequently considered at the end of life. Last, they often have limited knowledge of palliative care and hospice services. Prior to designing an intervention targeting those who make visits, we recognized the need to assess their attitudes and perceptions about EOL care. We conducted a focus group study to ascertain the spiritual and other perspectives that influence choices and preferences for palliative care and hospice among African American church members who commonly visit and support persons at the EOL. Our specific aims were to elicit their perceptions, beliefs, and attitudes about: (1) the relation between faith beliefs and EOL care, (2) emotional and family influences on EOL decision-making, (3) palliative care and hospice resources and services, and (4) opportunities to improve communication among lay persons and health professionals and within families.

Methods
Participants and recruitment procedures
After a dialogue about palliative care and hospice with the pastors of several African American churches in Philadelphia, we partnered with two African American churches to conduct this phase of our research because of their interest in improving access to information about palliative care and hospice services for their congregants and their interest in participating in research about palliative care and hospice. Each church identified a representative to join the research team and to assist with identifying and recruiting focus group participants. We targeted members of the churches' health- and bereavement-related ministries and deacons and deaconesses, who routinely visit and support persons with life-limiting illnesses. Pastors of the churches endorsed the project but were excluded from the focus groups because of their potential influence on the views of other participants.

The 7 focus groups comprised 51 persons who frequently made visits to persons with (life-limiting illnesses). Of this group, 27 persons were deacons or deaconesses, 17 were members of health or bereavement ministries, and the other 7 were members of the general congregation. Participants ranged in age from 45 to 80 years of age and 32 were women.

Development of focus group guide and focus group procedures
Members of the university staff and the church representatives developed a focus group guide. Topics and questions were informed by literature review, the views of the church representatives, and the research team's experiences with palliative care and hospice and community-based research. The focus group opened with a statement that "Our goal is to find out what would help you communicate more effectively with people in your congregation who are making end-of-life decisions because of illnesses." We referred to the end of life rather than alternative expressions such as "serious illness" so that participants would convey their thoughts and feelings about death and dying. We used open-ended questions such as "What would you say are the major concerns of persons and their families as they face the end of life?" Other key questions are shown in the Results section.

We conducted three focus groups at one church and four at the other. Focus groups were conducted onsite at each church, and each group lasted approximately 90 minutes. All focus groups were moderated by a trained facilitator. One member of the research team took notes to capture broad themes. Another member of the team served as an observer to describe and record group dynamics and to note which questions and topics generated the most active discussions or caused discomfort. All groups were audio-recorded and transcribed; participants were informed of the recording and provided written informed consent. The study was reviewed and approved by the University of Pennsylvania Institutional Review Board. Focus group participants received a $25.00 gift card.

Data analysis
Three members of the research team analyzed the focus group transcripts. First, members of the team read each transcript and then met to develop major coding categories (domains) and subcategories (components of each domain).

Domains and subcategories were defined, revised, and refined through a series of consensus meetings. Themes and patterns were identified within each domain, and illustrative quotes were selected to represent and capture each major theme related to the study aims.

Results

Participants voiced a consensus that patients, caregivers, and family members of their churches need more knowledge about EOL care and that congregants harbor beliefs, perceptions, and feelings about death and dying that were often not communicated to their family members or to health care providers. Findings were grouped in five categories: (1) influence of faith on EOL decision making, (2) emotional burden, (3) family dynamics, (4) facts and myths about palliative care and hospice, and (5) communicating with health care professionals.

Influence of faith on EOL decision making

The participants were asked two questions about the role that faith has or can have when persons are facing death: (1) How have you found that persons with strong faith beliefs view death from illnesses? and (2) How does having faith help persons cope with death and dying? Participants said that having faith provides peace, calmness, acceptance, less fear of death, strength, endurance of the ups or downs of the illness, and less suffering. Participants described three aspects of faith: trust in the power of God, recognition that death is the beginning of a new life, and belief in a better life after death.

> No matter what it is. God is going to take care of me.
>
> Death is the end of the physical life and the beginning of spiritual life.
>
> When it was time for her to go, she said to me, I am going home to be with Jesus. Do not worry about me at all. I am ready.

Emotional burden

Participants identified many emotional responses experienced by both the patient and family: denial, anger, fear, grief, guilt, loneliness, loss of control, fear of loss, and fear of talking about and planning for EOL care. An exemplary statement by one person was, "feeling drenched in other people's emotions." Another feared the loneliness and loss of: "the break in the family chain."

Family dynamics

Participants were asked "How can communication about EOL be improved within families?" Participants acknowledged that long-standing family dynamics influence EOL decisions.

Conflicts ranged from denial of the pending deaths by the patient, the family, or both; different views over decision-making authority; and potentially conflicting faith beliefs (e.g., Christian parent of an adult child of Islam faith). Two participants stated:

> In my family . . . they just cannot make decisions.
>
> And the last thing that resonated with me from my father was I know it was very important to him that his family be together, but we were not all at the same place.

Participants recognized that when family members are at odds, the dignity of the patient can be overlooked. One participant said:

> A lot of folks—the family member wants to have their dignity and the family may want this and this and the dignity piece is often overlooked.

Facts and myths about palliative care and hospice

We asked participants questions to elicit information about their knowledge, attitudes and perceptions of palliative care and hospice: What do you think of when you hear the terms "palliative care" and "hospice care?" Many participants were unfamiliar with the term "palliative care," although they referred to a desire of patients, caregivers, and family members for comfort and support as important EOL goals. Some persons were either unsure what hospice meant or knew other persons who were unsure. Several positive attributes ascribed to hospice were (1) offers a chance to say good-bye, (2) assists patient and family with closure, (3) provides the comfort, support, and care the patient needs, (4) brings joy if enrolled in "the right hospice program," (5) provides support to family, and (6) restores dignity, especially if offered in the home. One participant stated that experience with hospice was likely to induce positive feelings.

> I know if they have the right hospice program, it is a wonderful, wonderful, wonderful way to end life . . . it is so much less painful because they [hospice personnel] are truly there. . .

Participants expressed the need for factual information about hospice services and how to access those services before seeing hospice as a viable option. As one person said:

> When hospice came in to talk to me about you know letting them take care of him, I had no idea what hospice was. I put my guards up. But once the hospice people came and talked (to) me and explained to me, I trusted them.

The Impact of Faith Beliefs on Perceptions of End-of-Life Care and Decision Making by Jerry Johnson et al.

63

For other participants, particularly those with no exposure to hospice services, hospice meant "no hope . . ."; "You're on your death bed; you're on your way out." They expressed negative feelings or reported that they knew people who felt negatively about hospice:

> When I hear somebody is in hospice, it is almost like somebody just slapped me in the face. It is always a shock no matter who it is, no matter.

Communication with health professionals

We asked: "How can communication between health care professionals and persons with life-limiting illnesses or their families be improved?" Participants perceived that many of their fellow congregants harbor beliefs, perceptions, and feelings about death and dying that were often not communicated to family members or to health care providers. A majority of the participants responded that communications with health care professionals were unsatisfactory.

One person lamented the brevity of discussions, saying that the time with the health care professional "was often limited to 15 minutes." Participants want health professionals to use terms that they can understand and they want "not to be ignored or feel ignored when being given information about their condition."

Discussion

We conducted a focus group study of members of African American churches who visit and support their fellow congregants with life-limiting illnesses on behalf of the church. Our goal was to determine their perceptions, beliefs, and attitudes about the relationship between faith beliefs and EOL care; emotional and family influences on EOL decision making; palliative care and hospice resources and services; and opportunities to improve communication among lay persons and health professionals and within families. We found that faith beliefs, emotional issues and family dynamics, and insufficient knowledge of palliative care and hospice are intertwined. Our findings confirm the influence of faith beliefs on decisions about palliative care and hospice. We found that faith beliefs can support discussions about palliative care and hospice. However, we also found significant emotional distress (sometimes couched in spiritual terms) regarding acceptance of death. Health care providers should not be surprised when the same person views death as a transition to a better life and as something to be avoided by obtaining medical interventions. We found that for many African Americans, "palliative care" is an unfamiliar and confusing term. On the other hand, persons held strong beliefs about hospice, whether or not those beliefs were accurate. Supportive views about hospice were often expressed

by persons with prior experience with hospice. Participants expressed uncertainty as to how to approach health care providers and what questions to ask. These views confirm the need to improve communication about palliative care and hospice and EOL decision making and an opportunity to use the African American church as a venue to attain this goal.

Our findings are consistent with other studies that reveal the challenges of communicating with African Americans about EOL care. These studies demonstrate the complex interplay of historical and social experiences, faith beliefs, and lack of information that shape patients' views and preferences about EOL care.[30] The studies reveal a lower likelihood of preparing living wills, less knowledge about palliative care and hospice and advance directives, lack of trust in health care systems, and a significant influence of spirituality and faith beliefs on end of life decision making.[10,11,29,31,32] A study of the influence of culture on communication among persons near the end of life because of cancer showed that African Americans often requested spiritual-focused information and desired to have a spiritual leader participate in EOL decision making.[10] In another study, some African Americans viewed pain and suffering as a spiritual obligation, a view that might dissuade the use of palliative care and hospice services.[33] In contrast, our findings suggest that professionals can embrace the faith beliefs of their African American patients as an asset rather than a barrier.

African American churches have participated in studies about EOL decision making and care, particularly in efforts to recruit research participants.[34] Several studies examined the views and attitudes of church members about advance directives, palliative care, or hospice.[29] In response to questions about advance directives, 75% of the focus group participants in 12 churches in rural North Carolina rejected the offer to complete an advance directive, largely because of spiritual beliefs.[25] A survey of members of 11 churches in North Carolina found that most participants thought advance directives were not needed and also demonstrated a general lack of knowledge of the benefits provided by hospice.[35] Similar to our study, the church survey emphasized the significance of the family in making EOL decisions. Last, a few studies have queried pastors and found them to be receptive to increasing their knowledge and that of their congregants about opportunties to improve EOL care.[27,36]

African Americans recruited through churches have served as lay or peer advisors for persons who were characterized as having serious illnesses.[28] In this study, lay persons, many of them from the church community, working alone as visitors, expressed discomfort and a lack of preparedness to assume roles as health visitors for persons at the end of life. This study found a support team model of visitations more effective. Support team members most often provided practical (e.g., meals and errands), emotional (shared time and visits), and spiritual (praying) support. However, they did not undertake the challenges of bridging the communication gaps about EOL care and rarely provided information about palliative care. We conclude that new models are required to prepare African American church members to assist their fellow church members overcome the communication challenges about palliative care and hospice and that the church provides a venue to increase awareness and knowledge.

We note two significant limitations of our study. First, all of our focus group participants were Baptists. Members of other denominations may have different views based on church doctrine or have different structures to support persons with life-limiting illnesses. We note that the Baptist faith is the dominant faith among African Americans with 45% of African Americans considering themselves Baptist.[37] Second, we did not involve pastors and ministers in our focus groups because of concern that they would influence the views of the other participants. We note that most visits to persons with life-limiting illnesses are conducted by church members other than pastors, such as the persons enrolled in this study. Nevertheless, more EOL research should target the African American ministers and pastors because of their role in establishing chuch policies and their significance to congregants.

The Initiative to Improve Palliative and End of Life Care in the African American Community, an interdisciplinary work group of African American scholars and professionals, voiced the need for new care delivery models and education of health professionals and lay persons in the care of African Americans at the end of life.[33] Our findings from church members and ministries charged with visiting African Americans with life-limiting illnesses add insights necessary to develop and evaluate new church based models of care sensitive to the beliefs and attitudes of African Americans. Our findings suggest several directions for future research: (1) testing alternative approaches to affirming faith beliefs while accepting palliative care and hospice as an option for care; (2) testing the impact of framing palliative care and hospice as part of good care along the spectrum of illness severity and pointing out that hospice care may have a survival benefit for persons who are at the EOL; (3) encompassing prior experiences of church members who have had a favorable experience with hospice as a means of focusing on selecting the right hospice rather than focusing on hospice care versus non-hospice care; and (4) can churches be aligned with hospice programs that are viewed favorably by church members? Although the vehicle, or to use the language of community based participatory research, the "unit of identity," for our research is the church, lessons learned from working within the church structure are applicable to communications with African Americans about EOL decision making, irrespective of their church affiliations. For example, the

meaning of comfort vs. suffering, when considering intensive treatments at the end of life, has faith based connotations that can be explored in many settings. This body of research will enrich our understanding of the influence of faith beliefs on EOL decision making among African Americans and position health professionals to bridge the current communications gap about palliative care and hospice services.

References

1. Torke AM, Garas NS, Sexson W, et al.: Medical care at the end of life: Views of African American patients in an urban hospital. *J Palliat Med* 2005;8:593–602.
2. Waters CM: Understanding and supporting African Americans' perspectives of end-of-life care planning and decision making. *Qual Health Res* 2001;11:385–398.
3. Hospice Care in America Facts and Figures: National Hospicre and Palliative Care Organization: 2012.
4. Unroe KT, Greiner MA, Johnson KS, et al.: Racial differences in hospice use and patterns of care after enrollment in hospice among Medicare beneficiaries with heart failure. *Am Heart J* 2012;163:987–993 e983.
5. Braun UK, Beyth RJ, Ford ME, et al.: Voices of African American, Caucasian, and Hispanic surrogates on the burdens of end-of-life decision making. *J Gen Intern Med* 2008;23:267–274.
6. Peereboom K, Coyle N: Facilitating goals of care discussions for patient with life-limiting disease-communication strategies for nurses. *J Hosp Palliat Care Nurs* 2012;14:251–258.
7. Kelley AS, Deb P, Du Q, et al.: Hospice enrollment saves money for Medicare and improves care quality across a number of different lengths-of-stay. *Health Aff* (Millwood) 2013;32:552–561.
8. Quill TE: Perspectives on care at the close of life. Initiating end-of-life discussions with seriously ill patients: Addressing the "elephant in the room." *JAMA* 2000;284:2502–2507.
9. Wright AA, Zhang B, Ray A, et al.: Associations between end-of-life discussions, patient mental health, medical care near death, and caregiver bereavement adjustment. *JAMA* 2008;300:1665–1673.
10. Shrank WH, Kutner JS, Richardson T, et al.: Focus group findings about the influence of culture on communication preferences in end-of-life care. *J Gen Intern Med* 2005;20:703–709.
11. Wicher CP, Meeker MA: What influences African American end-of-life preferences? *J Health Care Poor Underserved* 2012;23:28–58.
12. Weeks JC, Catalano PJ, Cronin A, et al.: Patients' expectations about effects of chemotherapy for advanced cancer. *N Engl J Med* 2012;367:1616–1625.
13. Crawley LM: Palliative care in African American communities. *J Palliat Med* 2002;5:775–779.
14. Crawley LM, Marshall PA, Lo B, et al.: Strategies for culturally effective end-of-life care. *Ann Intern Med* 2002;136:673–679.
15. Duffy S, Jackson F, Schim S, et al.: Cultural concepts at the end of life. *Nurs Older People* 2006;18:10–014.

The Impact of Faith Beliefs on Perceptions of End-of-Life Care and Decision Making by Jerry Johnson et al.

65

16. Krakauer EL, Crenner C, Fox K: Barriers to optimum end-of-life care for minority patients. *J Am Geriatr Soc* 2002;50:182–190.

17. Cnaan RA, Boddie SC, Kang J: Religious congregations as social services providers for older adults. *J Gerontol Soc Work* 2005;45:105–130.

18. Miller WR. Thoresen CE: Spirituality, religion, and health. An emerging research field. *Am Psychol* 2003;58:24–35.

19. Neighbors HW, Musick MA, Williams DR: The African American minister as a source of help for serious personal crises: Bridge or barrier to mental health care? *Health Educ Behav* 1998;25:759–777.

20. Williams DR, Sternthal MJ: Spirituality, religion and health: Evidence and research directions. *Med J Aust* 2007;186(10 Suppl):S47–50.

21. Taylor RJ, Chatters LM, Levin J: *Religion in the Lives of African Americans: Social, Psychological, and Health Perspectives.* Thousand Oaks, CA: Sage Publications, Inc.; 2004.

22. Koenig H, George L, Titus P, et al.: Religion, spirituality, and acute care hospitalization and long-term care use by older patients. *Arch Intern Med* 2004;164:1579–1585.

23. Levin JS, Taylor RJ. Chatters LM: Race and gender differences in religiosity among older adults: Findings from four national surveys. *J Gerontol* 1994;49:S137–145.

24. Taylor RJ, Chatters LM: Nonorganizational religious participation among elderly black adults. *J Gerontol* 1991;46:S103–111.

25. Bullock K: Promoting advance directives among African Americans: A faith-based model. *J Palliat Med* 2006;9:183–195.

26. Perkins HS: Ethics expertise and cultural competence. *Virtual Mentor* 2006;8:79–83.

27. Green MA, Lucas J, Hanson LC, et al.: Carrying the burden: Perspectives of African American pastors on peer support for people with cancer. *J Relig Health* 2014;53:1382–1397.

28. Hanson LC, Armstrong TD, Green MA, et al.: Circles of care: development and initial evaluation of a peer support model for African Americans with advanced cancer. *Health Educ Behav* 2013;40:536–543.

29. Johnson KS, Kuchibhatla M, Tulsky JA: What explains racial differences in the use of advance directives and attitudes toward hospice care? *J Am Geriatr Soc* 2008;56:1953–1958.

30. True G, Phipps EJ, Braitman LE, et al.: Treatment preferences and advance care planning at end of life: The role of ethnicity and spiritual coping in cancer patients. *Ann Behav Med* 2005;30:174–179.

31. Johnson KS, Kuchibhatla M, Tulsky JA: Racial differences in self-reported exposure to information about hospice care. *J Palliat Med* 2009;12:921–927.

32. Perkins HS, Geppert CM, Gonzales A, et al.: Cross-cultural similarities and differences in attitudes about advance care planning. *J Gen Intern Med* 2002;17:48–57.

33. Crawley L. Payne R, Bolden J, et al.: Palliative and end-of-life care in the African American community. *JAMA* 2000;284:2518–2521.

34. Payne R, Payne TR: The Harlem Palliative Care Network. *J Palliat Med* 2002;5:781–792.

35. Yancu CN, Farmer DF, Leahman D: Barriers to hospice use and palliative care services use by African American adults. *Am J Hosp Palliat Care* 2010;27:248–253.

36. Reese DJ, Ahern RE, Nair S, et al.: Hospice access and use by African Americans: Addressing cultural and institutional barriers through participatory action research. *Soc Work* 1999;44:549–559.

37. Sahgal N, Smith G: A religious portrait of African Americans. In: *The Pew Forum on Religion and Public Life, Volume 389.* Washington, D.C.: Pew Research Center, 2009, pp. 1–5.

Critical Thinking

1. What are some of the issues surrounding religious beliefs of African Americans as compared to others in the United States regarding end-of-life issues?
2. Describe the Initiative to Improve Palliative and End-of-Life Care in the African American community. How would you rate its success based on the findings in the article?
3. What is a focus group and how can such be effective in gaining ideas/opinions from a group of individuals?

Internet References

EthnoMed
   https://ethnomed.org/clinical/end-of-life/cultural-relevance-in-end-of-life-care/
Medscape
   http://www.medscape.com/viewarticle/726462

Acknowledgments—The work underlying this article could not have been conducted without the support of the First African Baptist Church and The Pinn Memorial Baptist Church.

Author Disclosure Statement—No competing financial interests exist.

Unit 4

UNIT

Prepared by: George E. Dickinson, *College of Charleston*
Michael R. Leming, *St. Olaf College*

Ethical Issues of Dying and Death

One of the concerns about dying and death that is pressing hard upon our consciences is the question of helping the dying to die sooner with the assistance of the physician. Public awareness of the horrors that can visit upon us by artificial means of ventilation and other support measures in a high-tech hospital setting has produced a literature that debates the issue of euthanasia—a "good death." As individuals think through their plans for care when dying, there is a steady increase in the demand for control of that care. Another controversial issue is physician-assisted suicide. Is it the function of the doctor to assist patients in their dying—to actually kill them at their request? This has become commonplace in the Netherlands and there is much debate concerning the spread of this model of care to the United States. Many are concerned about the so-called "slippery slope," where physician aid in dying will be extended to the disabled, vulnerable adults, and even to children.

Legislative action has been taken in some states (Montana, Oregon, Vermont, and Washington), to permit this, and the issue is pending in a number of others. We are in a time of intense consideration by the courts, by the legislatures, and by the medical and nursing professions of the legality and the morality of providing the means by which a person can bring about their own death. Is this the role of healthcare providers? The pro and contra positions are presented in several of the unit's articles. Although the issue is difficult and personally challenging, as a nation we are in the position of being required to make difficult choices. There are no "right" answers; the questions pose dilemmas that require choices based upon moral, spiritual, and legal foundations.

Key Points to Consider

The question, "What is a good death?" has been asked for centuries. What would constitute a good death in this time of high-tech medical care? Does the concept of a good death include the taking of a life? Defend your answer.

Does the role of the healthcare provider include taking life or providing the means for others to do so? Why or why not?

Are constraints required to prevent the killing of persons we do not consider worthwhile contributors to our society? Explain.

Should limits be placed on the length of life as we consider the expenses involved in the care of the elderly and the infirm?

Article   Prepared by: George E. Dickinson, *College of Charleston*
Michael R. Leming, *St. Olaf College*

Ethics and Life's Ending

An Exchange

ROBERT D. ORR AND GILBERT MEILAENDER

Learning Outcomes

After reading this article, you will be able to:

- Understand the difference between a durable power of attorney and a living will.

- Understand the importance of having a living will and the limitations of such legal documents.

- Gain an appreciation for the difficulty in determining issues surrounding the relationship between extra-ordinary and ordinary measures of treating patients and withholding and withdrawing life support.

Feeding tubes make the news periodically, and controversies over their use or non-use seem unusually contentious. But feeding tubes are not high technology treatment; they are simple, small-bore catheters made of soft synthetic material. Nor are they new technology; feeding tubes were first used in 1793 by John Hunter to introduce jellies, eggs, sugar, milk, and wine into the stomachs of patients unable to swallow. Why does this old, low-tech treatment generate such controversy today? The important question is not whether a feeding tube *can* be used, but whether it *should* be used in a particular situation.

Too often in medicine we use a diagnostic or therapeutic intervention just because it is available. This thoughtless approach is sometimes called the technological imperative, i.e., the impulse to do everything we are trained to do, regardless of the burden or benefit. Kidney failure? Let's do dialysis. Respiratory failure? Let's use a ventilator. Unable to eat? Let's put in a feeding tube. By responding in this way, the physician ignores the maxim "the ability to act does not justify the action." Just because we know how to artificially breathe for a patient in respiratory failure

doesn't mean that everyone who cannot breathe adequately must be put on a ventilator. Such a response also represents a failure to do the moral work of assessing whether the treatment is appropriate in a particular situation.

The moral debate about the use or non-use of feeding tubes hinges on three important considerations: the distinction between what in the past was called "ordinary" and "extraordinary" treatments; the important social symbolism of feeding; and a distinction between withholding and withdrawing treatments.

It was recognized many years ago that respirators, dialysis machines, and other high-tech modes of treatment are optional. They could be used or not used depending on the circumstances. However, it was commonly accepted in the past that feeding tubes are generally not optional. Part of the reasoning was that feeding tubes are readily available, simple to use, not very burdensome to the patient, and not very expensive. They were "ordinary treatment" and thus morally obligatory.

Ordinary [versus] Extraordinary

For over four hundred years, traditional moral theology distinguished between ordinary and extraordinary means of saving life. Ordinary means were those that were not too painful or burdensome for the patient, were not too expensive, and had a reasonable chance of working. These ordinary treatments were deemed morally obligatory. Those treatments that did involve undue burden were extraordinary and thus optional. This distinction was common knowledge in religious and secular circles, and this language and reasoning was commonly applied in Western society.

As medical treatments became more complicated, it was recognized that this distinction was sometimes not helpful. The problem was that the designation appeared to belong to the treatment itself, rather than to the situation. The respirator and dialysis machine were categorized as extraordinary while antibiotics and feeding tubes were classed as ordinary. But real-life situations were not that simple. Thus began a change in moral terminology first officially noted in the *Declaration on Euthanasia* published in 1980 by the Catholic Church's Sacred Congregation for the Doctrine of the Faith in 1980: "In the past, moralists replied that one is never obligated to use 'extraordinary' means. This reply, which as a principle still holds good, is perhaps less clear today, by reason of the imprecision of the term and the rapid progress made in the treatment of sickness. Thus, some people prefer to speak of 'proportionate' and 'disproportionate' means."

This newer and clearer moral terminology of proportionality was used in secular ethical analysis as early as the 1983 President's Commission report, *Deciding to Forgo Life-Sustaining Technologies*. The "ordinary/extraordinary" language, however, continues to be seen in the medical literature and heard in the intensive care unit. Reasoning on the basis of proportionality requires us to weigh the burdens and the benefits of a particular treatment for a particular patient. Thus, a respirator may be proportionate (and obligatory) for a young person with a severe but survivable chest injury, but it may be disproportionate (and thus optional) for another person who is dying of lung cancer. The same is true for (almost) all medical treatments, including feeding tubes. There are two treatments that always remain obligatory, as I shall explain below.

A second aspect of the discussion about the obligation to provide nutritional support, especially in secular discussions but also in religious debate, was the symbolism of food and water—feeding is caring; nutrition is nurture; food and water are not treatment, and therefore they are never optional. The reasoning commonly went as follows: we provide nutritional support for vulnerable infants because this is an important part of "tender loving care." Shouldn't we provide the same for vulnerable adults as well?

Certainly when a patient is temporarily unable to swallow and has the potential to recover, artificially administered fluids and nutrition are obligatory. Does that obligation change if the prognosis is poor?

This aspect of the debate continued through the 1970s and 1980s. It appeared to be resolved by the U.S. Supreme Court in its 1990 decision in *Cruzan v. Director, Missouri Department of Health* when five of the nine Justices agreed that artificially administered fluids and nutrition are medical treatments and are thus optional. Since *Cruzan* medical and legal professions have developed a consensus that feeding tubes are not always obligatory. This debate is ongoing, however, and in some minds the symbolism of feeding remains a dominant feature.

Starvation

A parallel concern to the symbolism entailed in the use of fluids and nutrition is the commonly heard accusation, "But you will be starving him to death!" when discontinuation of a feeding tube is discussed. This is incorrect. Starvation is a slow process that results from lack of calories and takes several weeks or months. When artificially administered fluids and nutrition are not used in a person who is unable to swallow, that person dies from dehydration, not starvation, and death occurs in five to twelve days. Dehydration is very commonly the last physiologic stage of dying, no matter what the cause.

"But that is no comfort! Being dehydrated and thirsty is miserable." Yes and no. Being thirsty is miserable, but becoming dehydrated need not be. The only place in the body where thirst is perceived is the mouth. There is good empirical evidence that as long as a person's mouth is kept moist, that person is not uncomfortable, even if it is clear that his or her body is becoming progressively dehydrated.

I said earlier that there are two treatments that are never optional: these are good symptom control and human presence. Therefore, when a person is becoming dehydrated as he or she approaches death, it is obligatory to provide good mouth care, along with other means of demonstrating human caring and presence, such as touching, caressing, gentle massage, hairbrushing, talking, reading, and holding.

Withholding [versus] Withdrawing

A third feature of the debate over feeding tubes is the issue of withholding versus withdrawing therapy. Thirty years ago, it was common teaching in medicine that "it is better to withhold a treatment than to withdraw it." The thinking was that if you stop a ventilator or dialysis or a feeding tube, and the patient then dies from this lack of life support, you were the agent of death. Therefore, it would be ethically better not to start the treatment in the first place. Then, if the patient dies, death is attributable to the underlying disease and not to your withdrawal of life support.

Slowly, with help from philosophers, theologians, attorneys, and jurists, the medical profession came to accept that there is no moral or legal difference between withholding and withdrawing a treatment. In fact, it may be ethically better to withdraw life-sustaining treatment than it is to withhold it. If there is a treatment with a very small chance of helping the patient, it is better to give it a try. If it becomes clear after a few days or weeks that it is not helping, then you can withdraw the treatment without the original uncertainty that you might be quitting too soon, and now with the comfort that comes from knowing you are not the agent of death.

However, even if there is no professional, moral, or legal difference, it still may be psychologically more difficult to withdraw a treatment that you know is postponing a patient's death than it would have been not to start it in the first place. Turning down the dials on a ventilator with the expectation that the patient will not survive is more personally unsettling than is merely being present with a patient who is actively dying. Withdrawal of a feeding tube can be even more unsettling, especially if the professional involved has any moral reservations about the distinction between ordinary and extraordinary means or about the symbolism of artificially administered fluids and nutrition.

Some develop this part of the debate with moral concern about intentionality. They contend that your intention in withdrawing the feeding tube is that the patient will die, and it is morally impermissible to cause death intentionally. In actuality, the intention in withdrawing any therapy that has been proven not to work is to stop postponing death artificially.

With these aspects of the debate more or less settled, where does that leave us in making decisions about the use or non-use of feeding tubes? The short-term use of a feeding tube for a patient who is unable to swallow adequate fluids and nutrition for a few days, because of severe illness or after surgery or trauma, may be lifesaving and is almost always uncontroversial. Such usage may even be morally obligatory when the goal of treatment is patient survival and a feeding tube is the best way to provide needed fluids and nutrition.

A feeding tube is sometimes requested by a loved one as a last-gasp effort to postpone death in a patient who is imminently dying and unable to swallow. This is almost always inappropriate. Good mouth care to maintain patient comfort and hygiene is obligatory, but in such cases maintenance of nutrition is no longer a reasonable goal of treatment. In fact, introduction of fluids may even lead to fluid overload that can cause patient discomfort as the body's systems are shutting down.

Long-Term Use

The situation that can generate ethical quandaries, front-page news, and conflicts in court is the long-term use of feeding tubes. And these situations are not as neatly segregated into proportionate or disproportionate usage.

Long-term use of a feeding tube remains ethically obligatory for a patient who is cognitively intact, can and wants to survive, but is permanently unable to swallow, an example being a patient who has been treated for malignancy of the throat or esophagus. Protracted use of a feeding tube is also morally required in most instances when it is uncertain whether a patient will regain awareness or recover the ability to swallow—for instance, immediately after a serious head injury or a disabling stroke.

Long-term use of a feeding tube becomes controversial in patients suffering from progressive deterioration of brain function (e.g., Alzheimer's dementia) or in patients with little or no likelihood of regaining awareness after illness or injury (e.g., the permanent vegetative state). Thus, the most perplexing feeding-tube questions involve patients who are unable to take in adequate fluids and nutrition by themselves but who have a condition that by itself will not soon lead to death. The reasoning is, the patient has no fatal condition; he or she can be kept alive with the simple use of tube feedings; therefore, we are obligated to use a feeding tube to keep this person alive.

Alzheimer's dementia is the most common type of brain deterioration, afflicting five percent of individuals over sixty-five and perhaps as many as 50 percent of those over eighty-five. It is manifested by progressive cognitive impairment, followed by physical deterioration. This process generally takes several years, often a decade, and is ultimately fatal. In its final stages, it almost always interferes with the patient's ability to swallow. Eventually the individual chokes on even pureed foods or liquids. Continued attempts at feeding by mouth very commonly result in aspiration of food or fluid into the airway, frequently leading to pneumonia. Aspiration pneumonia will sometimes respond to antibiotics, but other times it leads to death. Such respiratory infections are the most common final event in this progressive disease.

Feeding tubes have been commonly used in the later stages of Alzheimer's. The reasoning has been that this patient is not able to take in adequate fluids and nutrition and he is not imminently dying. Several assumptions then follow: a feeding tube will improve his comfort, will prevent aspiration pneumonia, and will ensure adequate nutrition which will in turn prevent skin breakdown and thus postpone his death. However, empirical evidence, published in the *Journal of the American Medical Association* in 1999, has shown each of these assumptions to be incorrect: using a feeding tube in a patient with dementia does not prevent these complications, nor does it prolong life.

In addition, there are several negative aspects to using a feeding tube in a person with advanced cognitive impairment. There are rare complications during insertion, some merely uncomfortable, some quite serious. Having a tube in one's nose is generally uncomfortable; even having one coiled up under a dressing on the abdominal wall can be annoying. Because the demented patient doesn't understand the intended purpose of the feeding tube, he or she may react by trying to remove it, requiring either repeated re-insertions or the use of hand restraints. In addition, using a feeding tube may deprive the patient of human presence and interaction: hanging a bag of nutritional fluid takes only a few seconds, as opposed to the extended time of human contact involved in feeding a cognitively impaired person.

End Stage Alzheimer's

There is a slowly developing consensus in medicine that feeding tubes are generally not appropriate for use in most patients nearing the end stage of Alzheimer's disease. This belief can be supported from a moral standpoint in terms of proportionality. And yet feeding tubes are still rather commonly used. A recently published review of all U.S. nursing home patients with cognitive impairment found that an average of 34 percent were being fed with feeding tubes (though there were large state-to-state variations, from nine percent in Maine, New Hampshire, and Vermont to 64 percent in Washington, D.C.).

The cases we read about in the newspaper—in which families are divided and court battles fought—most often involve patients in a permanent vegetative state (PVS). This is a condition of permanent unawareness most often caused by severe head injury or by the brain being deprived of oxygen for several minutes. Such deprivation may be the result of successful cardiopulmonary resuscitation of a patient whose breathing or circulation had stopped from a cardiac arrest, near-drowning, strangulation, etc. In a PVS patient, the heart, lungs, kidneys, and other organs continue to function; given good nursing care and artificially administered fluids and nutrition, a person can live in this permanent vegetative state for many years.

A person in a PVS may still have reflexes from the spinal cord (grasping, withdrawal from pain) or the brain stem (breathing, regulation of blood pressure), including the demonstration of sleep-wake cycles. He may "sleep" for several hours, then "awaken" for a while; the eyes are open and wander about, but do not fix on or follow objects. The person in a PVS is "awake, but unaware" because the areas of the upper brain that allow a person to perceive his or her environment and to act voluntarily are no longer functioning.

Uncertainty

Some of the clinical controversy about nutritional support for persons in a PVS is due to uncertainty. After a head injury or resuscitation from a cardiac arrest, it may be several weeks or months before a patient can rightly be declared to be in a PVS—months during which the provision of nutritional support via feeding tubes is often very appropriate. Loved ones usually remain optimistic, hoping for improvement, praying for full recovery. The length of time from brain damage to declaration of a PVS can extend, depending on the cause of the brain injury, from one month to twelve months. And just to muddy the waters even further, there are rare instances of delayed improvement after many months or even a few years, so that the previously unaware patient regains some ability to perceive his or her environment, and may even be able to say a few words. These individuals are now in a "minimally conscious state." More than minimal delayed improvement is exceedingly rare. (Treatment decisions for persons in a minimally conscious state are perhaps even more controversial than are those for PVS patients, but that discussion must wait for another time.)

The greatest ethical dilemma surrounding the use or non-use of nutritional support for persons in a PVS arises from the fact that they are not clearly dying. With good nursing care and nutrition, individuals in this condition have survived for up to thirty-five years. Those who advocate continued nutritional support argue thus: this person is alive and not actively or imminently dying; it is possible to keep him alive with minimal effort; this human life is sacred; therefore, we are obligated to continue to give artificially administered fluids and nutrition.

It is hard to disagree with the various steps in this line of reasoning. (Some utilitarians do disagree, however, claiming that a patient in a PVS is "already dead" or is a "non-person." Those who believe in the sanctity of life must continue to denounce this line of thought.) Let us stipulate the following: the person in a PVS is alive; he can be kept alive for a long time; his life is sacred. But does the obligation to maintain that severely compromised human life necessarily follow from these premises?

Let's first address the issue of whether he is dying. One could maintain that his physical condition is such that he will die soon but for the artificial provision of fluids and nutrition. Thus the permanent vegetative state could be construed to be lethal in and of itself. However, that fatal outcome is not inevitable since the saving treatment is simple. How does this differ from the imperative to provide nourishment for a newborn who would die without the provision of fluids and nutrition? There are two differences. Most newborns are able to take in nutrition if it is placed in or near their mouths. PVS patients can't swallow, so the nutrition must be delivered further down the gastrointestinal tract. As for sick or premature infants, they have a great potential for improvement, growth, and development. The PVS patient has no such potential.

Kidney Failure

Rather than a newborn, a better analogy for this aspect of the discussion would be a person with kidney failure. The kidney failure itself is life-threatening, but it is fairly easily corrected by dialysis three times a week. If the person has another condition that renders him unaware of his surroundings, or a condition that makes life a continuous difficult struggle, most would agree that the person is ethically permitted to stop the dialysis even if that means he will not survive. The ultimate cause of death was treatable, so that death could have been postponed, possibly for years. However, other mitigating circumstances may make the dialysis disproportionate, and so one should be allowed to discontinue this death-postponing treatment in a person who is not imminently dying.

Someone coming from a mechanistic perspective can easily and comfortably decide that a person in a PVS with no potential for recovery has no inherent value and is even an emotional drain on loved ones and a financial drain on society. But what about a person of faith? Does the sanctity of life, a basic tenet of Christianity, Judaism, and Islam, dictate that life must always be preserved if it is humanly possible to do so? Our moral intuitions tell us the answer is no.

It might be possible to postpone the death of a patient from end-stage heart failure by doing one more resuscitation. It might be possible to postpone the death of someone with end-stage liver disease by doing a liver transplant. It might be possible to postpone the death of someone with painful cancer with a few more blood transfusions or another round of chemotherapy. But these therapies are often not used—because the burden is disproportionate to the benefit. Thus the timing of death is often a matter of choice. In fact, it is commonly accepted that the timing of 80 percent of deaths that occur in a hospital is chosen.

Believers do not like to use the words "choice" and "death" in the same sentence. Doing so recalls acrimonious contests about the "right to life" versus the "right to choose" that are the pivotal point in debates about abortion, assisted suicide, and euthanasia. And certainly belief in the sanctity of human life obligates believers to forgo some choices. But does this belief preclude all choices? No: life is full of difficult choices. This is true for believers and nonbelievers alike. Believers may have more guidance about what choices to make and perhaps some limits on options, but we still are faced with many choices—such as choices about the use or non-use of feeding tubes.

When engaging in moral debate on matters of faith, it is important not to focus exclusively on one tenet of faith to the exclusion of others. In debating the use of feeding tubes—or of any mode of treatment for that matter—one must not ignore the concepts of finitude and stewardship by focusing only on the sanctity of life.

If belief in the sanctity of human life translated automatically into an obligation to preserve each human life at all costs, we would not have to debate proportionate and disproportionate treatments. We would simply be obligated to use all treatments available until they failed to work. However, because of the Fall, human life is finite. All of us will die. Since that is inevitable, God expects us to care wisely for our own bodies and for those of our loved ones, and also for our resources. Healthcare professionals similarly must be wise stewards of their skills and services.

Taking into consideration the scriptural principle of stewardship and the tradition of proportionate treatment, I conclude that there must be some degree of discretion in the use or non-use of feeding tubes. There are clearly situations where a feeding tube must be used. There are other situations where a feeding tube would be morally wrong. But there are many situations where the use of a feeding tube should be optional. And this means that one

individual of faith might choose to use a tube when another might choose not to use it.

Personal Values

Because of the patient's personal values, someone might choose to continue artificially administered fluids and nutrition for a loved one in a permanent vegetative state for many years. Another might choose to continue for one year and then to withdraw it if there was no sign of awareness. Still another might choose to stop after three months or one month.

What might those discretionary personal values include? Such things, among others, as an assessment of how to deal with uncertainty, concern about emotional burden on loved ones, and cost of care. Though beliefs in the sanctity of human life and in the obligation to care for vulnerable individuals are not optional for persons of faith, an assessment of whether or not to use a given technology requires human wisdom and thus entails some discretion.

Gilbert Meilaender

There is much to agree with in Robert D. Orr's measured discussion of the moral issues surrounding the use of feeding tubes, there are a few things that seem to me doubtful or in need of clarification, and then there is one major issue that requires greater precision.

Accepted Claims

It may be useful to note first some claims of Dr. Orr that few would dispute.

- Feeding tubes are a rather low-tech form of care.
- Our ability to do something does not mean that we should do it.
- Any distinction between "ordinary" and "extraordinary" care (if we wish to use that language) cannot simply be a feature of treatments but must be understood as patient-relative. What is ordinary treatment for one patient may be extraordinary for another, and what is ordinary treatment for a patient at one point in his life may become extraordinary at another point when his illness has progressed to a new stage.
- There is no crucial moral difference between withholding or withdrawing a treatment. (Dr. Orr actually writes that there is "no moral or legal difference" between these. The issue of legality is, I suspect, sometimes more complicated, but I take him to be correct insofar as a strictly moral judgment is involved.)

- There are circumstances, some noted by Dr. Orr, in which the use of feeding tubes seems clearly required and is relatively uncontroversial.
- Patients in a persistent vegetative state are not dying patients. (I don't quite know how to combine this with Dr. Orr's statement a few paragraphs later that the permanent vegetative state "could be construed to be lethal in and of itself." In general, I don't think his article ever really achieves clarity and precision on this question, and it will turn out to be a crucial question below.)
- A commitment to the sanctity of human life does not require that we always do everything possible to keep a person alive.

There are also places where Dr. Orr's discussion seems to me to be doubtful or, at least, underdeveloped. Among these are the following:

- The idea that the terms "proportionate" and "disproportionate" are more precise than the (admittedly unsatisfactory) language of "ordinary" and "extraordinary" is, at best, doubtful. On what scale one "weighs" benefits and burdens is a question almost impossible to answer. Even more doubtful is whether we can "weigh" them for someone else. My own view is that when we make these decisions for ourselves, we are not in fact "weighing" anything. We are deciding what sort of person we will be and what sort of life will be ours. We are making not a *discovery* but a *decision*. And if that is true, then it is obvious that we have not discovered anything that could necessarily be transferred and applied to the life of a different patient. In general, the language of "weighing" sounds good, but it is almost impossible to give it any precise meaning.
- No *moral* question was resolved by the Supreme Court's *Cruzan* decision. It established certain legal boundaries, but it did no more than that.
- I suspect that—despite the growing consensus, which Dr. Orr correctly describes—he is too quick to assume that the "symbolism" issue can be dispensed with, and too quick to assume that feeding tubes are "treatment" rather than standard nursing care. A consensus may be mistaken, after all. It is hard to see why such services as turning a patient regularly and giving alcohol rubs are standard nursing care while feeding is not. To take an example from a different realm of life, soldiers are combatants, but the people who grow the food which soldiers eat are not combatants (even though the soldiers could not continue to fight without

nourishment). The reason is simple: they make not what soldiers need to fight but what they need, as we all do, in order merely to live. Likewise, we might want to think twice before endorsing the view that relatively low-tech means of providing nourishment are treatment rather than standard nursing care.

Intention

- Dr. Orr's discussion of the role of "intention" in moral analysis is, putting it charitably, imprecise. Obviously, if a treatment has been shown not to work, in withdrawing it we do not intend or aim at the patient's death. We aim at caring for that person as best we can, which hardly includes providing treatment that is useless. But the crucial questions will turn on instances in which the treatment is not pointless. If we stop treatment in such cases, it is harder to deny that our aim is that the patient should die.
- Dr. Orr's seeming willingness to allow the state of a patient's cognitive capacities to carry weight—or even be determinative—in treatment decisions is troubling. Obviously, certain kinds of higher brain capacities are characteristics that distinguish human beings from other species; however, one need not have or be exercising those capacities in order to be a living human being. Allowing the cognitive ability of a patient to determine whether he or she is treated will inevitably lead to judgments about the comparative worth of human lives.

If Dr. Orr is correct in arguing that the use of feeding tubes in end-stage Alzheimer's patients is of no help to those patients and may sometimes be burdensome to them, we would have no moral reason to provide them with tube feeding. This judgment, however, has nothing at all to do with "proportionality." It has to do, simply, with the two criteria we ought to use in making treatment decisions—usefulness and burdensomeness. If a treatment is useless or excessively burdensome, it may rightly be refused.

This brings us to the most difficult issue, which clearly troubles Dr. Orr himself, and which is surely puzzling for all of us; the patient in a persistent vegetative state. We cannot usefully discuss this difficult case, however, without first getting clear more generally on the morality of withholding or withdrawing treatment. As I noted above, on this issue, the language of proportionality is unlikely to be of much use for serious moral reflection.

Morality of Treatment

At least for Christians—though, in truth, also much more generally for our civilization's received medical tradition—we begin with what is forbidden. We should never aim at the death of a sick or dying person. (Hence, euthanasia, however good the motive, is forbidden.) Still, there are times when treatment may rightly be withheld or withdrawn, *even though* the patient may then die more quickly than would otherwise have been the case. How can that be? How can it be that, as a result of our decision, the patient dies more quickly, yet we do not aim at his death? This is quite possible—and permissible—so long as we aim to dispense with the treatment, not the life. No one need live in a way that seeks to ensure the longest possible life. (Were that a moral requirement, think of all the careers that would have to be prohibited.) There may be many circumstances in which we foresee that decisions we make may shorten our life, but we do not suppose that in so deciding we are aiming at death or formulating a plan of action that deliberately embraces death as a good. So in medical treatment decisions the question we need to answer is this: Under what circumstances may we rightly refuse a life-prolonging treatment without supposing that, in making this decision, we are doing the forbidden deed of choosing or aiming at death?

The answer of our medical-moral tradition has been the following: we may refuse treatments that are either *useless* or *excessively burdensome*. In doing so, we choose not death, but one among several possible lives open to us. We do not choose to die, but, rather, how to live, even if while dying, even if a shorter life than some other lives that are still available for our choosing. What we take aim at then, what we refuse, is not life but treatment—treatment that is either useless for a particular patient or excessively burdensome for that patient. Especially for patients who are irretrievably into the dying process, almost all treatments will have become useless. In refusing them, one is not choosing death but choosing life without a now useless form of treatment. But even for patients who are not near death, who might live for a considerably longer time, excessively burdensome treatments may also be refused. Here again, one takes aim at the burdensome treatment, not at life. One person may choose a life that is longer but carries with it considerable burden of treatment. Another may choose a life that is shorter but carries with it less burden of treatment. Each, however, chooses life. Neither aims at death.

Rejecting Treatments

It is essential to emphasize that these criteria refer to treatments, not to lives. We may rightly reject a treatment that is useless. But if I decide not to treat because I think a person's life is useless, then I am taking aim not at the treatment but at the life. Rather than asking, "What if anything can I do that will benefit the life this patient has?" I am asking, "Is it a benefit to have such a life?" If the latter is my question, and if I decide not

to treat, it should be clear that it is the life at which I take aim. Likewise, we may reject a treatment on grounds of excessive burden. But if I decide not to treat because it seems a burden just to have the life this person has, then I am taking aim not at the burdensome treatment but at the life. Hence, in deciding whether it is appropriate and permissible to withhold or withdraw treatment—whether, even if life is thereby shortened, we are aiming only at the treatment and not at the life—we have to ask ourselves whether the treatment under consideration is, for this patient, either useless or excessively burdensome.

Against that background, we can consider the use of feeding tubes for patients in a persistent vegetative state. (I set aside here the point I noted above—that we might want to regard feeding simply as standard nursing care rather than as medical treatment. Now we are asking whether, even on the grounds that govern treatment decisions, we have good moral reason not to feed patients in a persistent vegetative state.)

Is the treatment useless? Not, let us be clear, is the life a useless one to have, but is the treatment useless? As Dr. Orr notes—quite rightly, I think—patients "can live in this permanent vegetative state for many years." So feeding may preserve for years the life of this living human being. Are we certain we want to call that useless? We are, of course, tempted to say that, in deciding not to feed, we are simply withdrawing treatment and letting these patients die. Yes, as Dr. Orr also notes, these patients "are not clearly dying." And, despite the sloppy way we sometimes talk about these matters, you cannot "let die" a person who is not dying. It is hard, therefore, to make the case for treatment withdrawal in these cases on the ground of uselessness. We may use those words, but it is more likely that our target is a (supposed) useless life and not a useless treatment. And if that is our aim, we had better rethink it promptly.

Is the treatment excessively burdensome? Alas, if these patients could experience the feeding as a burden, they would not be diagnosed as being in a persistent vegetative state. We may wonder, of course, whether having such a life is itself a burden, but, again, if that is our reasoning, it will be clear that we take aim not at a burdensome treatment but at a (presumed) burdensome life. And, once more, if that is our aim, we had better rethink it promptly.

Choosing Life

Hence, although these are troubling cases, Dr. Orr has not given us good or sufficient arguments to make the case for withdrawing feeding tubes from patients in a persistent vegetative state. I have not suggested that we have an obligation always and at any cost to preserve life. I have simply avoided all comparative judgments of the worth of human lives and have turned aside from any decisions which, when analyzed carefully, look as if they take aim not at a dispensable treatment but at a life. "Choosing life" does not mean doing whatever is needed to stay alive as long as possible. But choosing life clearly means never aiming at another's death—even if only by withholding treatment. I am not persuaded that Dr. Orr has fully grasped or delineated what it means to choose life in the difficult circumstances he discusses.

Critical Thinking

1. Why are each of these a problem: the distinction between extraordinary and ordinary treatments? the social symbolism of feeding? and the distinction between withholding and withdrawing of treatments?
2. Why do real-life situations complicate the distinction between extraordinary and ordinary treatments?

3. What does the author argue are never optional treatments for the dying?

Internet References

BBC—Ethics: Euthanasia and physician assisted suicide
www.bbc.co.uk/ethics/euthanasia/

Ethical Key Issues—Euthanasia
www.life.org.nz/euthanasia/euthanasiaethicalkeyissues/

The Ethical Debate
https://www.health.ny.gov/regulations/task_force/reports_publications/when_death_is_sought/chap5.htm

Mr. Orr is the Director of Ethics and a professor of family medicine at the University of Vermont College of Medicine. **Mr. Meilaender** is a member of the President's Council on Bioethics. From "Ethics & Life's Ending: An Exchange," by Robert D. Orr and Gilbert Meilaender, *First Things*, August/September 2004, pages 31–38.

Prepared by: George E. Dickinson, *College of Charleston*
Michael R. Leming, *St. Olaf College*

Article

Apostolate of Death

AARON KHERIATY

Learning Outcomes

After reading this article, you will be able to:

- Understand some of the complex issues related to having a terminal illness, and the right to die with physician assistance.

- Understand the problematic nature of passing laws that would provide physician assistance to terminally ill patients.

- Understand that sometimes suicide and the desire for physician-assisted dying are very different things.

On November 1, after posting a Facebook message stating, "Today is the day I have chosen to pass away with dignity in the face of my terminal illness, this terrible brain cancer," twenty-nine-year-old Brittany Maynard took a lethal dose of barbiturates, prescribed by an Oregon physician, and ended her own life. One newspaper opinion columnist spoke with almost religious awe when she noted that "Maynard has ascended to martyr-saint status as an advocate for the right to suicide in the throes of terminal illness."

In the wake of her death, bills to legalize physician-assisted suicide are being considered in at least twelve states (California, Colorado, Illinois, Indiana, Iowa, Minnesota, Nevada, New Mexico, Pennsylvania, Rhode Island, Wisconsin, and Wyoming). The public is clearly not yet sold, as these efforts follow on the heels of failed attempts to legalize assisted suicide in three other states (Connecticut, Massachusetts, and New Hampshire).

The claim to a right to physician-assisted suicide raises many questions, not the least of which is this: If there is such a right, why would it be restricted to those in the throes of terminal illness? What about the elderly person suffering a slow but nonterminal decline? What about the adolescent or young adult in the throes of depression, demoralization, or despair?

Once we adopt the principle that suicide is acceptable, then the fences that legislators might try to erect around it—having six months to live, or having mental capacity, for example—are inevitably arbitrary. These restrictions will eventually be abandoned, as the situation with assisted suicide in Belgium and the Netherlands demonstrates.

In Belgium, assisted suicide has been granted to a woman with "untreatable depression"; in the Netherlands, assisted suicide has been granted to a woman because she did not want to live in a nursing home. We see evidence here of not only a *practical* slippery slope but also a relentlessly *logical* slide from a cancer patient with six months to live to people who are merely unhappy, demoralized, dejected, depressed, or desperate. If assisted suicide is a good, why limit it only to a select few?

Recent debates on physician-assisted suicide have largely ignored research in psychiatry and the social sciences. It is important to appreciate what motivates suicidal behavior, which individuals are at risk for suicide, and how suicide risk can be lowered. We know, for example, that suicide is typically an impulsive and ambivalent act.

One suicide "hot spot" is the Golden Gate Bridge in San Francisco, where fourteen hundred people have died, while only a handful have survived the jump. A journalist tracked down a few of these survivors and asked them what was going through their minds in the four seconds between jumping off the bridge and hitting the water. All of them responded that they regretted the decision to jump, with one saying, "I instantly realized that everything in my life that I'd thought was unfixable was totally fixable—except for having just jumped." This small sample is consistent with larger studies of suicide survivors: Ten years after attempted suicide, nearly all survivors no longer wish to die but are pleased to be alive. To abandon suicidal individuals in the midst of a crisis—under the guise of respecting their autonomy—is socially irresponsible: It undermines sound medical ethics and erodes social solidarity.

Suicidal individuals typically do not want to die; they want to escape what they perceive as intolerable suffering. When comfort or relief is offered, in the form of more-adequate treatment for depression, better pain management, or more-comprehensive palliative care, the desire for suicide wanes. We know that the vast majority of suicides are associated with clinical depression or other treatable mental disorders; yet alarmingly, less than 6 percent of the 752 reported cases of individuals who have died by assisted suicide under Oregon's law were referred for psychiatric evaluation prior to their death. This constitutes gross medical negligence.

We also know that there is a "social contagion" aspect to suicide, which leads to copycat suicides. In 1933, on the Japanese island of Izu Oshima, a twenty-one-year-old student named Kiyoko Matsumoto jumped into the volcano of Mount Mihara from an observation point overlooking the molten lava. Her death became a media sensation across Japan as newspapers reprinted her poignant suicide note and turned her into an overnight celebrity. Nine hundred forty-four people subsequently jumped into the volcano's crater in 1933 alone. In the years that followed, thousands more made the one-way trip to the volcano, including, every year, dozens of suicide-pact couples who plunged into the lava together. The Tokyo Bay Steamship Company set up a daily line to the island's volcano rim, which became known as "Suicide Point," to ferry victims and spectators: Some passengers bought one-way tickets to the destination, while others traveled there round-trip to watch people jump. This suicide epidemic ended only after officials made it a criminal offense to purchase a one-way ticket to the island and placed a barrier at the observation point.

Many recent commentators have called Maynard's death "courageous" and "inspiring," but we should worry that her death will indeed "inspire" others to follow her example. Assisted-suicide advocates might insist that her death was a purely private decision or merely an exercise in personal autonomy; but given what we know about suicide's social effects, and given the media portrayal of her death, we can anticipate that her decision will influence other vulnerable individuals.

Suicide rates now constitute a public-health crisis: According to the Centers for Disease Control, suicide is currently the third leading cause of death among adolescents and young adults and the tenth leading cause of death overall for individuals over the age of ten. Not all suicides can be prevented, but many can, and our collective efforts have the capacity to save many lives. Studies show that when we intervene during a crisis—for example, during the months of difficult adjustment after a new diagnosis of a serious or terminal disease—we can substantially lower the person's risk of suicide.

Refusing to legitimate suicide helps those in need. The practice of physician-assisted suicide—by whatever name one calls it—sends a message that some lives are not worth living. The law is a teacher: If assisted suicide is legalized, this message will be heard by everyone who is afflicted by suicidal thoughts or tendencies.

While a causal relationship is difficult to establish with the available data, it is perhaps relevant that the overall suicide rates in Oregon rose dramatically in the years following the legalization of physician-assisted suicide in that state in 1997: According to data from Oregon Public Health, after the state's suicide rates declined in the 1990s, they increased significantly between 2000 and 2010, and are now 35 percent higher than the national average.

Many advocates of assisted suicide try to redefine it as something else—indeed, to redefine human dignity and human life itself. Maynard has become a sort of secular saint for the cause, and the media have provided her hagiography. Maynard herself wrote: "If I'm leaving a legacy, it's to change this health-care policy or be a part of this change of this health-care policy so it becomes available to all Americans. That would be an enormous contribution to make, even if I'm just a piece of it." CNN named Maynard one of its "11 Extraordinary People of 2014" for her decision to define death "on her own terms." Another columnist wrote that Maynard in her choice for self-inflicted death employed her "own definitions of life and dignity."

This echoes the famous "mystery clause" of Supreme Court justice Anthony Kennedy: "At the heart of liberty is the right to define one's own concept of existence, of meaning, of the universe, and of the mystery of human life." Such a notion of liberty and human dignity can only lead to incoherence and absurdity; life and death are not ours to define but are objective realities to which we must adapt. There is a great irony in all of this empty talk about controlling the timing and circumstances of our death, since death is the singular event that finally and completely announces our lack of complete mastery and control.

The euphemistically renamed Compassion and Choices (formerly the Hemlock Society) trades on this supposed "right" to redefine human life and death, claiming that "physician aid in dying" is *not really suicide,* simply because the means employed—taking a deadly drug—are "nonviolent" and "peaceful." This Orwellian attempt to manipulate language, and to do an end-run around hard realities, is irresponsible and deceptive.

Evil is always parasitic on, and derivative of, the good: It cannot generate anything of its own, but only distorts and corrupts what is already given. Perhaps this explains the pseudo-religious tones of the assisted-suicide movement's latest iteration. It borrows from mystical or religious language to cast itself as a "compassionate" spirituality.

The most striking example can be seen in Fernand Melgar's prize-winning 2005 documentary film *Exit: Le Droit de Mourir* (Exit: The Right to Die), recently made available with English subtitles on YouTube. This simultaneously mesmerizing and terrifying film follows the work of the Swiss-assisted suicide association EXIT, which provides volunteer "escorts" who help usher people to their deaths. These escorts show remarkable dedication to their work and demonstrate an intense drive to proselytize. They advocate tirelessly for the legalization of assisted suicide in other countries.

In one striking scene, filmed in a way that evokes Da Vinci's *The Last Supper*, twelve escorts gather around a U-shaped dining table with EXIT's president, Dr. Jérôme Sobel, seated in the center. The seasoned escorts share tricks of the trade and offer guidance to the new recruits. One woman suggests using two large straws for those patients who can no longer hold a glass to down the pills. The same woman then notes that she cannot take on any new cases as she already has four "self-deliverances" scheduled before the end of the year. Another escort describes the case of an elderly couple who wish to die together by "self-deliverance," which ushers in a conversation about whether the escorts can assist them. One pleads that this couple is "entitled to this departure together because they've spent a lifetime together" and argues that "this forms part of our philosophical mandate," while another regretfully notes that the current law will not allow them to assist because only one member of the couple has a terminal illness. As the conversation continues, their leader, Dr. Sobel, speaks to his disciples in warm and encouraging tones. He acknowledges that their work is emotionally exhausting—"we have to rest between two missions, recharge our batteries; this is not something you can do as regularly as clockwork." He encourages them to persevere in their work

nonetheless: "It is an exceptional act, every single time," he tells them. "I'm exhausted after every assisted suicide." He then states that from now on he will no longer call what they do voluntary work; it is a vocation. The final scene of the film shows Dr. Sobel asking a woman several times whether she is certain she wants to die. After she consents, he prepares the deadly potion and hands her the glass, instructing her to drink it down to the last drop. "May the light guide you and lead you to peace," he tells her as she ingests the poison. Then he bids her farewell: "Bon voyage, - Micheline." We watch this woman, on camera, lie back on her bed and die.

Some people thought St. John Paul II was speaking metaphorically when he wrote about our "culture of death." But he meant that this quite literally: A culture that honors and exalts those who deliberately reject life is a culture that eventually will come to worship death.

Critical Thinking

1. Why was Brittany Maynard ascended to martyr-saint status as an advocate for the right to suicide in the throes of terminal illness?
2. How do bills guaranteeing assisted suicide eventually lead to a slippery slope?
3. How does assisted suicide for terminally ill patients encourage suicides for non-terminal people?

Internet References

BBC—Ethics—Euthanasia: Ethical Problems of Euthanasia
www.bbc.co.uk/ethics/euthanasia/overview/problems.shtml

BBC—Ethics—Euthanasia: Religion and Euthanasia
www.bbc.co.uk/ethics/euthanasia/religion/religion.shtml

Pew Research Center
http://www.pewforum.org/2013/11/21/religious-groups-views-on-end-of
-life-issues/

Religious Views on Euthanasia—Wikipedia
https://en.wikipedia.org/wiki/Religious_views_on_euthanasia

Aaron Kheriaty is associate professor of psychiatry at University of California Irvine School of Medicine.

Prepared by: George E. Dickinson, *College of Charleston*
Michael R. Leming, *St. Olaf College*

Article

As We Lie Dying

A Necessary Protocol for End-of-Life Care

GERALD COLEMAN AND MARGARET R. MCLEAN

Learning Outcomes

After reading this article, you will be able to:

- Come to understand that Physician Orders for Life Sustaining Treatment (POLST) is different from mercy killing and physician aid in dying.

- Understand why you need Physician Orders for Life Sustaining Treatment (POLST) created by advanced directives.

- Come to understand that POLST, used properly, supports the Catholic commitment to human dignity and patient centered care without offering mercy killing or physician assisted dying.

W e all die, and most of us understand that it is best to be prepared. Yet most of us remain woefully unprepared for life's final transition. One way of addressing this problem is the Physician Orders for Life Sustaining Treatment (POLST) paradigm, which provides an opportunity for patients with advanced illness to understand their illness and their treatment options and to have their wishes for these options known and followed.

POLST is not without critics. Some criticisms address clear misuses of the paradigm—as when, for instance, the process fails to include face-to-face physician conversations with the patient, or when POLST is used for someone who is medically stable with a life expectancy of years. But others are more fundamental. Some critics, including some Catholic bishops, assert that POLST elevates patient autonomy to the level of an overarching, enforceable legal right, allowing patients to mandate nontreatment in a way that constitutes voluntary euthanasia. It is, of course, important to guard against opening any

doors to euthanasia but worries about POLST in that regard are unwarranted.

Let's consider the theoretical case of Max, an active septuagenarian. When he turned seventy-five Max received a diagnosis of aortic stenosis, a gradual narrowing of the heart's aortic valve that slowly closes the main pipeline for blood flow to the body. Over time, Max's heart muscle would weaken, leading to severe problems and, if left untreated, death. Max carefully considered his options—open-heart surgery to replace the failing valve or increasing frailty as the valve slowly closed. He weighed his alternatives and concluded that he wanted his life and death to progress naturally. Declining surgery, he completed an "advance directive"—not a POLST—documenting his desire for a natural death. He shared his wishes with his family, who accepted his decision.

Five years later, and increasingly frail, Max collapsed from heart failure on the golf course. An ambulance was called, and Max's wife arrived fifteen minutes later to find the ambulance crew attempting to resuscitate her husband's lifeless body—exactly the scenario he had diligently sought to avoid. Brandishing Max's advance directive, which she faithfully kept in her purse, she pleaded with the EMTs to stop, but without medical orders from a physician, they could not. Max's advance directive was useless, since the EMTs were legally required to do whatever necessary to stabilize Max—even things he would abhor—in the absence of an order from a physician. Advance directives, it turns out, work better in the hospital than on a golf course.

Max's story is an example of the limitations of advance directives and surrogate decision makers in directing medical care in an urgent non-hospital setting. This hypothetical story served as the centerpiece of testimony given by Amy Vandenbroucke to the Senate Special Committee on Aging on June 26, 2013.

Vandenbroucke, executive director of the National POLST Paradigm Program Task Force, explained that Max's story would have had a different ending—an ending in keeping with his wishes—if the emergency personnel responding to the 911 call had had a physician's order on a POLST form to direct his medical care. In that case, the EMTs would not have attempted resuscitation, Max would have gotten the natural death he desired, and his family would have been comforted by the knowledge that he had died on his own terms.

POLST is a tool for translating a patient's wishes into a medical order documented on an easily recognizable form. Unlike an advance directive, POLST is explicitly designed to function across care settings, from a grassy fairway to the front porch to the ICU. Oregon pioneered the protocol, and currently forty-five states have some kind of POLST program (the only places that don't are Alabama, Arkansas, Mississippi, Oklahoma, South Dakota, and Washington D.C.). Several states have registries for POLST forms intended to ensure that emergency personnel and health-care professionals have quick and reliable access to the treatment wishes of patients.

POLST is much more than a set of instructions taped to the refrigerator door or stored in a medical-records database. The paradigm is both a holistic method of planning for end-of-life care and a specific set of medical orders designed to carry out patient wishes. It explicitly supports not only free consent but also *informed* consent, requiring meaningful discussions between patients, loved ones, and medical professionals. These planning conversations—aimed at understanding diagnosis, prognosis, available treatment options, patient goals, and treatment preferences—are the hallmark of the approach. A health-care professional (usually a physician, but in some states a nurse practitioner or physician assistant) must talk with the patient—or the patient's legally authorized medical decision-maker—about the medical interventions and procedures listed on the POLST form. These include cardiopulmonary resuscitation, the continuum of medical intervention from "comfort measures only" to "full treatment," and medically administered nutrition. POLST encourages the careful weighing of the benefits and burdens of end-of-life treatment options.

Completing a POLST means more than just filling out a form. It is a process, typically requiring a number of discussions, during which patient values and wishes are identified, and patients, families, and decision-makers come to understand end-of-life care options in light of current medical circumstances and likely outcomes. Only at the end of this process is the form signed, by both the physician and the patient or decision-maker. Though many states also grant signature authority to nurse practitioners

and physician assistants, no facility administrator may sign a POLST form. (In some states, the signature of the patient or decision-maker is not required—an oversight that needs immediate correction in the interest of protecting patient dignity, values, and choice.)

The POLST is designed only for patients who are living with a serious progressive illness. A valid form documents the decisions of a competent person faced with advanced illness or of someone who is frail or chronically ill. Once completed, it travels with the patient, wherever he or she may go. If Max's wife had had a POLST in hand, the EMTs could have granted his wish to die a natural death.

There are two key principles underlying POLST. First, it is completely voluntary. Second, it can be easily modified, amended, revoked, or voided in response to changing circumstances. As treatments succeed or as disease or infirmity progress, a patient's desire for certain medical interventions may change. Research has shown that the use of POLST results in treatment consistent with a patient's wishes more than 90 percent of the time, significantly reduces unwanted hospitalizations, and decreases medical errors.

Of particular significance for Catholics is the fact that, although a POLST form may record a patient's wish to limit medical intervention, it is never the intent for the orders to be written with the goal of hastening death. POLST recognizes that allowing natural death to occur is not the same as intentionally shortening life and provides the unique opportunity for those with serious life-limiting illness to think through medical interventions common at the end of life and to discuss them with a physician. Some patients nearing the end of life wish to stop burdensome medical interventions and focus on comfort; others do not. Notably, POLST requires that comfort measures be provided to all patients.

It is lamentable that some Catholics—including members of the Catholic Medical Association and the bishops from Wisconsin and Minnesota—are calling for Catholic hospitals to refuse to comply with POLST and for Catholics to refrain from completing POLST. We share their concern about coercion and inappropriate use; where these things occur they require immediate correction. Certainly, when a POLST conflicts with Catholic teaching, it should not be honored. But to send POLST packing because of *potential* abuses allows seriously ill patients to die in ways inimical to their values and faith.

Negative critiques tend to conclude that POLST is intrinsically flawed and should not be used in Catholic health-care settings. Such critiques err. Instead of throwing the baby out with the bathwater, it would be better to correct the shortcomings, misunderstandings, and actual and potential abuses of the protocol. This goal can be realized if all POLST users follow the guidelines of the National POLST Paradigm Program. That program should require the signature of the patient or decision-maker on every POLST in every state.

While everyone can benefit from an advance directive, only those facing an illness likely to result in death within the year should have a POLST. The protocol provides concrete and practical help for those approaching the end of life, supporting the real-time medical decision-making so necessary for those who are critically ill. As Cardinal Elio Sgreccia has noted, proxy and treatment directives are "inevitably abstract . . . in comparison with the real situation of sickness"—which is why it is vitally important for Catholic health care to support POLST, since, unlike an advance directive, it is about the here and now. We agree with the Louisiana Conference of Catholic Bishops who state in "The Final Journey" that Louisiana's version of POLST "adheres to all the official teachings of the Catholic Church with regard to end-of-life decisions."

The U.S. Conference of Catholic Bishops' Ethical and Religious Directives affirm that "Christ's redemption and saving grace embraces the whole person, especially in his or her illness, suffering, and death. The Catholic health-care ministry faces the reality of death with the confidence of faith." We believe that POLST, used properly, supports the Catholic commitment to human dignity and patient-centered care.

Critical Thinking

1. What is the Physician Orders for Life Sustaining Treatment (POLST) paradigm?

2. What are the objections to the Physician Orders for Life Sustaining Treatment (POLST) paradigm?

3. What are the limitations of advance directives and surrogate decision-makers in directing medical care in an urgent non-hospital setting? What are the advantages of the Physician Orders for Life Sustaining Treatment (POLST) paradigm?

Internet References

Physician Orders for Life-Sustaining Treatment (POLST)
www.chcf.org/projects/2013/polst

POLST California
http://capolst.org/

State-by-State POLST Forms | Everplans
https://www.everplans.com/articles/state-by-state-polst-forms

What is POLST?—National POLST
www.polst.org/about-the-national-polst-paradigm/what-is-polst

REV. GERALD COLEMAN is vice president for corporate ethics, Daughters of Charity Health System, and adjunct professor at Santa Clara University.

MARGARET R. MCLEAN is associate director of the Markkula Center for Applied Ethics and a senior lecturer in Religious Studies at Santa Clara University.

Prepared by: George E. Dickinson, *College of Charleston*
Michael R. Leming, *St. Olaf College*

Article

Dying Dutch: Euthanasia Spreads Across Europe

In the Netherlands, euthanasia is legal and becoming increasingly popular. Other nations may soon follow suit.

Winston Ross

Learning Outcomes

After reading this article, you will be able to:

- Understand the Dutch perspective on euthanasia and physician-assisted dying.

- See that the Dutch perspective is quite different from the American quest of the right to die with physician assistance.

- Realize that Dutch laws allow for suicide and creates the slippery slope that many fear as national policy in the United States.

In one of the last photographs my family took of my grandmother, she looks as if she's been in a fistfight. Jean Bass Tinsley is lying in a hospital bed in Athens, Georgia, wearing a turquoise button-up shirt and staring blankly at the camera. A bandage obscures her fractured skull, along with the bridge of her bloodied nose. She is 91 years old.

My grandmother essentially did this to herself. In June 2013, she fell out of her wheelchair headfirst, after ignoring her caregivers' warnings not to get out of bed without help. Earlier that year, she'd broken both of her hips, in separate falls. Before that, her pelvis—all while trying to do what for most of her life she'd managed just fine on her own: walk.

In her last year, dementia crept into my grandmother's mind. The staff at her long-term-care facility plotted ways to protect her from herself. It's against the law in Georgia to restrain patients in such facilities, so they lowered her bed to the floor and put a pad down next to it. They even installed an alarm that went off if she left her mattress. My grandmother disabled the alarm, moved the pad and freed herself, repeatedly. In the end, she was both too weak and too strong.

Four months before Grandma died, my mother moved to Georgia to be with her. To prevent her from getting out of bed, nurses at my grandmother's facility began medicating her so heavily that she barely seemed alive. My mom insisted they stop drugging her, at which point Grandma's resolve (and penchant for injury) returned. Several times a week, Mom would call me, bawling, with the latest in my grandmother's saga. At one point, Grandma told my Aunt Cindy that she didn't want to "do this" anymore. That she was ready to die.

From across the country, I listened to these stories and wondered aloud if perhaps my grandmother had lived too long. Doctor-assisted suicide is illegal in Georgia, and even in my home state of Oregon, no physician would have helped her; she was no longer consistently lucid. My point was moot, but Grandma clearly wasn't going to recover. All that was left of her life was pain, confusion and suffering.

Give Me Liberty, Give Me Death

Last month, while traveling through Europe, I met a 65-year-old woman in Amsterdam determined never to wind up like my grandmother. Jannie Willemsen is in near-perfect health, but as we sat down at a small café, she showed me papers that laid out the circumstances under which she no longer wants to live: if she's severely and permanently lame; if she can no longer leave the house on her own; if she's dependent on others to eat, drink, shower and put on her clothes; if she goes blind or deaf or is suffering from dementia—most of what my grandmother experienced in her final months. "I'm an autonomous person," Willemsen says. "For me, it seems a disaster not to be able to go out and visit friends, to a concert, to the theater."

A kind and lively woman, Willemsen is now retired from her career as a biologist. She and her husband signed their power of attorney papers in 1997, just after doctors diagnosed him with intestinal cancer. Neither had any interest in living longer than what felt natural; they wanted to decide for themselves when they would go. Willemsen's husband died in 2004, not from cancer but a heart problem. He was "lucky," she says, because he didn't suffer for long. After his second operation to remove intestinal tumors, his heart stopped. Willemsen had to produce his papers, she says, to convince the doctors not to resuscitate him. "They said, 'Our first concern is keeping him alive,'" she recalls. But that's not what he wanted. It's not what she wants, either.

What she wants, if the circumstances merit it, is doctor-assisted euthanasia, which is booming in the Netherlands. In 2013, according to the latest data, 4,829 people across the country chose to have a doctor end their lives. That's one in every 28 deaths in the Netherlands, and triple the number of people who died this way in 2002. The Dutch don't require proof of a terminal illness to allow doctors to "help" patients die. Here, people can choose euthanasia if they can convince two physicians they endure "unbearable" suffering, a definition that expands each year. Residents here can now choose euthanasia if they're tired of living with Lou Gehrig's disease, multiple sclerosis, depression or loneliness. The Dutch can now choose death if they're tired of living.

That act is technically illegal in the Netherlands. Those who aid in euthanasia can face up to four and a half years in prison. But since the early 1970s, the Dutch government has treated assisted suicide much the same way it handles cannabis users: by looking the other way, honoring the public's overwhelming view that people in the Netherlands should have the right to die. Since 2002, euthanasia has officially been decriminalized here, so long as certain criteria are met.

Other countries are now edging closer to the Dutch model. On February 6, the Supreme Court of Canada struck down a ban on doctor-assisted suicide, joining Luxembourg, Belgium and Switzerland on the list of Western countries where euthanasia is fully legal. Switzerland has allowed assisted suicide since 1942, so long as patients "participate" in the administration of life-ending drugs (by ingesting them). The law doesn't require that a patient be a Swiss national, which has encouraged "suicide tourists" from other countries to book one-way tickets there.

In France, lawmakers are debating a bill that would give doctors the right to place patients into a deep, painless and permanent sleep. In the U.K., legislators are now considering an "assisted dying bill" that would legalize euthanasia for the first time. "I think in 10 or 15 years, a lot of Western European countries are going to have a law, one way or another," says Fione Zon-neveld, communications director for Right to Die-Netherlands, an Amsterdam-based organization that lobbies for the expansion of euthanasia laws. "It's a snowball."

Assisted suicide has long been taboo in the U.S., thanks in large part to Jack Kevorkian, the Michigan euthanasia activist who claimed to have assisted in the suicides of at least 130 people. Today, more than 15 years after Kevorkian's conviction on charges of second-degree murder, Americans are taking a second look. Assisted suicide is legal in Oregon, Washington and Vermont; in New Mexico and Montana, doctors are permitted to prescribe medication to end patients' lives. Last year, a 29-year-old California woman with terminal brain cancer moved to Oregon so she could legally end her life. A newlywed, Brittany Maynard wrote articles and appeared on television to discuss her decision. Some lauded her as brave; others condemned what they called her cowardice. Since Maynard died on November 1, lawmakers in six states have proposed right-to-die laws, and politicians have promised to do so in eight others. A Gallup poll conducted last May showed that nearly seven in 10 Americans believe physicians should be able to "legally end a patient's life by some painless means." The figure has bounced between 65 and 75 percent since 1996, after a steady climb from 36 percent in 1950.

The march toward euthanasia mirrors a trend spanning continents today: a growing number of countries are placing more value on individual freedom. This worries religious leaders, ethicists, and disability advocates. Assisted suicide may ease suffering, they say, but it threatens our most vulnerable citizens—the elderly and the disabled, who already struggle to justify their lives. "I like autonomy very much," says Theo Boer, a professor of ethics at the Theological University Kampen in the Netherlands. "But it seems to have overruled other values, like solidarity, patience, making the best of things. The risk now is that people no longer search for a way to endure their suffering. Killing yourself is the end of autonomy."

The Wrong Way to Die

Last year, within the span of a few weeks, both of my parents sent me a story in *The Atlantic* by American oncologist Ezekiel Emanuel. The headline was "Why I Hope to Die at 75." My mother added in a note: "I think 80 is my number."

It wasn't the first time my parents dropped a morbid little bomb on me. In 2011, my mom emailed me with the subject line "I want to go on record," and the body read, "If I die at the hand of another, I don't want anyone taking a life to avenge my death." My dad used to tell me he wanted to be pushed out on an ice block when it was time for him to go. (I get it, OK? You guys are both going to die someday. Can I go back to watching Breaking Bad now?) They want to be sure I understand that they won't cling to life when there's nothing in it worth clinging to.

On suicide, however, they disagree. My father is convinced he'll find a way to die peacefully, even if by his own hand. "I'll take some aspirin, drink some fine whiskey and it'll be done," he told me recently. My mother insists she will never commit suicide. Her father shot himself in the head when she was 29 so he wouldn't have to undergo surgery to repair a ruptured vein in his esophagus. "It's a selfish act," she told me between tears. "It denies your loved ones the ability to be with you and take care of you."

Around the world, there are many who don't see it that way, and they've found plenty of like-minded physicians to guide them toward death. But it's not exactly a comfortable practice. Most doctors find euthanasia counterintuitive to the Hippocratic oath and terrifying. It's irreversible.

For Bert Keizer, that fear has subsided with time. He's a Dutch physician who has, in 33 years of practicing medicine, assisted the deaths of dozens of patients—mostly without regret. His first few cases were difficult, he told me in a phone interview, because they made him afraid. Not of prosecution but because of the finality of the act. "The fear is of doing something to a person you know can never be rescinded," Keizer says. "I never had an easy [death]." But over time, he says, that angst subsided. Keizer has grown increasingly at ease with injecting patients with a lethal dose of sodium thiopental and then a muscle relaxant, knowing he is bringing suffering to an end.

When Keizer agrees to help someone, he says it's usually obvious it's the right thing to do. The last patient he euthanized was an American expatriate who had lived in the Netherlands for 15 years. The man was 78 and had suffered a cerebral hemorrhage; he was unable to walk and barely able to speak. His wife had died a year earlier, which is why the first time the man asked Keizer for help, the doctor refused. "You have to come to terms with the fact you're mourning your wife," he told his patient. Eight months later, the man changed Keizer's mind. He could no longer wash himself, was incontinent and his condition was unlikely to improve. In summer 2013, Keizer agreed to help the man die. He's confident that was the right thing to do.

It's common for a physician to say no to a first request, Keizer says, in part because people sometimes change their minds. "I know we planned on it just before Christmas, but I'd like to hang on until February," he's had patients tell him. "If someone says that, as a doctor, you think, Oh my God, what am I doing? And I have to say, 'Look, I'm sorry, but this is the end of the line for me. I'm no longer willing to talk to you about euthanasia.'"

Every doctor who assists a suicide is likely to have at least one case he wishes he could take back. For Keizer, it was a 55-year-old man with lung cancer. The man had already undergone chemotherapy and radiation; oncologists "put him through the paces," Keizer says, "and at the end of the line he was still going to die. He was furious with his doctors that they had led him astray all these years." When the man asked for Keizer's help 25 years ago, it was out of "an anger against life. I helped him, supplied him with an overdose, but years later I realized it wasn't right. It was a revengeful act. He died not with a smile on his face but with this bitter expression. That's not the way you should die."

Death Is Contagious

In the Netherlands, there are hundreds of people dying for reasons never anticipated when the law was passed. To understand why, I went to see Zonneveld at Right to Die-Netherlands. Her organization also helps members draft living wills and power of attorney papers, like the ones Willemsen showed me. Taped to the dry erase board in her newly refurbished office is a Dutch comic strip. "I consider my life completed, and want to die," a patient says. A doctor responds "OK" and produces a pistol. "Oh, no, I meant a soft death," the patient says. "Ah," the doctor says, and attaches a silencer to the gun.

Beneath that comic is a chart that shows a huge spike in the group's membership, from about 120,000 in 2010 to 160,000 today. On average, between 30 and 50 Dutch citizens sign up daily. Members pay 17 euros a year in exchange for end-of-life counseling and help with their documents. Last year, Right to Die-Netherlands used its funding surplus to open a mobile clinic. Twenty-three nurse-doctor teams now stand ready to be dispatched to people's homes—to dispatch those people.

In the first few years after the Netherlands decriminalized euthanasia in 2002, the number of cases declined. Then, in 2007, the statistics began a steady climb, an average jump of 15 percent a year. Keizer admits he "didn't see it [this growth] coming." The situation has put him and other doctors in the country in an ethical quandary. "It's a feeling of not being quite certain about where you're going," he says, though he adds, "We're talking about 5,000 people out of 140,000. That's not an epidemic."

He figures Dutch autonomy has the most to do with the steady increase in assisted suicide. More than 90 percent of Dutch citizens polled say they support the law, though only 20 percent say they would choose to die that way. But euthanasia has in some form been passively allowed here for decades. There had to be other reasons for the surge.

Boer, the ethicist, has some theories. Once a supporter of euthanasia, he's now one of its most vocal critics. Among the reasons for the euthanasia boom, Boer suggests, is propaganda. Over the past decade, he says, Dutch journalist Gerbert van Loenen has been tracking a series of documentary films that depict euthanasia in a wholly positive light. "They do ask certain questions," Boer says. "But they systematically ignore most critical questions, so that the general public is presented with an opinion that is completely good, and has no risks. This is contagious."

Another key factor: It's getting easier each year to qualify for euthanasia. In the beginning, most of those eligible were terminally ill. Now doctors are helping people die if they no longer want to bear depression, autism, blindness, or even being dependent on the care of others. "There are increasing numbers of double euthanasia—one of the partners is terminal and the other partner is care-dependent, they don't want to live alone," says Boer. One in 10 of the past 500 dossiers he has read contains some reference to "loneliness," he adds. "Those are the cases where I have become increasingly uneasy."

The numbers support Boer. In 2012, 13 patients were euthanized after convincing a doctor they were suffering unbearably from mental illnesses ranging from depression to schizophrenia. The following year, the figure more than tripled, to 44. The number of patients with dementia who killed themselves grew from 43 in 2012 to 97 in 2013. "I'm afraid," Boer says, "the situation in the Netherlands is out of control."

In 2005, lawmakers decriminalized another form of euthanasia—for babies. In recent years, the number of cases of newborn euthanasia has declined—because parents are acting sooner. The country introduced a new system of prenatal screening that allows parents to terminate pregnancy if ultrasound results reveal severe congenital malformations within 20 weeks of conception.

The Dutch didn't stop at babies. Minors in the Netherlands are now allowed to choose euthanasia, too. Children ages 12 to 15 may ask to die if they can get parents' permission. After age 16, young people can make the decision with only "parental involvement."

Pediatrician Eduard Verhagen helped establish the Dutch euthanasia guidelines for infants. He says the law should go further. "If we say the cutoff line is age 12, there might be children of 11 years and nine months who are very well capable of determining their own fate and making their own decisions, but they're not allowed to ask for euthanasia."

It is hard to imagine an American pediatrician making that argument. But no one envisioned euthanasia in the Netherlands would expand the way it has in the past 13 years. Perhaps the U.S. isn't far behind.

Doubts and Double Suicides

The euthanasia debate is often reduced to horrifying anecdotes. A doctor in Switzerland is under investigation for helping French twins with schizophrenia kill themselves. In Belgium, where assisted suicide cases rose in 2013 by 27 percent to 1,816, a Brussels man arranged the "double euthanasia" of his

parents so they no longer had to be alone. My grandmother's last days, on the other hand, are seemingly easy fodder for assisted suicide supporters. The reason France is discussing euthanasia is partly because of two cases from 2013: both double suicides, both couples in their 80s. One of the couples ended their lives in a luxury hotel in Paris, ordering room service and then asphyxiating themselves by putting plastic bags over their heads. Hotel staff discovered them holding hands, with a note next to them that claimed "the right to die with dignity." The other couple died in a hospital: The 84-year-old man shot his terminally ill wife in her bed, then turned the gun on himself.

But it's dangerous, euthanasia opponents say, to view the issue solely from the perspective of a few individuals determined to end their lives. There are great risks associated with allowing doctors to help people check out early, they say. Paramount among them, says Wesley J. Smith, a California lawyer and consultant for the International Task Force on Euthanasia and Assisted Suicide, is that people have forgotten the meaning of suffering. "There is a new view of suffering, that it's the worst of all possible experiences," Smith told me in a phone interview, "and that the role of society is to prevent it, as opposed to mitigating it."

Financial considerations could also creep into discussions that should never involve money. In the Netherlands, as in many developed countries, the number of elderly citizens is expected to increase by 30 to 40 percent in the coming two decades. Euthanasia, critics say, adds a dangerous option in this context: a way for societies to nudge the elderly to quicker deaths.

In the U.S., euthanasia opponents contend the profit-driven health care system and its slow takeover by cost-cutting managed-care companies pose major ethical risks. "There's a lot of pressure in the system already," says Diane Coleman, the president and CEO of Not Dead Yet, a disability rights group that lobbies against the legalization of assisted suicide and euthanasia. "We see people denied the care they need for economic reasons. Assisted suicide is the cheapest kind of treatment that could be offered by the system. These pressures are a reason for concern."

In 2008, Oregon Medicaid officials sent a letter to Barbara Wagner and Randy Stroup after the couple sought treatment for her lung cancer and his prostate cancer. The state denied their (costly) treatment, but on a list of alternative options, it offered to pay for assisted suicide. The couple went public and the state changed its mind, but Smith contends that the more we embrace euthanasia, the more government officials will back away from paying to treat its weakest members.

Accountability is a huge problem with assisted suicide, critics say. In the Netherlands, a doctor must report the cause of such deaths to the coroner. The case is then reviewed by one of five regional Euthanasia Committees, consisting of a doctor, a lawyer and an ethicist. But that review happens after the patient is dead, and it's only to determine whether a doctor might be charged with a crime. The review committees have deemed about five cases per year to be illegal since 2002, but no physicians have been prosecuted. "The doctors always promised not to make the same mistake again," Boer says.

In light of the Dutch experiment, critics say there is no way to legalize assisted suicide without accepting the risk that vulnerable people will be pushed to their deaths—by the health care system, by their own guilt or by abusive family members or caregivers. "We don't think any set of safeguards is sufficient," Coleman says. "We need to respond to the desire to die with the message, 'No, how can we help you? How can we be with you?' That's the real compassion people deserve."

As the euthanasia movement grows, critics in America and beyond are calling for a better approach to the way we end our lives. In November, the surgeon and writer Atul Gawande published *Being Mortal,* a groundbreaking book that argues for wholesale change in the philosophy of health care, a departure from the American fixation on survival to a focus instead on enabling "well-being."

As for euthanasia, Gawande is torn. He acknowledges that people "want to end their stories on their own terms," and that "we inflict deep gouges at the end of people's lives and then stand oblivious to the harm done." He also points out that American doctors rightly allow people to refuse food, water, medication, and treatments (and therefore end their lives). But the Dutch model is "a measure of failure," he writes, because it forgets that the ultimate goal should be "not a good death but a good life to the very end. The Dutch have been slower than others to develop palliative care programs that might provide for it. One reason, perhaps, is that their system of assisted death may have reinforced beliefs that reducing suffering and improving lives through other means is not feasible when one becomes debilitated or seriously ill."

Instead of suicide assistance, Coleman argues, doctors should offer better suicide prevention. When asked why they want to end their lives, people invariably check the same boxes: They've lost autonomy or don't want to be a burden on friends and family. But allowing physicians to help patients commit suicide is a cheap out, she says. What they should do instead is to help people make their lives livable, even if that's just for the last few weeks.

"The majority of Jack Kevorkian's victims were people with disabilities who were not terminal," Coleman says. "I saw him on TV once say, 'Well, they need it more, because they're going to suffer long.'"

Coleman has herself confronted this so-called need. After a lifelong battle with congenital myopathy, a neuromuscular disorder, she was hospitalized in 2012 with acute respiratory failure

after a bout with viral pneumonia. On her way to the hospital, one of the EMTs asked her husband if she had a do-not-resuscitate order. "Something about the way they asked the question led him to not only say 'No' but also to explain to them that I have a full-time job," she wrote later. "He felt that this changed their tone." A month later, Coleman was again hospitalized with chest congestion, and one of her doctors questioned whether she wanted it treated. "He looked at me in my wheelchair with what I'm sure he viewed as sympathy for my condition and a genuine concern to be sure that he knew what I wanted. But I also felt sure that he wouldn't have spoken that way to a nondisabled woman at age 58." Again, Coleman said, "I have a full-time job," and "he backed off, stopped talking and left."

Who's Ready to Die?

The day we met, Jannie Willemsen was on her way to visit an old friend who lives about 40 miles outside of Amsterdam. Each of these gatherings may as well be the first, she tells me. Willemsen's friend is 87 and suffering from dementia. She remembers nothing of their past encounters, nothing of their four decades of friendship, not even Willemsen's name. "It's so nice that you come to visit me," her friend said when she got there, as she ate in the restaurant of her nursing home and nibbled on chocolates. "She's still very kind. But she doesn't recognize me."

Willemsen dutifully visits anyway, but less often now. If she derives something from these encounters, it's a reminder that she is determined never to be swallowed by such a haze, never to spend even a day bumbling around a nursing home. "I'm happy there is an end of life," she says. "Some people believe God has given us life and that he should be the one to take it. I think when you get older and older, there comes a time when you don't feel at home in this world, where you don't understand it any longer, where you can't explain it."

My grandmother reached that point, but it's not how I remember her. Once, on a sticky summer day in 1998, I surprised her, sneaking over to her century-old Craftsman house in Calhoun, Georgia. I was 21 and hadn't seen her in a decade. How funny would it be, I thought, for me to walk up her driveway unannounced? I was halfway through my first internship at a small newspaper in Alabama, only a few hours' drive to her place, so one Saturday I printed out a set of MapQuest directions, journeyed across the border, parked down the block and sauntered toward the screen door to the back porch, full of mirth and mischief, anticipating the stunned look on Grandma's face. Would she even recognize me? As I went to knock, she emerged, shot me half a glance and said, "I have to run to the store. I'll see you in a bit." She walked right past me, got in her car and drove off.

This is how I will always remember my grandmother, as a tough woman to rattle. I wasn't there when she died and didn't participate in the decisions my family had to make about her final days. It was easy for me to judge from afar that Grandma had lived too long. My mom didn't see it that way.

"It made me so angry at the time, when people suggested that she was ready to die and I should just give up on her," she recently told me. "Those last days were brutally hard, but rich with meaning. I taught her to knit again, to try and keep her busy and take her mind off the boredom and discomfort of being confined to a wheelchair. One afternoon we went through her old photo albums, and she told me about her high school days, remembering the names of people and events. It was amazing, and I'll never forget it."

My mother says she would never have chosen euthanasia; not for her mom, not for herself. But she had to make difficult decisions throughout my grandmother's final months. After Grandma stopped eating on her own, my mom and her siblings decided against feeding her intravenously, but they didn't reject fluids. "I'm not going to let my mom die of dehydration," she told a doctor.

Someday I may be faced with the same impossible choices about my own parents. Both recently turned 70.

Critical Thinking

1. Explain doctor-assisted suicide as practiced in the Netherlands.
2. Is euthanasia legal in the Netherlands? How does the Dutch government deal with euthanasia?
3. How is the Dutch model of dealing with physician aid in dying spreading throughout the world?

Internet References

Assisted Dying: How Does It Work in a Dutch End-of-life Clinic?
http://www.theguardian.com/lifeandstyle/2015/sep/11/assisted-dying-dutch-end-of-life-netherlands-unbearable-suffering

Euthanasia, Assisted Suicide and Non-resuscitation on Request
https://www.government.nl/topics/euthanasia/contents/euthanasia-assisted-suicide-and-non-resuscitation-on-request

Lessons From the Dutch Experience
www.life.org.nz/euthanasia/abouteuthanasia/history-euthanasia11/

Rise in Euthanasia Requests Sparks Concern as Criteria for Help Widen
http://www.dutchnews.nl/features/2015/07/rise-in-euthanasia-requests-sparks-concern-as-criteria-for-help-widen/

Prepared by: George E. Dickinson, *College of Charleston*
Michael R. Leming, *St. Olaf College*

Article

Dutch Pediatricians Want to Euthanize Children

WESLEY J. SMITH

Learning Outcomes

After reading this article, you will be able to:

- Realize that Dutch laws allow for physician-assisted dying for children of any age, creating the slippery slope that many fear as national policy in the United States.

- See that the implementation of the Dutch laws related to the right to die leads to a lack of protection of the most vulnerable people—children, the disabled, the poor, and the elderly.

- See that while Dutch law is very progressive and meets the needs of many dying patients, this model is dangerous regarding the change in the United States national policy dealing with terminal patients.

There is no limit to the culture of death once it is fully off the leash.
Dutch law allows euthanasia for children age 12 and over. But now a prominent pediatrician wants the age limits erased. From the AFP story:

> Terminally ill children in unbearable suffering should be given the right to die, the Dutch Paediatricians Association said on Friday, urging the suppression of the current 12-year age limit. "We feel that an arbitrary age limit such as 12 should be changed and that each child's ability to ask to die should be evaluated on a case-by-case basis," said Eduard Verhagen, paediatrics professor at Groningen University who is on the association's ethics commission.

Kill, kill, kill, kill, kill! And don't think the "terminal illness" restriction would last two weeks.

Dutch law does not require that people be dying to be euthanized.

It should be noted that [Eduard] Verhagen—who co-authored the Groningen Protocol—commits infanticide. (The GP is a bureaucratic protocol under which doctors kill newborn babies born with disabilities and terminal illnesses.)

Think that will never happen? It's already the law in Belgium.

As I said, there is no limit to the culture of death once it is fully off the leash.

Editor's note. This appeared on Wesley's great blog (www. nationalreview.com/human-exceptionalism/420046/dutch -pediatricians-want-euthanize-children-wesley-j-smith).

Critical Thinking

1. What age does a child have to be for a physician in the Netherlands to assist in his or her death?
2. Explain doctor-assisted euthanasia as practiced in the Netherlands relative to children.
3. Is euthanasia for children legal in the Netherlands? How does the Dutch government deal with euthanasia?

Internet References

Background about Euthanasia in The Netherlands | Patients Rights Council
http://www.patientsrightscouncil.org/site/holland-background/
Euthanasia.com
www.euthanasia.com/page18.html
Euthanasia in Holland—Patients Rights Council
www.patientsrightscouncil.org/site/holland/

Prepared by: George E. Dickinson, *College of Charleston*
Michael R. Leming, *St. Olaf College*

Article

At the Bottom of the Slippery Slope

Where euthanasia meets organ harvesting.

WESLEY J. SMITH

Learning Outcomes

After reading this article, you will be able to:

- Understand the problematic nature of organ harvesting and physical aid in dying for national policy in the United States.

- See that coupling organ harvesting with mercy killing creates a strong emotional inducement to suicide, particularly for people who are culturally devalued and depressed.

- See that in coupling organ harvesting and euthanasia, a marketplace will be created for organ purchase where the wealthy can exploit the poor in meeting their medical needs.

In 1992, my friend Frances committed suicide on her 76th birthday. Frances was not terminally ill. She had been diagnosed with treatable leukemia and needed a hip replacement. Mostly, though, she was depressed by family issues and profoundly disappointed at where her life had taken her.

Something seemed very off to me about Frances's suicide. So I asked the executor of her estate to send me the "suicide file" kept by the quintessentially organized Frances and was horrified to learn from it that she had been an avid reader of the (now defunct) *Hemlock Quarterly,* published by the aptly named Hemlock Society (which was since merged into the assisted-suicide advocacy group, Compassion and Choices). The HQ taught readers about the best drugs with which to overdose and gave precise instructions on how to ensure death with a plastic bag—the exact method used by Frances to end her life.

I was furious. Frances's friends had known she was periodically suicidal and had intervened to help her through the darkness. The Hemlock Society had pushed Frances in the other direction, giving her moral permission to kill herself and then teaching her how to do it. This prompted the first of the many articles I have written over the years against assisted-suicide advocacy. It appeared in the June 28, 1993, *Newsweek* and warned about the cliff toward which assisted-suicide advocacy was steering our society:

We don't get to the Brave New World in one giant leap. Rather, the descent to depravity is reached by small steps. First, suicide is promoted as a virtue. Vulnerable people like Frances become early casualties. Then follows mercy killing of the terminally ill. From there, it's a hop, skip, and a jump to killing people who don't have a good "quality" of life, perhaps with the prospect of organ harvesting thrown in as a plum to society.

The other shoe—"organ harvesting"—has now dropped. Euthanasia was legalized in Belgium in 2002. It took six years for the first known coupling of euthanasia and organ harvesting, the case of a woman in a "locked in" state—fully paralyzed but also fully cognizant. After doctors agreed to her request to be lethally injected, she asked that her organs be harvested after she died. Doctors agreed. They described their procedure in a 2008 issue of the journal *Transplant International*:

This case of two separate requests, first euthanasia and second, organ donation after death, demonstrates that organ harvesting after euthanasia may be considered and accepted from ethical, legal, and practical viewpoints in countries where euthanasia is legally accepted. This possibility may increase the number of transplantable organs and may also provide some comfort to the donor and her family, considering that the termination of the patient's life may be seen as helping other human beings in need for organ transplantation.

The idea of coupling euthanasia with organ harvesting and medical experimentation was promoted years ago by the late Jack Kevorkian, but it is now becoming mainstream. Last year, the Oxford bioethicist Julian Savulescu coauthored a paper in *Bioethics* arguing that some could be euthanized, "at least partly to ensure that their organs could be donated." Belgian doctors, in particular, are openly discussing the nexus between euthanasia and organ harvesting. A June 10 press release from Pabst Science Publishers cited four lung transplants in Leuven from donors who died by euthanasia.

What's more, Belgian doctors and bioethicists now travel around Europe promoting the conjoining of the two procedures at medical seminars. Their PowerPoint presentation touts the "high quality" of organs obtained from patients after euthanasia of people with degenerative neuro/muscular disabilities.

Coupling organ donation with euthanasia turns a new and dangerous corner by giving the larger society an explicit stake in the deaths of people with seriously disabling or terminal conditions. Moreover, since such patients are often the most expensive for whom to care, and given the acute medical resource shortages we face, one need not be a prophet to see the potential such advocacy has for creating a perfect utilitarian storm.

Some might ask, if these patients want euthanasia, why not get some good out of their deaths? After all, they are going to die anyway.

But coupling organ harvesting with mercy killing creates a strong emotional inducement to suicide, particularly for people who are culturally devalued and depressed and, indeed, who might worry that they are a burden on loved ones and society. People in such an anguished mental state could easily come to believe (or be persuaded) that asking for euthanasia and organ donation would give a meaning to their deaths that their lives could never have.

And it won't stop there. Once society accepts euthanasia/organ harvesting, we will soon see agitation to pay seriously disabled or dying people for their organs, a policy that Kevorkian once advocated. Utilitarian boosters of such a course will argue that paying people will save society money on long-term care and allow disabled persons the satisfaction of benefiting society, while leaving a nice bundle for family, friends, or a charitable cause.

People with serious disabilities should be alarmed. The message that is being broadcast with increasing brazenness out of Belgium is that their deaths are worth more than their lives.

Critical Thinking

1. How did this article link organ harvesting with Kevorkian's campaign to give patients the "right to die"?
2. How does physician aid in dying give society a stake in the deaths of people with seriously disabling terminal conditions?
3. How does organ donation give those who would seek physician aid in dying a meaning for their suicides?

Internet References

Number of Dutch Killed by Euthanasia Rises by 13 Per Cent
http://www.telegraph.co.uk/news/worldnews/europe/netherlands/10330823/Number-of-Dutch-killed-by-euthanasia-rises-by-13-per-cent.html

Lessons From the Dutch Experience
www.life.org.nz/euthanasia/abouteuthanasia/history-euthanasia11/

Assisted Dying: How Does It Work in a Dutch End-of-life Clinic?
http://www.theguardian.com/lifeandstyle/2015/sep/11/assisted-dying-dutch-end-of-life-netherlands-unbearable-suffering

Euthanasia, Assisted Suicide and Non-resuscitation on Request
https://www.government.nl/topics/euthanasia/contents/euthanasia-assisted-suicide-and-non-resuscitation-on-request

WESLEY J. SMITH is a senior fellow at the Discovery Institute's Center on Human Exceptionalism, a lawyer for the Patients Rights Council, and a special consultant for the Center for Bioethics and Culture.

Prepared by: George E. Dickinson, *College of Charleston*
Michael R. Leming, *St. Olaf College*

Article

How Doctors Die

What's unusual about medical professionals is not how much treatment they get when faced with a terminal illness—but how little.

KEN MURRAY

Learning Outcomes

After reading this article, you will be able to:

- Gain an appreciation for the difficulty in determining issues surrounding the relationship between extra-ordinary and ordinary measures of treating patients and withholding and withdrawing life support.

- Make distinctions between providing medical treatment for illness and providing end of life care.

- Understand that while doctors are often involved intimately with dying patients, their own deaths are a matter of a different order because they have so much involvement.

Years ago, Charlie, a highly respected orthopedist and a mentor of mine, found a lump in his stomach. He had a surgeon explore the area, and the diagnosis was pancreatic cancer. This surgeon was one of the best in the country. He had even invented a new procedure for this exact cancer that could triple a patient's five-year-survival odds—from 5 percent to 15 percent—albeit with a poor quality of life. Charlie was uninterested. He went home the next day, closed his practice, and never set foot in a hospital again. He focused on spending time with family and feeling as good as possible. Several months later, he died at home. He got no chemotherapy, radiation, or surgical treatment. Medicare didn't spend much on him.

It's not a frequent topic of discussion, but doctors die, too. And they don't die like the rest of us. What's unusual about them is not how much treatment they get compared to most Americans, but how little. For all the time they spend fending off the deaths of others, they tend to be fairly serene when faced with death themselves. They know exactly what is going to happen, they know the choices, and they generally have access to any sort of medical care they could want. But they go gently.

Of course, doctors don't want to die; they want to live. But they know enough about modern medicine to know its limits. And they know enough about death to know what all people fear most: dying in pain and dying alone. They've talked about this with their families. They want to be sure, when the time comes, that no heroic measures will happen—that they will never experience, during their last moments on earth, someone breaking their ribs in an attempt to resuscitate them with CPR (that's what happens if CPR is done right).

Almost all medical professionals have seen too much of what we call "futile care" being performed on people. That's when doctors bring the cutting edge of technology to bear on a grievously ill person near the end of life. The patient will get cut open, perforated with tubes, hooked up to machines, and assaulted with drugs. All of this occurs in the Intensive Care Unit at a cost of tens of thousands of dollars a day. What it buys is misery we would not inflict on a terrorist. I cannot count the number of times fellow physicians have told me, in words that vary only slightly, "Promise me if you find me like this that you'll kill me." They mean it. Some medical personnel wear medallions stamped "NO CODE" to tell physicians not to perform CPR on them. I have even seen it as a tattoo.

To administer medical care that makes people suffer is anguishing. Physicians are trained to gather information without revealing any of their own feelings, but in private, among fellow doctors, they'll vent. "How can anyone do that to their family members?" they'll ask. I suspect it's one reason physicians have higher rates of alcohol abuse and depression than professionals in most other fields. I know it's one reason I stopped participating in hospital care for the last 10 years of my practice.

How has it come to this—that doctors administer so much care that they wouldn't want for themselves? The simple, or not-so-simple, answer is this: patients, doctors, and the system.

To see how patients play a role, imagine a scenario in which someone has lost consciousness and been admitted to an emergency room. As is so often the case, no one has made a plan for this situation, and shocked and scared family members find themselves caught up in a maze of choices. They're overwhelmed. When doctors ask if they want "everything" done, they answer yes. Then the nightmare begins. Sometimes, a family really means "do everything," but often they just mean "do everything that's reasonable." The problem is that they may not know what's reasonable, nor, in their confusion and sorrow, will they ask about it or hear what a physician may be telling them. For their part, doctors told to do "everything" will do it, whether it is reasonable or not.

The above scenario is a common one. Feeding into the problem are unrealistic expectations of what doctors can accomplish. Many people think of CPR as a reliable lifesaver when, in fact, the results are usually poor. I've had hundreds of people brought to me in the emergency room after getting CPR. Exactly one, a healthy man who'd had no heart troubles (for those who want specifics, he had a "tension pneumothorax"), walked out of the hospital. If a patient suffers from severe illness, old age, or a terminal disease, the odds of a good outcome from CPR are infinitesimal, while the odds of suffering are overwhelming. Poor knowledge and misguided expectations lead to a lot of bad decisions.

But of course it's not just patients making these things happen. Doctors play an enabling role, too. The trouble is that even doctors who hate to administer futile care must find a way to address the wishes of patients and families. Imagine, once again, the emergency room with those grieving, possibly hysterical, family members. They do not know the doctor. Establishing trust and confidence under such circumstances is a very delicate thing. People are prepared to think the doctor is acting out of base motives, trying to save time, or money, or effort, especially if the doctor is advising against further treatment.

Some doctors are stronger communicators than others, and some doctors are more adamant, but the pressures they all face are similar. When I faced circumstances involving end-of-life choices, I adopted the approach of laying out only the options that I thought were reasonable (as I would in any situation) as early in the process as possible. When patients or families brought up unreasonable choices, I would discuss the issue in layman's terms that portrayed the downsides clearly. If patients or families still insisted on treatments I considered pointless or harmful, I would offer to transfer their care to another doctor or hospital.

Should I have been more forceful at times? I know that some of those transfers still haunt me. One of the patients of whom I was most fond was an attorney from a famous political family. She had severe diabetes and terrible circulation, and, at one point, she developed a painful sore on her foot. Knowing the hazards of hospitals, I did everything I could to keep her from resorting to surgery. Still, she sought out outside experts with whom I had no relationship. Not knowing as much about her as I did, they decided to perform bypass surgery on her chronically clogged blood vessels in both legs. This didn't restore her circulation, and the surgical wounds wouldn't heal. Her feet became gangrenous, and she endured bilateral leg amputations. Two weeks later, in the famous medical center in which all this had occurred, she died.

It's easy to find fault with both doctors and patients in such stories, but in many ways all the parties are simply victims of a larger system that encourages excessive treatment. In some unfortunate cases, doctors use the fee-for-service model to do everything they can, no matter how pointless, to make money. More commonly, though, doctors are fearful of litigation and do whatever they're asked, with little feedback, to avoid getting in trouble.

Even when the right preparations have been made, the system can still swallow people up. One of my patients was a man named Jack, a 78-year-old who had been ill for years and undergone about 15 major surgical procedures. He explained to me that he never, under any circumstances, wanted to be placed on life support machines again. One Saturday, however, Jack suffered a massive stroke and got admitted to the emergency room unconscious, without his wife. Doctors did everything possible to resuscitate him and put him on life support in the ICU. This was Jack's worst nightmare. When I arrived at the hospital and took over Jack's care, I spoke to his wife and to hospital staff, bringing in my office notes with his care preferences. Then I turned off the life support machines and sat with him. He died two hours later.

Even with all his wishes documented, Jack hadn't died as he'd hoped. The system had intervened. One of the nurses, I later found out, even reported my unplugging of Jack to the authorities as a possible homicide. Nothing came of it, of course; Jack's wishes had been spelled out explicitly, and he'd left the paperwork to prove it. But the prospect of a police investigation is terrifying for any physician. I could far more easily have left Jack on life support against his stated wishes, prolonging his life, and his suffering, a few more weeks. I would even have made a little more money, and Medicare would have ended up with an additional $500,000 bill. It's no wonder many doctors err on the side of over-treatment.

But doctors still don't over-treat themselves. Almost anyone can find a way to die in peace at home, and pain can be managed better than ever. Hospice care, which focuses on providing terminally ill patients with comfort and dignity rather than on futile cures, provides most people with much better final days. Amazingly, studies have found that people placed in hospice care often live longer than people with the same disease who are seeking active cures. I was struck to hear on the radio recently that the famous reporter Tom Wicker had "died peacefully at home, surrounded by his family." Such stories are, thankfully, increasingly common.

Several years ago, my older cousin Torch (born at home by the light of a flashlight—or torch) had a seizure that turned out to be the result of lung cancer that had gone to his brain. I arranged for him to see various specialists, and we learned that with aggressive treatment of his condition, including three to five hospital visits a week for chemotherapy, he would live perhaps four months. Ultimately, Torch decided against any treatment and simply took pills for brain swelling. He moved in with me.

We spent the next eight months doing a bunch of things that he enjoyed, having fun together like we hadn't had in decades. We went to Disneyland, his first time. We hung out at home. Torch was a sports nut, and he was very happy to watch sports and eat my cooking. He even gained a bit of weight, eating his favorite foods rather than hospital foods. He had no serious pain, and he remained high-spirited. One day, he didn't wake up. He spent the next three days in a coma-like sleep and then died. The cost of his medical care for those eight months, for the one drug he was taking, was about $20.

Torch was no doctor, but he knew he wanted a life of quality, not just quantity. Don't most of us? If there is a state of the art of end-of-life care, it is this: death with dignity. As for me, my physician has my choices. They were easy to make, as they are for most physicians. There will be no heroics, and I will go gentle into that good night. Like my mentor Charlie. Like my cousin Torch. Like my fellow doctors.

Critical Thinking

1. Do medical doctors die like the rest of us?
2. How is their behavior related to their own dying different from the way in which they treat their patients? Why?
3. How do doctors die? What information do they have to help them make decisions for themselves that others do not receive?

Internet References

Beyond Advance Directives: Personal Autonomy and the Right To Refuse Life-Sustaining Medical Treatment
https://www.nhbar.org/publications/display-journal-issue.asp?id=349

Patient Refusal: What to Do When Medical Treatment and Transport Are Rejected
www.jems.com/articles/1969/12/patient-refusal-what-do-when-m.html

Taking No for an Answer: Refusal of Life-Sustaining Treatment
http://journalofethics.ama-assn.org/2010/06/ccas2-1006.html

The Right to Treatment and the Right to Refuse Treatment
http://careforyourmind.org/the-right-to-treatment-and-the-right-to-refuse-treatment/

KEN MURRAY, M.D., is a retired clinical assistant professor of family medicine at University of Southern California.

Unit 5

UNIT

Prepared by: George E. Dickinson, *College of Charleston*
Michael R. Leming, *St. Olaf College*

Funerals

Decisions relating to the disposition of the body after death often involve feelings of ambivalence—on one hand; attachments to the deceased might cause one to be reluctant to dispose of the body, on the other hand, practical considerations make the disposal of the body necessary. Funerals or memorial services provide methods for disposing of a dead body, remembering the deceased, and helping survivors accept the reality of death. They are also public rites of passage that assist the bereaved in returning to routine patterns of social interaction. In contemporary America, approximately 58 percent of deaths involve earth burial and 42 percent involve cremation. However, there are great differences regarding the frequency of these occurrences from state to state. The states with the fewest cremations are Mississippi, Alabama, Kentucky, and Louisiana (approximately 20 percent). The states with the most cremations are Nevada, Washington, Oregon, Hawaii, and Montana (approximately 70 percent). These public behaviors, along with the private process of grieving, comprise the two components of the bereavement process.

This unit on the contemporary American funeral begins with a general article on the nature and functions of public bereavement behavior by Michael Leming and George Dickinson. Leming and Dickinson provide an overview of the present practice of funeralization in American society, including traditional and alternative funeral arrangements. They also discuss the functions of funerals relative to the sociological, psychological, and theological needs of adults and children. The remaining articles in this section reflect upon the many alternative ways in which funerals, rituals, and final dispositions for the deceased may be constructed.

Key Points to Consider

Describe how the funeralization process can assist in coping with grief and facilitate the bereavement process. Distinguish between grief, bereavement, and funeralization.

Discuss the psychological, sociological, and theological/philosophical aspects of the funeralization process. How does each of these aspects facilitate the resolution of grief?

Describe and compare each of the following processes: burial, cremation, environmentally friendly alternatives, cryonics, and body donation for medical research. What would be your choice for final disposition of your body? Why would you choose this method, and what effects might this choice have upon your survivors (if any) and the stewardship for the earth's resources? Would you have the same or different preferences for a close loved one such as a spouse, child, or parent? Why or why not?

Article

Prepared by: George E. Dickinson, *College of Charleston*
Michael R. Leming, *St. Olaf College*

The Contemporary American Funeral

Meeting the Needs of the Bereaved

MICHAEL R. LEMING AND GEORGE E. DICKINSON

Learning Outcomes

After reading this article, you will be able to:

- Understand the social functions of the funeral.

- Know how the needs of the bereaved are served by the funeral.

- Come to understand how one can help children when they attend funerals.

Paul Irion (1956) described the following needs of the bereaved: reality, expression of grief, social support, and meaningful context for the death. For Irion, the funeral is an experience of significant personal value insofar as it meets the religious, social, and psychological needs of the mourners. Each of these must be met for bereaved individuals to return to everyday living and, in the process, resolve their grief.

The psychological focus of the funeral is based on the fact that grief is an emotion. Edgar Jackson (1963) indicated that grief is the other side of the coin of love. He contended that if a person has never loved the deceased—never had an emotional investment of some type and degree—he or she will not grieve upon death. Evidence of this can easily be demonstrated by the number of deaths that we see, hear, or read about daily that do not have an impact on us unless we have some kind of emotional involvement with those deceased persons. We can read of 78 deaths in a plane crash and not grieve over any of them unless we personally knew the individuals killed. Exceptions to the preceding might include the death of a celebrity or other public figure, when people experience a sense of grief even though there has never been any personal contact.

In his original work on the symptomatology of grief, Erich Lindemann (1944) stressed this concept of grief and its importance as a step in the resolution of grief. He defined how the emotion of grief must support the reality and finality of death. As long as the finality of death is avoided, Lindemann believed, grief resolution is impeded. For this reason, he strongly recommended that the bereaved persons view the dead. When the living confront the dead, all of the intellectualization and avoidance techniques break down. When we can say, "He or she is dead, I am alone, and from this day forward my life will be forever different," we have broken through the devices of denial and avoidance and have accepted the reality of death. It is only at this point that we can begin to withdraw the emotional capital that we have invested in the deceased and seek to create new relationships with the living.

On the other hand, viewing the corpse can be very traumatic for some. Most people are not accustomed to seeing a cold body and a significant other stretched out with eyes closed. Indeed, for some this scene may remain in their memories for a lifetime. Thus, they remember the cold corpse, not the warm, responsive person. Whether or not to view the body is not a cut-and-dried decision. Many factors should be taken into account when this decision is made.

Grief resolution is especially important for family members, but others are affected also—the neighbors, the business community in some instances, the religious community in most instances, the health care community, and the circle of friends and associates (many of whom may be unknown to the family). All of these groups will grieve to some extent over the death of their relationship with the deceased. Thus, many people are affected by the death. These affected persons will seek not only a means of expressing their grief over the death but also a network of support to help cope with their grief.

Sociologically, the funeral is a social event that brings the chief mourners and the members of society into a confrontation with death. The funeral becomes a vehicle to bring persons of all walks of life and degrees of relationship to the deceased together for expression and support. For this reason, in our contemporary culture, the funeral becomes an occasion to which no one is invited but all may come. This was not always the case, and some cultures make the funeral ceremony an "invitation only" experience. It is perhaps for this reason that private funerals (restricted to the family or a special list of persons) have all but disappeared in our culture. (The possible exception to this statement is a funeral for a celebrity—in which participation by the public may be limited to media coverage.)

At a time when emotions are strong, it is important that human interaction and social support become high priorities. A funeral can provide this atmosphere. To grieve alone can be devastating because it becomes necessary for that lone person to absorb all of the feelings into himself or herself. It has often been said that "joy shared is joy increased"; surely grief shared is grief diminished. People need each other at times when they have intense emotional experiences.

A funeral is in essence a one-time kind of support group to undergird and support the grieving persons. A funeral provides a conducive social environment for mourning. We may go to the funeral home either to visit with the bereaved family or to work through our own grief. Most of us have had the experience of finding it difficult to discuss a death with a member of the family. We seek the proper atmosphere, time, and place. It is during the funeral, the wake, the shivah, or the visitation with the bereaved family that we have the opportunity to express our condolences and sympathy comfortably.

Anger and guilt are often deeply felt at the time of death and will surface in words and actions. They are permitted within the funeral atmosphere as honest and candid expressions of grief, whereas at other times they might bring criticism and reprimand. The funeral atmosphere says in essence, "You are okay, I am okay; we have some strong feelings, and now is the time to express and share them for the benefit of all." Silence, talking, feeling, touching, and all means of sharing can be expressed without the fear of their being inappropriate.

Another function of the funeral is to provide a theological or philosophical perspective to facilitate grieving and to provide a context of meaning in which to place one of life's most significant experiences. For the majority of Americans, the funeral is a religious rite or ceremony (Pine, 1971). Those grievers who do not possess a religious creed or orientation will define or express death in the context of the values that the deceased and the grievers find important. Theologically or philosophically, the funeral functions as an attempt to bring meaning to the death and life of the deceased individual. For the religiously oriented person, the belief system will perhaps bring an understanding of the afterlife. Others may see only the end of biological life and the beginning of symbolic immortality created by the effects of one's life on the lives of others. The funeral should be planned to give meaning to whichever value context is significant for the bereaved.

"Why?" is one of the most often asked questions upon the moment of death or upon being told that someone we know has died. Though the funeral cannot provide the final answer to this question, it can place death within a context of meaning that is significant to those who mourn. If it is religious in context, the theology, creed, and articles of faith confessed by the mourners will give them comfort and assurance as to the meaning of death. Others who have developed a personally meaningful philosophy of life and death will seek to place the death in that philosophical context.

Cultural expectations typically require that we dispose of the dead with ceremony and dignity. The funeral can also ascribe importance to the remains of the dead. In keeping with the specialization found in most aspects of American life (e.g., the rise of professions), the funeral industry is doing for Americans that necessary task they no longer choose to do for themselves.

Critical Thinking

1. What are the three basic needs of the bereaved according to Paul Iron?
2. Explain the following quote by Edgar Jackson, "Grief is the other side of the coin of love."
3. How can one help children when they attend funerals?

Internet References

All You Need To Know About Cremation | Everplans
www.everplans.com/articles/all-you-need-to-know-about-cremation

How Is A Body Cremated? | Cremation Resource
www.cremationresource.org/cremation/how-is-a-body-cremated.html

Shopping for Funeral Services | Consumer Information
www.consumer.ftc.gov/articles/0070-shopping-funeral-services

Prepared by: George E. Dickinson, *College of Charleston*
Michael R. Leming, *St. Olaf College*

Article

Good Mourning

A death forces us to pause and reflect—something our fast-paced culture avoids. But Catholic funeral and burial practices are worth keeping alive.

KATIE BAHR

Learning Outcomes

After reading this article, you will be able to:

- Become a critical reader of research related to the grieving process.

- Understand how changes in the social environment will have effects on the bereavement process.

When Alexander Edelen lost his grandmother in 2013 he faced a difficult choice. Though he wanted to attend her funeral, his boss would not give him a day off for bereavement. "I guess, from an employer's perspective, a funeral is taking away a day that an employee is productive," he says. "But a person only lives once."

As a child Edelen spent a lot of time with his grandmother. On holidays her house was where relatives would gather. Other times she would watch him when his parents were at work. Because her illness was sudden, Edelen couldn't spend much time with her before she died. When he got married, she was too sick to attend the wedding.

Edelen, a parishioner at Most Blessed Sacrament Catholic Church in Baton Rouge, Louisiana, was determined to attend his grandmother's funeral. His family planned a traditional funeral Mass at the parish where his grandmother belonged for decades. Even though he could not get a bereavement day, Edelen still went.

"For me, the funeral and the wake were my last chance to see my grandmother and to say goodbye to her," he says. "Some things are more important than a Saturday at the office."

Though Edelen was surprised at his employer's expectation that he should skip a close relative's funeral, his experience is indicative of a shift in how society handles death. According to data from the National Funeral Directors Association, funerals in recent decades have become shorter and less religious. More people choose cremation, and a growing number choose not to hold services at all.

Deacon George Kelder, a funeral director for 30 years and assistant executive vice president of the New Jersey State Funeral Directors Association, has experienced these changes firsthand—even among Catholics. In his diocese of Trenton, New Jersey, it has become more common for families to skip parts of the funeral, particularly the wake or committal if cremation is involved. Other times, they might hold the service at a funeral home or other location instead of a church. In Kelder's words, it's "Catholic funeral lite."

The un-churched may not understand the significance of the funeral rite, Kelder says, while those who are not religious would often prefer to not have Mass at all. But even among practicing Catholics Kelder has seen the ceremonial connections become less of a priority. "Have you ever been in a funeral home (for a vigil) when the clergy arrives and everyone hightails it out prior to the prayers starting, so as not to overstay their welcome? It's almost comic."

Kelder believes the changes in funerals are a troubling reflection of the changes in society. By focusing more on careers and worldly success, he thinks some people no longer have time for relationships and personal affairs, even when someone has died. "It's the reality of where we are," he says. "The living have to get back to their lives."

Many Catholics may not realize how much they lose by skipping the ceremonial steps along the way. "A good funeral gets the dead where they need to be and the living where they need to be, but our clocks are getting in the way," Kelder says.

No Time for Goodbyes

Traditionally funerals within the Catholic Church have followed the *Order of Christian Funerals,* which has three distinct parts: the vigil service (also known as the wake), a time for visitation, prayer, and remembrance; the funeral Mass, a time to offer prayers for the repose of the deceased s soul; and the Rite of Committal, in which the body is committed to its final resting place. Father Edward Hathaway, pastor of St. Mary Parish in Alexandria, Virginia, believes that when done right Catholic funerals can be an awe-inspiring expression of the faith. They are also a source of comfort and familiarity in a time of loss and dramatic change; a place where Catholics can be reminded of their union with God and one another.

"Funerals can be a very profound moment for people to confront their own mortality as well as the immortal life Jesus won for us on the cross," Hathaway says. "Were confronted with the beauty of God, and that's what can give us hope if we lose a loved one."

Though most of his parishioners still follow church traditions when it comes to death, Hathaway has noticed some changes since he was ordained in 1991. Today people dress more casually for funerals. Eulogies and nontraditional music are more common. And visitation hours are much shorter—it was once common practice for wakes to take place the day before the funeral Mass from 2 to 4 p.m. and then again from 6 to 8 p.m.

"Now with everyone working," Hathaway says, "who can come to the afternoon wake? People are commuting. They get home late. They will still come out for a wake in the evening, but now a lot of it is centered on the social thing of comforting the family. You don't always see prayer."

The busyness of life has also affected priests, Kelder says. In larger parishes especially, pastors are often overloaded with work. In some cases, a funeral can become just another task to be crossed off an ever-growing to-do list. When priests are rushed, Kelder believes it can be detrimental to the service. If they try to put the elements into place without talking to the family, it can cause more harm than good.

"We try to make a point of reaching out to families and asking what's important, what needs to be said and, more importantly, what doesn't need to be said," Kelder explains. "You don't want to go into an environment with a fractured family and talk to them about what a loving mother she was."

He adds that funerals should be flexible in accommodating the needs of the family and friends of the deceased. "When you push them away from participating in it at all, before you know it, there's no benefit to them," he says.

Occasionally, Hathaway says he experiences a culture clash when devout parents die and their nonpracticing children decide a traditional funeral service is unnecessary. "Sometimes it's money-driven. Sometimes it's about a decrease in faith, and sometimes it shows a lack of awareness for how the sacrifice of the Mass is a benefit to the souls who preceded us," he says.

For these reasons, Hathaway feels strongly about providing education around funerals. He also thinks the funerals themselves can be strong teaching tools, giving people who don't normally enter church the opportunity to ask the big questions about life, death, and their own mortality. In his own life, Hathaway says it was his father's funeral that helped him cement his faith.

"I was 21 years old and I was confronted with those questions, which were very important to my vocation," he says. " 'What am I doing?' 'What is the meaning of life?' I decided, 'If it's supernatural, let me focus more on that than I have been.'"

Discomfort with the Dead

Other changes to funerals over the years have more complicated causes than packed calendars. Mark T. Higgins, a Catholic and co-owner of Hall-Wynne Funeral Service and Crematory in Durham, North Carolina, says he's noticed an increasing discomfort when it comes to death in recent years. "We're looking at a generation that doesn't want to look at death," he says. "People want to make it simple; they want to get the body disposed of quickly. The same people who are in the delivery room when the baby is born, when they are around death, they don't want anything too graphic."

In the 2013 book *The Good Funeral: Death, Grief, and the Community of Care* (Westminster John Knox) coauthors Thomas Lynch, a Catholic poet and funeral director, and Thomas Long, a Presbyterian minister and theologian, trace the modern discomfort with death back to the origins of the funeral industry, which began soon after the Civil War. For most of human history, when a person died their family or friends would prepare the body and take care of the funeral preparations by themselves. The body would be laid for visitation in the parlor of the family home. When it was time for burial, the deceased would often be laid to rest in a family cemetery.

"When funeral directors began to take over the embalming of the dead, they disappeared from our sight and we began to become disconnected from the process," Long says. "We decided that we didn't really like or couldn't tolerate the dead."

This distance from death was a departure from other cultural traditions, Lynch says. "In most cultures, a corpse can be a bit of an encumbrance. Someone has to help dress the person and move the body, someone has to cook and prepare a meal. Everybody has a part to play because they know that nobody is going to bury the body for you. But in this culture, you can get on the phone, call your undertaker, and he returns with a box of ashes. We can disappear the dead without much trouble."

Lynch and Long both say they are troubled by how this disconnect plays out in the funerals they see—people seem so afraid of death that they refuse to acknowledge it. Fewer people choose to accompany the body to the gravesite or the crematory. And while it is still expected for the remains to be present in a Catholic funeral Mass if at all possible, more and more non-Catholics are choosing to hold memorial services in which the bodies are not present. "We're the first people in the history of the world for which the dead are no longer welcome at their own funerals," Long says.

Lynch has stronger words. He believes funerals at which the body is purposely not present are not just misguided but "inhuman."

"Those are the bodies we fought for, slept with, loved, sat with, got comfort from, and lived with," he says. "If we're going to dispatch them to the ground, we should go to the cemetery. If we're going to burn them, we should go with them to the fire. . . . Any church that has forgotten how to deal with the dead is of no use to the living."

Kelder has noticed the disconnect with death in some Catholic burials, where the Rite of Committal might take place in a tented area of a cemetery surrounded by astroturf, with the actual burial happening later. "Our burials can sometimes be so sanitized that we lose the aspects of what we're doing and that connection is severed," he says. "Sometimes because it's such a painful thing to work through, you have to get your hands dirty."

He and others find hope in the recent interest in farm-to-table eating and home births. Just as more people are hoping to reconnect with where their food comes from and how people are born, they think people should be willing to reconnect with how people die. "Hospice is a good step to equate us to dying," Kelder says. "We may not like it, but it happens to all of us. Witnessing our spouse's death, our parents' or children's deaths, I think, is very vital to the process."

A Loss of Faith?

While a lack of connection to the dead is bad, Long believes the changes in funerals are reflective of an even bigger problem—a lack of faith across society. "Sometimes we clergy have the sense that funeral directors somehow 'took over' the funeral from the church. But I don't think funeral directors could have taken this job over if we were not so willing to give it up," he says.

Long points to significant theological and cultural changes at the end of the 19th century that he says caused Christians to lose their grasp on the idea of heavenly hope. One cause of this shift was the Civil War, which presented challenging images of mass deaths. "Many Americans had a very individualistic and literalistic picture of 'my loved one going to heaven and being welcomed by Jesus,'" Long says. "But this deeply personal image became difficult to maintain with over a half million dead lying on the battlefields of Virginia and Pennsylvania."

That, combined with a more scientific worldview, caused many Christians to doubt their earlier ideas of heaven and the afterlife. As Americans grew wealthier and more enchanted by the pleasures of this world, they began to lose interest in the joys of the next, Long says. "The more you like this life, the less intriguing the next one becomes," Long says. "When the dead aren't going anywhere, we have to figure out some other way to find meaning about them."

This led to a transition, moving funerals from being a ritual to accompany the dead on their way to heaven to being focused on getting mourners to a place of healing. "Funerals shifted from dealing with both the dead and the living to dealing almost exclusively with the living, and they became all about grief management," Long says.

Outside the Catholic Church, many Christian and secular funerals have morphed into highly personalized celebrations of life, in which multiple people who knew the deceased person will share stories and anecdotes about his or her life. Lynch thinks those funerals can cause harm if they force mourners into false emotions. "A good funeral should allow for the entire emotional register," he says. "It should allow for the grin to give way to a wince, and nobody should be shocked by that. . . . The problem with a celebration of life is that it says, 'We're here for the good laugh, but not as much for the good cry.'"

Father Hathaway believes problems arise in funerals when people replace the primary purpose—praying for the souls of their loved ones—with the secondary purpose of providing comfort for those left behind. In his parish, Hathaway has seen an increased push for eulogies, which are not traditionally a part of the Catholic funeral Mass. (Many parishes around the country have forbidden eulogies from the funeral Mass, while others allow them only occasionally.) While there should be time for families and friends to reminisce and laugh about the deceased person, Hathaway believes the funeral Mass should be primarily about prayer.

"For me, the most disappointing thing at funerals is when someone makes a long eulogy with no reference to the person as a child of God or a person of faith, or sometimes even talks about things that are contrary to the faith, like how much beer they could drink," he says. "Sometimes the emotions can run the whole show. We do need to acknowledge our emotions, but what's beautiful about the church's liturgy is that when we don't know what to say, it provides us with the words."

Though celebrations of life are not encouraged in the Catholic Church, Higgins says he has heard of churches loosening their restrictions to allow multiple eulogies, secular music, or even special events like balloon releases at the wake service. Within the funeral Mass itself, Higgins thinks churches should be more careful. "If there's one too many things, the service can get hijacked and become all about the person and their particular interests and quirks," he says. "That's not the witness of the funeral Mass.

"The appeal for a celebration of life service is strong because somehow it's not as sad, not as in your face, but I think people who go to a well-done funeral will constantly comment on the beauty and the transcendence and the power of that funeral through its timeless ritual," Higgins says. "We've been doing this a long time, and it doesn't require a lot of embellishment."

A Faithful Farewell

One funeral Higgins can remember that reached the level of transcendence was that of Terence McCann, who passed away in 2012. When Terence's wife, Bodie, was planning the funeral at Immaculate Conception Church in Durham, she wanted it to reflect some of her husband's lifelong passions while also remaining true to Catholic rituals.

The couple met in the church choir, so it was fitting that the funeral Mass have the beautiful choral music he loved. Bodie also wanted the funeral to reflect Terence's love of God, his family, and the parish—all elements of his life that she took into account when preparing his funeral.

During the funeral, chosen hymns reflected Terence's Irish heritage and naval career. Over the course of the funeral's three parts, Bodie says she had time to socialize with friends and family at the wake and to pray in a Mass that reflected who her husband was. And she had time to say goodbye.

"It was very respectful of his life, and I think it really honored who he was and what he stood for," she says. "I believe that ritual is supportive in grief and can be supportive in lots of life's passages."

Though she has been to many different kinds of funerals through the years, Bodie said she was happy she went the traditional Catholic route. "I experienced the arc, the whole story, and that was very important to me," she says. "I have seen people not want to do this or that, for fear of it being uncomfortable or too sad, but in the long run that would have been a mistake for me. I would have regretted not being part of the send-off that he deserved."

According to Higgins, one of the reasons Terence's funeral was so successful had to do with the way it was both personal and prayerful. By combining all aspects of her husband—the physical, the emotional, and the spiritual—Bodie was able to say goodbye in a way that honored him completely.

Terence's funeral is an example of how other Catholics can proceed when it comes to death. Just as Catholics find themselves face-to-face with Jesus' suffering every time they see a crucifix, they should be prepared to face death when it shows up in their lives. And if Catholics truly believe in life after death, they need to accept that the souls of deceased loved ones still remain. Having a funeral that honors both who the person was and offers prayers for where he or she has gone can be one final way to show love.

"When a funeral is done well, these are some of the finest moments for the church," says Higgins. "The purpose is to get the dead person where they need to go and to usher that person physically as a community of faith. When we do that, when we act out that play, we are getting ourselves to a more solid ground."

Critical Thinking

1. How are the changes in funerals a troubling reflection of the changes in society?
2. What does one have to lose by skipping the funeral or making the funeral non-significant?
3. How is personalization related to "Good Mourning"?

Internet References

An Overview of Catholic Funeral Rites
    www.usccb.org/prayer-and-worship/bereavement-and-funerals/overview-of-catholic-funeral-rites.cfm

Burying the Dead: Catholic Funerals
    www.fisheaters.com/funerals.html

Catholic Funeral Traditions
    www.everplans.com/articles/catholic-funeral-traditions

Article

Prepared by: George E. Dickinson, *College of Charleston*
Michael R. Leming, *St. Olaf College*

The Viewing

BRIAN DOYLE

Learning Outcomes

After reading this article, you will be able to:

- Be better prepared for the viewing when attending a funeral.

- Understand ways in which one can assist others who are approaching the experience of the "viewing."

- Understand the advantages and disadvantages of viewing the dead body as part of the grieving experience.

Walked into the chapel at dusk last night, and there she was, in the casket off to the left, with her son standing sentinel. He is a priest and he was smiling a little in welcome as people walked up to him and hugged him, if they were young, or shook his hand, if they were older men. The older men who shook his hand would take his right hand with their right hands and then cover the two clasped hands with their left hands, I noticed. A sort of a paternal or protective gesture which moved me very much for some reason.

The casket was half open and she was wearing a lovely demure dress but you couldn't see if she had her best shoes on. I assume she had her best shoes on. A pink glass rosary was wrapped around her hands. It being Wednesday I assume she would be praying the Glorious Mysteries, during which we meditate particularly on resurrection, ascension, and assumption. She knew what Mysteries we meditated upon every day of the week. She had prayed the rosary every day since she was three years old, I believe. Even when she was very ill she prayed the rosary every day and even when she could no longer remember her son's face or name she would still run her fingers over her rosary. I believe you can pray the rosary even if you no longer know what the word rosary means. Perhaps that is when the rosary is prayed most piercingly of all.

Her hair was done beautifully in the bouffant style which long ago went out of style but most assuredly never went out of style for her. If there is a photograph of her in this world without her hair carefully elevated and frozen magically in place by mysterious elixirs, I have not seen it, and I cannot believe it exists. She is wearing her scapula, which I believe she wore every day of her life since she was a child, and she is wearing a Marian medal, because she and the Madonna were very close friends, and talked to each other continually, especially when she lost her husband and their other son.

Her surviving son is now moving toward the sacristy, for he will preside tonight over the vigil service for his mother, but it takes him a while to make his way to the sacristy to robe up, because people keep hugging him or shaking his hand. *I will gather you with care*, the chapel choir is singing. I stand by the casket for a while. *I will hold you close to my heart*, sings the choir. A child of about nine peers over the edge of the casket fearfully. *We will run and not grow weary*. I feel for the child, because it is unnerving to see a dead person supine in the chapel, and she sure looks like she is frozen solid, which may come from a faint dusting of powder on her face and hands. *We will rise again*. Her son the priest emerges from the sacristy and lines up with his altar servers. *Lift up your eyes and see who made the stars*. The congregation stands, rustling, and turns to watch the priest, their friend and companion, begin the service. He and his mother will go home to their native city tomorrow, by train, and there will be a rosary at night in their old parish, with their old neighbors and friends chanting back and forth in the dim candlelight, and a funeral Mass the next morning, and then she will be buried with her beloved husband and their other son. Her son the priest will not be buried with his brother and parents, but will someday sleep with his brother priests in a field with a low stone wall, along which students walk back and forth to class. I have seen the field and the stone wall and I have seen students run their hands gently along the wall as they walk past the hundreds of sleeping priests. *I know you, I call you each by name.* I pray with all my heart that this is so, and bless myself with water from the baptistry, and slip out of the chapel to be with my wife and children while yet we live; while yet we live.

Critical Thinking

1. How can you prepare for the "viewing"?
2. Why are people reluctant to view the dead body?
3. What are the advantages and disadvantages of viewing the dead body as part of the grieving experience?

Internet References

Chabad.org—Viewing the Remains
www.chabad.org/library/article_cdo/aid/281553/jewish/Viewing-the-Remains.htm

HG.org—Is There a Value in Viewing Your Loved One at a Funeral?
www.hg.org/article.asp?id=7287

Sudden
www.suddendeath.org/help-for-professionals/online-guidance/2-uncategorised/79-guidanceviewing

The Light Beyond—You Are Not Alone in Your Grief
www.thelightbeyond.com/death_of_a_loved_one_what_will_viewing_the_body_be_like_.html

BRIAN DOYLE, *is the editor of* Portland *magazine at the University of Portland, and the author most recently of* A Book of Uncommon Prayer *(Ave Maria).*

Article

Prepared by: George E. Dickinson, *College of Charleston*
Michael R. Leming, *St. Olaf College*

Green Burials Reflect Care for Earth, Family Finances

Lauren Markoe

Learning Outcomes

After reading this article, you will be able to:

- Come to understand the ecological, cultural, and financial advantages of green burials.

- Come to understand some of the ecological disadvantages of cremation.

- Come to understand that "green burials" are not a radical invention and are in keeping with many traditional customs for Jews, Muslims, and Americans of an earlier era.

Growing up in small-town Georgia, John B. Johnson had family friends who ran the funeral home down the street, so the particulars of a typical American funeral—the embalming, the heavy casket and remarks about how great the deceased's hair looked—were all familiar to him.

When the time came, he assumed, his funeral would look much the same.

But Johnson, now 44, envisions a different sort of send-off for himself: a "green burial" that draws upon both his faith and his commitment to the environment.

For Johnson and others like him, a green burial is a way to care for the earth. It is also a way of resisting the pomp of the average American funeral and of taking seriously the biblical reminder, "For dust thou art, and unto dust shalt thou return."

"It's the notion that Jesus was so humble," said Johnson, an Episcopalian, who lives in Washington, D.C. "I am a follower, and I want to follow that example. I want my death as humble as I think Jesus lived."

Johnson wants to skip the embalming fluid, which often contains methanol, ethanol, and formaldehyde—a suspected carcinogen. He wants a plain pine box. And he would just as soon skip the grand procession led by a gas-guzzling hearse.

There are no solid statistics on how many Americans choose green burial, but an indication of its rising popularity comes from a 2007 AARP study, which found that nearly one in five Americans age 50 and older who have planned for a funeral have considered a green one.

The stereotype of these people, said Joe Sehee, who founded the nonprofit Green Burial Council, is a "Prius-driving member of the eco-chic"—a person who is well educated, environmentally conscious, liberal and not too keen on organized religion.

But the stereotype, said Sehee, a former Jesuit lay minister, ignores a whole group of people who seek green burial in great part because of their religious or spiritual convictions. Sehee, whose group sets standards for green burials, has worked with Catholic priests, rabbis, and others who see it as an alternative to the funeral industry and a return to their religious traditions.

Green burial, Sehee said, recognizes that "there's death, but there's rebirth associated with it. And we don't see any connection between death and life in traditional death care."

Or, in the words of Maureen McGuinness, family service manager of upstate New York's Most Holy Redeemer Cemetery, green burial "is a way for families to talk about resurrection."

After fielding numerous requests from Catholics looking for a green burial, the Diocese of Albany set aside a wildflower-filled meadow at Most Holy Redeemer—one of its 16 cemeteries—and blessed it as a green resting place in September 2012. So far, 35 people have purchased grave sites, and about half of those have been used.

"When grandma dies and you come to this place, it's all filled with life," McGuinness said.

As in all Catholic cemeteries, all bodies interred in green graves at Most Holy Redeemer receive traditional Catholic rites.

But there is no embalming—or the embalming is with earth-friendly chemicals only—and the caskets are made of untreated wood or other natural materials. For grave markers, the deceased's name is sandblasted onto a cobblestone. Deer and wild turkey roam the meadow, which is named for Kateri Tekakwitha, the first Native American Catholic saint.

The price of green burial is often lower than typical burials, sometimes by hundreds or thousands of dollars, McGuinness said, because there is no embalming, and the casket—if there is one—is simple. Green burial also forgoes the concrete burial vaults into which caskets are placed.

The Green Burial Council has certified nearly 400 providers in 46 states. Some of them have religious orientations. And even some that are not certified consider themselves already green because their faiths have for millennia taken an ecologically friendly approach to death.

Muslims and Jewish traditions, for example, eschew embalming and require quick burials. A kosher casket is a plain wood box made without metal hardware. Muslim tradition specifies a simple shroud and does not require a casket.

Sehee says religious funeral professionals often fall short of embracing their green religious traditions. He knows of Jewish cemeteries that require burial vaults, and he has heard an imam lament that a funeral director serving his Muslim community pushes metal caskets.

"And there are Catholic cemeteries that won't accept a body in a shroud, even though Jesus was buried in a shroud," Sehee said.

Gilbert Becker was buried in a flannel shirt and overalls, the clothes he wore hunting, camping and fishing with his family. After he died last September, his Christian family placed his body in a casket carved by his son from a fallen tree and interred it in the woods at Green Acres Cemetery near Columbia, Missouri. It just made sense, said his wife, Suzanne.

"Gilbert and I always felt most close to God when we were out in the mountains or in the woods," she said. What "better place to camp out," she said, "until the good Lord brings us up."

Critical Thinking

1. What is a "green burial" and how does it differ from other types of burial? Why is it now becoming more popular in the United States?
2. Cremation is popular, but is it eco-friendly? Why is a "green burial" becoming a popular alternative to cremation?
3. Is "green burial" supported by most religions in the United States? What are the major obstacles to a "green burial" in the United States?

Internet References

Grave Matters: Green Burial: What You Need to Know
www.gravematters.us/faqs.html

Green Burial Council
https://greenburialcouncil.org/

Green Burial Council—What Is Green Burial?
https://greenburialcouncil.org/home/what-is-green-burial/

Green Burials: Return Naturally
http://www.greenburials.org/

Article

Prepared by: George E. Dickinson, *College of Charleston*
Michael R. Leming, *St. Olaf College*

A Proper Send-Off to the Great Beyond

"By becoming an informed consumer, you and your family are better equipped to make rational, considered decisions that create an appropriate and meaningful final tribute."

GEORGE C. CLARKE

Learning Outcomes

After reading this article, you will be able to:

- Come to understand the protections created by the Federal Trade Commission for consumers of funerals.

- Understand that planning and producing a funeral is an important part of grief work.

- Come to appreciate the role of itemization and personalization in the planning of funerals.

When a death occurs, those responsible for the funeral arrangements often do not know where to begin. Emotions, fears, and lack of experience in funeral planning all combine to produce confusion, apprehension, and feelings of vulnerability. By taking the following steps, however, it is possible to reduce the stress and arrive at decisions that meet your spiritual, cultural, emotional, and economic needs and preferences.

The first step is learning your rights as a consumer. In the U.S., the Federal Trade Commission regulates the funeral industry through its Funeral Rule, which requires a number of disclosures and actions on the part of the funeral provider, including:

- Provide price information by telephone when the caller requests it.

- Provide a copy of the funeral home's "General Price List" to anyone who inquires in person about funeral arrangements.

- Present casket and outer burial container (burial vault) price lists prior to review or selection of those items.

- Provide the purchaser with a "statement of funeral goods and services selected" prior to finalizing any purchases and payment.

- Disclose the fact that embalming rarely is required by law, and purchasers usually have the right to choose arrangements that do not require them to pay for it.

The FTC also mandates that the general price list be distributed at the beginning of any discussion about funeral arrangements.

In years past, the decision about which funeral home to call when a family member died probably was not a decision at all. For generations, one funeral home in the community had provided funerals for most, if not all, members of a given family, and the loyalty that developed was strong and enduring.

While such circumstances still exist, the mobility of today's society has left many people without a designated "family" funeral home. People may find themselves in a new community, suddenly faced with the unexpected death of a spouse, child, or other family member and are completely unfamiliar with the reputations and abilities of the funeral homes in the area.

If you have not determined which funeral home you would call in an emergency, consider the following steps:

- Do not wait. Start the process today, while you have time and before the need arises.

- Ask friends, coworkers, clergy, and other community professionals about their experiences.

- Telephone several funeral homes in your area. Ask questions, and try to get a sense of the staff's attitude, knowledge, courtesy, and professionalism. You also may inquire about the charges for various services the funeral home can provide.

After completing your initial telephone research, schedule an appointment with one or more of the funeral homes that you feel might be best for you. During the appointment, which usually is free of charge, you should take the opportunity to tour the facility, learn more about the options available to you, and get specific price information for the arrangements you are considering.

Most people are unfamiliar with the different components of a funeral, and can become quite confused when presented with the fees charged by funeral homes. It may help to remember that funeral expenses can be divided into three categories: professional services, merchandise, and cash advances.

Professional services include items such as the arrangements conference with the family; embalming and/or other preparation of the body; use of the facilities and staff for the ceremony and/or visitation; and the hearse or other motor vehicles. Typically, it is helpful to select the type of funeral arrangements desired and determine the charges for this category prior to selecting merchandise.

An important component of this category is the "Basic Services of the Funeral Director and Staff"—to which some funeral homes may add the words "and overhead." This item represents the fee the funeral home charges for virtually any type of arrangements it provides, whether it is a simple cremation with no ceremony, or a more traditional service. The FTC designates this fee as "nondeclinable," which means that, unlike other items on the General Price List that are subject to individual preferences, purchasers cannot opt to omit this charge, and it will apply in all cases.

This fee typically includes meeting with the family to determine the arrangements, and the "sheltering of the remains," or custody of the body, from the time of death until the time of the final disposition. Other services in this category include obtaining burial or cremation permits, and coordination with the cemetery or crematory. The fee also includes a proportionate share of the operating expenses of the funeral home, as allocated among the number of arrangements it provides each year.

Casket prices are determined primarily by the material from which they are constructed and can represent the single largest portion of the total cost of the funeral arrangements. Simply stated, caskets are divided into two categories: wood and metal. Wooden caskets can be made of particleboard covered with a veneer, or hardwoods such as pine, oak, cherry, mahogany, etc.

Metal caskets can be fabricated from steel, stainless steel, copper, or bronze. Within the category of steel casket, the price is determined primarily by the thickness of the steel. The manufacturers and funeral homes classify them as "protective" or "nonprotective." You also may hear the term "sealed," which refers to the same principle. A protective casket can be identified by the presence of a rubber gasket attached to the top of the base of the casket. There also is some form of locking device that, when the casket is closed, holds the main part of the casket and the lid firmly against the gasket.

There are two important points to consider about protective caskets: they will not permanently prevent the entrance of anything into the casket itself, and they do not in any way inhibit—and some claim they actually accelerate—the decomposition process. While people may think the combination of embalming, a protective casket, and a protective vault will preserve the remains forever, that simply is not the case.

The value of protective caskets is open to debate and is a personal decision. To some people, these qualities I have described are important and provide them with some comfort. Others have scoffed at the whole notion of protective caskets and are suspicious of casket manufacturers' attempt to provide some type of warranty when it is doubtful that anyone ever will know whether the casket has functioned as advertised.

In instances of traditional earth burial, cemeteries usually require that the casket be placed in an outer burial enclosure, also known as a grave liner or burial vault. These items usually are purchased from the funeral home and can be chosen through the use of display models illustrating the differences among those offered. Very few funeral homes have full-sized outer burial containers on display due to their size and weight.

In most instances, a grave liner will meet the cemetery's requirements. As an alternative, purchasers may choose a burial vault, which includes a method designed to resist the entrance of water or other substances.

A guest register is a book that attendees at the visitation or ceremony sign. There are a wide variety of registers from which to choose, from simple spiral-bound books with plastic covers to more expensive and ornate leather-bound varieties. Other items include acknowledgement cards the family can send to people who have attended the ceremony, or sent flowers or a memorial donation. Some funeral homes maintain a flower shop on the premises or near the funeral home.

Cremation urns are available for purchase from funeral homes, as are lockets or other forms of jewelry designed to contain a small portion of the deceased's cremated remains.

Cemetery monuments, also called headstones or grave markers, can be purchased directly from funeral homes or monument companies. Many funeral homes sell monuments, though in some states funeral homes are prohibited from owning monument companies.

Cash advances is the term used to describe the money the funeral home will distribute to third parties that provide services related to the funeral arrangements, as necessary. Examples of cash advances include the cost of preparing the grave at the cemetery or the fee for the cremation process; newspaper notices; fees paid to the clergy or other person officiating at the ceremony; and certified copies of the death certificate.

Policies regarding cash advances can vary by funeral home. Some funeral homes will assume responsibility for the payment of the cash advances to the providers, and the total of the cash advance items will appear on the "Statement of Funeral Goods and Services Selected" and the final bill. For reasons related to cash flow, other funeral homes will distribute the cash advances to the appropriate parties but will require you to pay for them at the time the SFGSS is presented to you, and some will provide you with a detailed list of the cash advances and require that you write checks to each of these providers, which the funeral home then will distribute.

When a death occurs, and arrangements have not been planned in advance, those responsible for the funeral arrangements may feel pressured into making decisions quickly. Decisions made without enough time to consider all available options may increase the potential for anxiety, confusion, and regret.

In most cases, family members should take whatever time is necessary to finalize funeral arrangements. Some religious denominations require burial or cremation of the deceased within a specific period of time following the death but, in the absence of those requirements, there generally is no need for decisions about funeral arrangements to be influenced by time pressure.

When arranging a funeral or other memorial tribute, it is important to remember that you usually have a number of options available to you that can be tailored to meet your needs and circumstances. For example, people usually have choices about: whether to include a visitation period (or "wake"); whether to have the body embalmed; where the ceremony will be held; whether the deceased's body will be present for the ceremony; and the method of final disposition of the body, which could be earth burial, cremation, entombment, or anatomical donation.

Today, people are placing much more emphasis on the personalization of memorial tributes. Baby boomers have grown accustomed to having things their way, from vacations to weddings to websites, and the trend toward unique end-of-life events is a natural extension of those desires.

Personalization does not need to be complicated, burdensome, or expensive. It can be as simple as arranging photographs of the deceased around the room where the visitation and/or ceremony will take place. Many funeral homes can arrange for the production of a video presentation of photographs that will be played continuously during these times. Various items that reflect the interests of the person who has died, such as fishing poles, baseball memorabilia, or even a motorcycle, can be placed near the casket (if there is one) or anywhere that visitors can see. These items often will be the catalyst for personal stories that evoke both sorrow and joy, both of which can be helpful in the emotional healing process.

By becoming an informed consumer, you and your family are better equipped to make rational, considered decisions that create an appropriate and meaningful final tribute.

Critical Thinking

1. How does the Federal Trade Commission (FTC) help families who wish a proper send-off?
2. How would you advise a family who wishes to have a proper send-off to plan and execute a funeral?
3. What can one do in personalizing a funeral? Is it difficult? What are the obstacles?

Internet References

Funeral Consumers Alliance
https://www.funerals.org/ and https://www.funerals.org/forconsumersmenu

Meaningful Funerals
www.meaningfulfunerals.com/ and www.meaningfulfunerals.com/meaningful-funerals/why-have-a-funeral/

GEORGE W. CLARKE *is author of* Nobody Wants to Talk About It—An Enlightening Guide to Planning a Funeral or Other Tribute, *from which this article is adapted.*

Article

Prepared by: George E. Dickinson, *College of Charleston*
Michael R. Leming, *St. Olaf College*

17 Behind-the-Scenes Secrets of Funeral Directors

CHRISTINE COLBY

Learning Outcomes

After reading this article, you will be able to:

- Come to understand the difficult demands placed on funeral directors by the community in common practice.

- Come to understand the special adoptions that funeral directors employ in their profession.

- Come to understand the life of the funeral director from the funeral director's personal point of view.

Practitioners of the "dismal trade"—whether known as funeral directors, morticians, or undertakers—likely have a more challenging day at the office than most people. Despite the fact that everyone will almost certainly need their services at some point in their lives, the specifics of their job duties often remain shrouded in mystery. We talked to several funeral directors to learn some little-known facts about the profession, from what happens behind the doors of the embalming room to the real reason you might want to think twice about that "protective" casket.

1. They Drive Minivans.

"The reason you don't see the dead being picked up in your daily life is because we're stealth like that," Jeff Jorgenson of Elemental Cremation & Burial in Seattle told *mental_floss*. "We are soccer moms and we are legion! Actually, we just use soccer-mom vehicles: Minivans are the transportation of the dead. We rarely drive hearses—those are ceremonial vehicles only."

2. That Sweet Look on the Deceased's Face Took Some Work.

Funeral directors say that the most important part of preparing a body for a viewing is the "setting of the features"—creating a peaceful facial expression with a pleasant smile. But while it might look nice at the end, the work creating that appearance can be grisly. Morticians stuff the throat and nose with cotton and then suture the mouth shut, either using a curved needle and thread to stitch between the jawbone and nasal cavity or using a needle injector machine to accomplish a similar job more quickly. Small spiked cups are also inserted under the eyelids to keep the lids closed and the eyes from caving in.

Of course, some bodies take more restoration than others. One mortician says that to prepare a corpse that has been decapitated for an open-casket viewing, he uses a wooden dowel to rejoin the head and body, then sutures the neck back together.

3. They Might Make a Trip to the Drugstore.

In her best-selling book *Smoke Gets In Your Eyes: And Other Lessons From the Crematory*, mortician Caitlin Doughty says: "If the usual methods of setting the features aren't sufficient to keep the eyes closed or the mouth shut, superglue is a secret weapon." In *Grave Matters*, author Mark Harris points out that superglue can also be used to close up any puncture marks from needles on a corpse. Brooklyn funeral director Amy Cunningham of Fitting Tribute Funeral Services told *mental_floss*: "if you need to keep a deceased person's hands folded neatly at their abdomen, but their arms keep falling down into the sides of the casket, you can gently bind their thumbs with a ponytail tie."

4. Comparison Shopping Is Key.

Sixth-generation funeral director Caleb Wilde, known for his popular blog Confessions of a Funeral Director, shares this story with *mental_floss*: "About a year ago, a husband and wife died about four months apart. The wife knew us, so we buried her, and the husband knew the funeral home in a neighboring town, so they buried him. They both had the same funeral, same casket, vault, etc. The family called us to let us know that the other funeral home charged $3000 more. Same value, different cost. Call around to different funeral homes. Shop. Ask for the GPL [General Price List]. Remember, cost doesn't always equal value."

5. You Might Want to Think Twice About "Protective" Caskets.

Some caskets that have vacuum-seal rubber gaskets are marketed as "protective" or resistant to the "entry of outside elements." As Harris details in *Grave Matters*, this creates conditions that encourage the growth of anaerobic bacteria, which break the body down by putrefying it, "turning soft body parts to mush and bloating the corpse with foul-smelling gas . . . Inside the sealed casket, the result is a funereal version of the decay that's found in swamp bottoms and the bowels of unturned compost piles."

6. Sometimes Caskets Explode.

In fact, the aforementioned buildup of methane gas can cause what people in the industry call "exploding casket syndrome," where the gas will literally blow the lids off of caskets and doors off of crypts. Some casket makers have added Tupperware-style "burping" features to their sealer models to release the accumulated gases. Harris spoke with a former cemetery owner who told him that those "protective" sealer caskets are "routinely unsealed after the family leaves . . . to relieve the inevitable buildup of gases within the casket." Staff may also just leave the caskets unlocked, not engaging the seal to begin with, in an attempt to avoid those "fetid conditions inside the casket."

7. Sometimes Pacemakers Explode, Too.

If a pacemaker is left in a body when cremated, "it can explode and can cause upward of $10,000 of damage to the retort [cremation machine]," Wilde says. "So, pacemakers need to be removed before cremation. And don't worry, the funeral directors/cremationists will do the removal for you."

8. Some Funeral Directors Rarely See the Dead.

Jorgenson says, "The bulk of what funeral directors do is paperpushing—filing death certificates, getting permits, editing obituaries, and sending them to the paper. [Some] will only see a dead person when they are delivered for a service. In the case of some funeral homes, a [corporate] funeral director could literally go *years* without seeing a dead person."

9. They See Things through Rose-colored Light Bulbs.

While the formaldehyde embalmers use does contain a rosy dye to restore color to graying, lifeless flesh, it's not always sufficient. According to Cunningham, "mortuary schools teach color theory and stage lighting—how to use colored gels over the ceiling lights." Doughty also mentions that bodies are often set out for visitation displayed under rose-colored light bulbs.

10. It All Goes Right Down the Drain.

You'd think all the chemicals and body fluids involved in embalming would be disposed of like biohazard, but it's industry practice to just wash it all off the table, right into the drain. Harris points out that just one embalming can generate 120 gallons of "funeral waste"—blood, fecal matter, and the former contents of internal organs, in addition to any chemicals in the preservation fluid itself—and it all ends up in the public sewer system, to be eventually released into waterways. Although, as Wilde points out, "Blood isn't any worse than the other things that go down the loo."

11. Formaldehyde Might Be Dying a Slow Death.

In addition to causing relatively minor problems, such as sinus issues and rashes (including one called "embalmer's eczema"), formaldehyde is a carcinogen. The U.S. National Toxicology Program, among other groups, have said that people with high levels of exposure—such as embalmers—are at a higher risk for nasopharyngeal cancer, myeloid leukemia, and other forms of cancers.

Usually, criticism comes from outside the death-care industry, but that's starting to change. In the May 2016 issue of *The Director*, the official publication of the National Funeral Directors Association, Carol Lynn Green, the NFDA's environmental-compliance counsel, writes, ". . . there is no dispute that formaldehyde poses a health risk." She says that the Occupational Safety and Health Administration is gearing up to make their workplace regulations stricter, and recommends that funeral homes start to transition to preservation products that don't use the dangerous gas.

12. You Can't Really Be Buried Under a Tree.

Some consumers who dislike the idea of embalming, or have environmental concerns, choose a "green" burial. Alongside that often comes a romantic idea about being buried beneath a favorite tree—perhaps a stately oak, for example. Sarah Wambold, an Austin funeral director and green burial expert, told *mental_floss*: "A body must be buried at least four feet from a tree to protect its roots system. It's a bit of an adjustment for people who are committed to the image of being buried under a tree, but that's not always the most green option for the tree. Wouldn't they rather allow the tree to continue to live?" You can, however, plant new trees or shrubs atop a grave after a burial, and the roots will grow down over the body.

13. At Least One Funeral Director Wants to Teach You to Prepare Dead Bodies Yourself.

Doughty, who runs a funeral home called Undertaking LA, told *WIRED* "I'm a licensed mortician, but I want to teach people that they don't need me." She advocates people learning to take care of their own dead at home, and says she wants the public to become comfortable with the way death looks naturally: "A chemically preserved body looks like a wax replica of a person. Bodies are supposed to be drooping and turning very pale and sinking in while decomposing. Within a day or so after they've died, you should be able to see that this person has very much left the building. That's the point. I think dead bodies should look dead. It helps with the grieving process."

Doughty encourages the idea of home funerals, which are legal in all 50 states (although 10 states require the involvement of a funeral director). For more information, check out the Home Funeral Alliance.

14. It's Hard to Be Their Friend.

Any friend might disappoint you once in a while, but funeral directors will probably do it more often, according to Wilde. "We might miss your birthday party; we might have to leave in the middle of dinner. Death has this way of keeping an untimely schedule, and as death's minions, we're tied to that schedule. Whether it be in the middle of the night, or in the middle of your wedding, when death calls, we have to respond."

15. No One Wants to Profit from the Deaths of Children.

"It is a tradition in the funeral industry to provide funerals to the families of stillborn babies and very young infants at cost," Cunningham says. "Funeral directors do not care to make a profit on the deaths of children, and in fact, the death of a young child saddens the whole firm more than almost anything else."

The funeral industry also includes a number of charitable projects devoted to helping parents after a child's death. A volunteer group called Little Angel Gowns makes burial garments for babies out of donated wedding dresses, and provides them at no cost to hospitals and funeral homes. The Tears Foundation assists grieving parents in paying for burial or cremation expenses after losing a baby. Eloise Woods, a natural burial ground in Texas, will bury infants at no charge.

16. Your Grandfather'S Hip Joint Might Become a New Road Sign.

According to Doughty, families can ask for replacement medical parts back after a cremation, but most do not. Hip and knee implants are often melted down and recycled for road signs and car parts, among other things. Unfortunately, she says, breast implants usually melt all over the cremation machine.

17. Some Funeral Homes Employ Therapy Dogs.

A large part of a funeral director's job is comforting the bereaved. Some use grief-therapy dogs to give the families a furry shoulder to cry on.

Critical Thinking

1. What are the special tools the funeral director uses in preparing the body for viewing?
2. Why might you want to think twice about "protective" caskets?
3. How can caskets or bodies explode? Why can't you be buried under a tree?

Internet References

5 Reasons Why Kids Should Grow Up To Be Funeral Directors
http://connectingdirectors.com/articles/48170-5-reasons-why-kids-should-grow-up-to-be-funeral-directors

Death and the Maidens: Women in Funeral Service
http://connectingdirectors.com/articles/48360-death-and-the-maidens-women-in-funeral-service

Meet Lulu—Our funeral service Goldendoodle
https://www.youtube.com/watch?v=g7Rw3G5X_Y4

Article   Prepared by: George E. Dickinson, *College of Charleston*
                                   Michael R. Leming, *St. Olaf College*

10 Burdens Funeral Directors Carry

I wrote this article over the weekend and I wasn't going to publish it until Wednesday, but since I just spent my entire night [11 PM to 5:45 AM] picking up three deceased persons, I thought it's probably appropriate to post it now. After I hit "publish," I'll be off to bed and back to work by noon. Ah, the joys of a small family business.

CALEB WILDE

Learning Outcomes

After reading this article, you will be able to:

- Come to understand the difficult demands placed on funeral directors by the community in common practice.
- Come to understand the special burdens of funeral directors in their profession.
- Come to understand the life of the funeral director from the funeral director's personal point of view.

The following burdens are not necessarily funeral service specific, but many, if not all, come with this profession. Those of us who stay in this profession do so because we find serving others in their darkest hour extremely rewarding, yet there are burdens to be borne. Here's ten.

One. A Lack of Personal Boundaries.

The phone rings at 3 AM in the morning with a hospice nurse on the other end of the line telling you that so-and-so has died, that so-and-so's family is requesting your services and that the family of so-and-so is ready for you to come and pick up so-and-so.

The phone rings at 6 PM the next day. Someone needs to see so-and-so . . . he simply can't believe so-and-so is dead and must come to the funeral home at once to see so-and-so.

Two. Depression.

While those of us who stay in this business do so because we love serving people, the lack of personal boundaries can lead to depression.

Depression, because my son's baseball game was at 6 PM, but somebody in so-and-so's family needed to see so-and-so this very minute. Depression because the emotional needs of others somehow always trump my personal life needs. And all of a sudden "I'm not a good father" and "I'm not happy with my life."

Three. Psychosis.

Psychologist Carl Rogers described how he "literally lost my 'self,' lost the boundaries of myself . . . and I became convinced (and I think with some reason) that I was going insane." When we in human service, and death service, become pulled into the whole narrative of death and dying, we can lose ourselves.

Four. Smells.

An iron stomach I have not. Putrid smells, this business has many. This is a burden that comes home with me . . . a burden that my wife often notices shortly after I walk through the door.

Five. Life Secrets, Death Secrets and Practice Secrets.

When a person commits suicide or dies from an overdose, there are times when the family simply wants to keep the manner of death a secret from the public.

I don't mind carrying the burden of a secret, but when you live in a small town where suspicion can run rampant, secrets can become heavy.

Some things we see will remain with us forever. They are so disturbing, so terrible that we do the world a favor by not sharing them.

Six. Isolation by Profession.

Death makes us different . . . not necessarily unique, just different. This difference creates a chasm between us and those not immersed in death. Sure, police, doctors, psychologist, etc. have chasms created by their professions, but ours—because of the fear, sadness and undefined hours of our practice—creates us into something other.

Seven. Death itself.

Death can be a beautiful experience in the life of a family. But when that death is tragic and unexpected, death is a heavy burden for both the family and for those who serve the family. Specifically, when the death is a young person, our entire staff becomes agitated and moody.

Eight. Workaholism.

Many funeral homes are small businesses that don't have enough staff for shift work. In order to serve our families (so that they'll return), we have learned that the way to overcome the depression and potential psychosis that can come with a lack of personal boundaries is to marry the business. We make the work our life. Such work addiction pleases the families we work for but can leave our personal families destitute.

And while many of us don't carry the burden of workaholism, we do carry the burden of fighting off the addiction.

Nine. Death Logistics Stress.

Every business has stress. Some more and some less. And while funeral service can't claim a quantitative difference in stress, it can claim to have its very own type of stress. To grasp the type of stress surrounding a funeral, imagine planning a wedding in five days, except where there's joy, sadness exists, and where there's usually a bride, a dead body lies in state.

Ten. Dress clothes . . .

. . . in the summer heat. Dress clothes in the dead of winter. We are one of the few—armed service members are the only others I can think of—professions that wears suits outdoors as a matter of practice. There's nothing like having sweat drip down your back and into your crack. Well, nothing except maybe freezing your dress shoe covered toes in a foot of snow.

10 Ways Funeral Directors Cope

*Here's 10 coping methods funeral directors use. The **first five** are coping methods that are negative or maladaptive techniques. The **last five** are positive coping methods. One or more of these methods MUST be used if a person is to stay in this profession AND maintain a healthy personal and family life.*

Negative Coping Methods

One. Displacement.

Funeral service is a business that is both uncontrollable and unpredictable. Since funeral directors can't control death and death's schedule, we attempt to control those things and/or people that we DO have power over. We too often take out our frustrations, fears and anger on those closest to us.

Two. Attack.

And we often displace those emotions on those closest to us with some kind of aggression. In an attempt to cope and find a sense of control in our uncontrolled and unpredictable world, we will often emotionally and verbally manipulate and control our family, co-workers, employees, associates and those closest to us, making us seem nearly bi-polar as we treat the grieving families that we serve with love and support and yet treat our staff and family with all the emotional turmoil that we're feeling inside.

Three. Emotional Suppression.

We are paid to be the stable minds in the midst of unstable souls. We withhold and withhold and withhold and then . . . then the floodgates open, turning our normally stable personality into a blithering, sobbing mess, or creating a monster of seething anger and rage. During different occasions, I have become both the mess and the monster. The difficulty is only compounded by the fact that you just cannot make your spouse or best friend understand how raising the carotid artery of a nine-month old infant disturbs your mind.

Four. Self-harm.

We cope with alcohol. I know a number who attempt to waste their troubles away with a bottle. Substance abuse. Sexual callousness. The sexual philandering that occurred in *Six Feet Under* was not just for higher TV ratings.

Five. Trivializing.

Compassion fatigue happens to all of us in funeral service. If we can't bounce back from the fatigue, we begin a journey down the road to callousness. Once calloused, we tell ourselves that "death isn't as bad as 'these people' are making it seem." Once we trivialize the grief and death we see, we can easily justify charging the hell out of the families we serve.

Positive Coping Methods

Six. Benefit-finding.

The funeral business contains many burdens. Yet, the good we can do and the beauty we can find around death—if we look for it—may outweigh the darkness. Learning to see the light in the darkness of death is a positive way we can cope.

Seven. Altruism.

Learn to love serving others. Probably the best means to cope with the funeral business is found in the people we serve. Love them intentionally and don't be afraid to find joy in meeting their needs. Don't be afraid to hear their stories and become a part of their family.

Eight. Problem-solve.

Don't be passive with the burdens you carry. Actively attempt to find positive ways to deal with your burden. Exercise. Eat better. Take a vacation. Go out with your friends. If you can't shed your burdens on your own, seek counseling. Find a psychologist. Find a psychiatrist. Talk out your problems with someone wiser than you.

Nine. Spiritual Community and Personal Growth.

Using religion as an opiate to ignore reality is something I speak AGAINST on a regular basis. Instead, seek a community where there's faith authenticity. Find people who can encourage you with their love and support as you worship together and ponder the mysteries and truths of a better world.

Ten. Avoidance.

If this business is wrecking your life and the lives of those around you, then salvage what you have left and quit this business. Quitting doesn't make you a failure. Quitting doesn't make you weak. You know more than anyone that you only have one life to live. Live it to its fullest by doing something that breathes life into your soul.

Critical Thinking

1. What are the special burdens that funeral directors carry?
2. What are negative coping mechanisms employed by funeral directors in dealing with the special burdens of funeral service?
3. What are positive coping mechanisms employed by funeral directors in dealing with the special burdens of funeral service?

Internet References

Confessions of a Mortician (Funeral Director)
http://www.aol.com/article/2011/02/04/confessions-of-a-mortician-funeral -director/19779287/

National Association of Funeral Directors
www.nafd.org.uk/**funeral**-advice/**the-role-of-a-funeral-director**/

National Funeral Directors & Morticians Association, Inc.
www.nfdma.com/

Article   Prepared by: George E. Dickinson, *College of Charleston*
Michael R. Leming, *St. Olaf College*

I'm Paid to Mourn at Funerals (And It's a Growing Industry)

EVAN V. SYMON

Learning Outcomes

After reading this article, you will be able to:

- Come to appreciate the advantages of paid mourners.

- Come to discover a job opportunity for your future, especially for college theater majors.

- Come to value an impression management involving lying right to people's faces, at a time when they're at their most vulnerable, in order to get the family through a difficult time.

A lot of you reading this are not going to believe this job is a real thing. But professional mourners—people paid to attend funerals and pretend to be friends and family of the deceased—are not only real, but common. Or they are in places like China; it's only just now starting to take off in Western countries. And we don't mean that they kind of stand by the graveside to fill out the crowd—they assume fake identities and fool the rest of the mourners into thinking they're one of the bereaved.

We spoke with Owen Vaughan, a professional mourner in London, to find out what it's like to have a job that honestly seems too ridiculous to be true. He says . . .

6. We Have To Do A Full Character Study In Advance

People like me get hired to play the part of mourners at funerals and wakes for any number of reasons. Maybe the family is worried about embarrassingly low attendance, or they want to make their deceased parent seem more important (or at least, popular). The only thing sadder than a funeral is a funeral that nobody shows up to, so the decision is generally coming from a good place.

Still, I am an actor playing a part. My job is to suspend the disbelief of the other people in the room. And because so many different kinds of people die (all of them, in fact), I need to take on a number of different characters. That's where it gets tricky. My background story needs to be effective and convincing, while simultaneously including valid reasons I would never have seen anybody at this funeral before. The family is often very helpful with this, but I have to do a lot of the study on my own. One time, I needed to learn some archery, because I was supposed to arrive as a deceased archery teacher's former protege, and there was a chance I'd actually have to fire off arrows.

Remember, socializing is a key part of mourning. We have to mingle with the crowd and play the part; that's why we're there. Most actors don't have a lot of experience interacting with their audience and improvising in character. Still, if you do enough character study, you end up knowing more about the deceased than some people who were truly close to them. I once sat next to an acquaintance of the deceased, in character as a former co-worker. I brought up a couple of funny stories and somehow slipped the deceased's middle name. This guy had known him pretty well, but had no clue what his middle name was.

And if that alone doesn't make it sound like a Daniel-Day-Lewis-level acting job, there's the part where we have to pretend to be emotionally devastated . . .

5. You Have To Trigger Sadness On Demand

Naturally, since I don't know the deceased, it can be hard to work up too many tears about them. Some professional mourners I know can cry on cue like a toddler at Toys "R" Us, but most of us keep a supply of tools to help us jerk out some tears on command. For example, if we know the person's occupation, we try to find the saddest or most depressing movie involving that profession and use that as a baseline.

Or I'll think about my own dad or my grandparents passing away to get the tears started or to help hit the tone of voice that only comes from a genuine loss. My go-to is rewatching *Schindler's List* beforehand. Remembering Liam Neeson's speech at the end is enough to get me going on a moment's notice. If I ever reach the point where I can't get emotional at the rescue of over a thousand Jews from Hitler's grasp, that's probably the point where I'll need a therapist.

Female mourners I know will often use *Titanic*. A few of the women I know track their menstrual cycles to know how much effort they're going to have to put into a good cry. Don't get me wrong—us guys can still get their cry on. It's just that it's already harder for us as men because we're psychologically conditioned not to. Thanks, *societal gender norms*.

4. Real Mourners Do Get Suspicious

I fully understand that getting paid to attend the funeral of a total stranger sounds like the plot of a forgettable *Seinfeld* episode. Yes, explaining this to people upsets them a lot of the time, and I can understand that. If you're not familiar with the practice, the whole thing sounds creepy and off-putting. If we get caught by the friends and family at the service, things can turn awkward fast.

Usually, it's the spouse or a child of the deceased who hired a bunch of strangers to come to the funeral, so they've got to be on patrol to back us up. ("You don't remember dad's crazy cousin Gunther? They used to be inseparable! Stop being so suspicious, Mom! Please?") I've only been caught once, but I was lucky. When I was confronted and forced to confess why I was there, their response was simply, "Aunt Eugenie *would* do something like this."

Other times, people we successfully convince that we knew the deceased will still get suspicious of us, but for the wrong reasons. This advance research we do can come off as phony if it's not done right. Relaying a bunch of factoids about the deceased can wind up sounding like a 14-year-old's book report on a novel they skimmed the night before. This makes people think—not that we're professionals, but that we're con artists there to muscle in on the will. I know from colleagues that nothing makes people flip out like thinking you're trying to con them out of their inheritance. And it's not like you can answer with the truth. Think about it. Which sounds more like a lie: That we're opportunistic strangers running a scam for cash, or that we're professional actors hired to help fill out the crowd?

3. You Need A Crash Course In How Different Groups— And Religions—Mourn

Most of the funerals I've gone to have been Christian, but I've also attend ones for Jewish, Muslim, and even Hindu and Buddhist folks. Most of the time, we need to pretend that we're of the same faith as the deceased so that we'll fit in at whichever church, synagogue, or mosque we're going to arrive at, and that can be interesting.

For one thing, there's avoiding unintentional rudeness. The noise level is something I've had to pay a surprising amount of attention to—some religions can have startlingly loud funerals, while others expect silent weeping. The Buddhist funeral I attended went from remembrances straight into cremation, and the tonal shifts of crying, silence, and prayers was quick and irregular.

But then there's the matter of knowing the rituals. I mentioned earlier that paid mourners are much more common and accepted in parts of Asia, and since London is very cosmopolitan, we are getting sent to funerals for an ever-increasing variety of faiths. If my character claims to be a guy "from church" or something, you better believe I'll need to know how a ceremony goes. If I kneel at the wrong time or don't seem to know what to do next, someone might question what exactly my deal is.

At a Conservative Jewish funeral I attended, I was chastised for not placing a rock on the grave—something which in retrospect I should've picked up from *Schindler's List*. I tried to defuse the situation by saying that my rabbi was much more casual about that tradition, but this only led to more and more questions about my identity. Finally, the son who had hired me stepped in to say that I was a Reform Jew, which was much more of a relief than I could have ever expected.

2. Families Are Very Specific—And Demanding—About Your Performance

Though the family members who hire us are usually very accommodating, in other cases, there are some odd mixed emotions. One time I was hired by the son of a recently deceased woman who made sure we knew how much he hated the people in my profession. He had hired us because he was out of options—his mother had wanted a ton of mourners, and after rounding up everyone she could possibly have known, he still needed more bodies. I know how to act around funerals, but he gave me so many restrictions that it was hard to be much of anything.

I was warned not to give any condolences to his siblings (who didn't know he was hiring us), not to eat at the reception, to stay only in a certain area, and to basically sit and look sad for two hours. He effectively hired extroverted actors to play socially-stunted outcasts for the duration of the funeral and reception, and we simply had to do it.

In other cases, the family members who hire us suddenly turn into Stanley Kubrick, giving us endless notes on our performance. By far my worst funeral (one in which I'd already refused to pretend to be a Naval officer, complete with uniform) was being run by a relative who kept coming to us *during the bloody funeral* to tell us what to do. He'd whisper "cry harder" or "moan louder," which are things that nobody wants to hear at a funeral (or in any other setting, if you think about it). It finally got so bad that it sounded fake, and a fellow mourner cried so hard that her eyelids swelled to the point where she couldn't physically see to drive to the reception.

1. Yes, It Really Can Help

Some of you are still firmly of the opinion that this is a sleazy business. After all, what we're doing involves lying right to people's faces, at a time when they're at their most vulnerable. But remember the part earlier about how when you hire us, you get the full mourner package—including mingling with the crowd and helping people talk through their grief. That is, after all, what funerals and wakes are for. People have been gathering to do this for as long as there have been people. Share stories, cry, get closure. I help people do that. It's why I took the job.

And we're really good at it—not only because of the sheer amount of practice (hundreds of ceremonies and thousands of conversations with mourners) but also because our heads *aren't* clouded by grief. I've done my research, so I can remind them of the good the deceased brought to the world. I can be a lot better to talk to than some distant relative who only showed up out of obligation; making people feel better is literally my job.

I remember one girl who had lost her grandmother. They were really close, and nobody other than her parents attempted to comfort her. When everyone at our table at the wake had stood up except the two of us, I spoke to her. I've done this enough to know that you don't tell children at a funeral that "Everything is going to be alright" or anything like that; movie cliches never work. Get on their level. Remember fun stories, talk about the good times they had with the deceased. When her parents came back, they were impressed and wanted to know how I'd gotten her to start talking again. I then learned that the

girl hadn't said anything in a few days, and that was her way of grieving. I told them what I'd said and left the table.

So yes, it is a very, very strange job. Yes, you're pretending to be someone else to fudge the crowd size at what should be a solemn, sacred event. But every once in a while, you get to be the mysterious stranger who can help alleviate some pain before disappearing into the crowd.

Critical Thinking

1. Why would families hire paid mourners? What is the appropriate role of the paid mourner?
2. What advice would you give to someone who wishes to be a paid mourner?
3. What is a positive role for a professional mourner? How can families benefit from hiring a professional mourner?

Internet References

Mourners-for-rent hired to blub at funerals—Telegraph
http://www.telegraph.co.uk/news/newstopics/howaboutthat/9955111/Mourners-for-rent-hired-to-blub-at-funerals.html

Professional Mourners: They Exist—Sowetan LIVE
http://www.sowetanlive.co.za/goodlife/2015/05/07/professional-mourners-they-exist

'Professional Sobbers' . . . Daily Mail
http://www.dailymail.co.uk/news/article-2299764/Professional-sobbers-charge-45-attend-strangers-funerals-pretend-mourn.html

Rent a Mourner
www.rentamourner.co.uk/

'Rent A Mourner' Helps You Look More Popular At Your Funeral
http://www.huffingtonpost.com/2013/03/27/rent-a-mourner_n_2964280.html

EVAN V. SYMON is the interview-finder for the Personal Experience Team at Cracked.

Article

Prepared by: George E. Dickinson, *College of Charleston*
Michael R. Leming, *St. Olaf College*

10 Amazing Things Your Ashes Can Do After You Die

AMANDA GREEN

Learning Outcomes

After reading this article, you will be able to:

- Come to understand some of the advantages of cremation.

- Come to see there are many options for what one might do with cremated remains that may be more personally satisfying that earth burials and cemetery obligations.

- Come to appreciate the ability to choose among the options created by cremation.

Ashes to ashes, dust to . . . diamonds? Here are 10 ways to give cremains a life after death.

1. An Hourglass

Time for some symbolism! Hourglass iconography on gravestones dates back to the Puritans. Now Lifetime Hourglass Urns can accommodate the ashes of one or two loved ones.

2. A Vinyl Record

Your cremated loved ones can't turn over in their graves, but they can spin right round on a record player. The British service And Vinyly presses ashes into vinyl so the dearly departed can rest in peace at 33 rpm. Families can provide the audio or have the service compose an original song, known as "bespook music."

3. A Diamond Ring

Human life is finite, but diamonds are forever. The memorial jewelry company LifeGem uses carbon from cremains to create diamonds of assorted cuts, colors, clarity, and carats. The gems can be used to make various pieces of jewelry, but we're thinking an engagement ring might be a little creepy.

4. A Teddy Bear

To paraphrase Yogi, this is more morbid than the average bear. The company Huggable Urns stores cremains inside the plush and cuddly body of a stuffed animal.

5. Tattoos

Commemorative tattoos don't just honor deceased loved ones. Some are made with them! Tattoo artists can sterilize cremains and then mix them with tattoo ink, so the dearly departed is always under your skin.

6. Something to Write With

Ink isn't for everyone. The Carbon Copies project by designer Nadine Jarvis turns cremains into a set of 240 pencils. Each is stamped with the departed's name and birth and death years. Pencils are accessed one at a time and sharpened into a wooden box. After each pencil is used, the box of shavings can be kept as an urn.

7. A Portrait

Now a painting of your late grandmother can really be of your grandmother. A number of artists mix cremains and paint to create a special memorial portrait, landscape, or still life.

8. Stained Glass

Let there be light. Stained glass pieces bonded with cremains are beautiful alt-urnatives, err, urn alternatives.

9. Human DNA trees

Here's a new twist on the tree of life. An art venture called Bio-presence claims to transcode human DNA into trees to create a leafy, living memorial that isn't technically genetically modified. Consult their helpful chart above if you have any questions. We're guessing it's not like Grandmother Willow in *Pocahontas*.

10. Fireworks

Go out with a bang! Companies like Heavenly Stars Fireworks transform ash scattering into a pyrotechnic extravaganza. Writer Hunter S. Thompson was memorialized this way in 2005. If ammo better suits the departed, a company called Holy Smoke turns cremains into shotgun shells.

Critical Thinking

1. List 10 things one can do with cremated remains?
2. Why would people want to do these things?
3. What are some of the social factors related to the need for ways of utilizing cremated remains?

Internet References

15 Unique Things to Do with Your Cremated Ashes when You Die
    http://www.al.com/business/index.ssf/2015/01/15_unique_things_to_do
_your_cr.html

Cremation Choices
    http://www.nfda.org/consumer-resources/planning-a-funeral/cremation
-options

Cremation Solutions | All About Cremation Ashes
    http://www.cremationsolutions.com/information/scattering-ashes/all-about
-cremation-ashes

National Cremation | Frequently Asked Cremation Questions
    https://nationalcremation.com/cremation-services/frequently-asked-cremation
-questions

Prepared by: George E. Dickinson, *College of Charleston*
Michael R. Leming, *St. Olaf College*

Article

Memorial Videos Give Lasting Farewell

Jeff Strickler

Learning Outcomes

After reading this article, you will be able to:

- Gain an appreciation for the opportunity to personalize with the creation of videos.
- Come to understand how video creation can lead to good mourning.
- Come to appreciate that the creation of a video before the person dies can create family memories and solidarity.

Shortly before Connie Dunlap died in October, she sat in front of a camera focused in a tight close-up and talked about her faith and how it shaped her battle against cancer.

"Our legacy is usually money or property that we pass down to our children and grandchildren," she says softly but earnestly. "But I think a legacy of faith and our life is much more valuable."

The Forest Lake resident, who was 68, had called the Rev. Alan Naumann and asked him to record a farewell message to be shared with her family after her death. "It was important for her to know that her grandchildren, who were too young to remember her, would one day get to know her," said Naumann, who also is a videographer.

Memorial videos are the latest twist on the video slide shows of snapshots chronicling a life that are often shown at funerals. Aging baby boomers, completely comfortable in the medium of video, are using it not only to look back but also to leave a final message for the future. They share insights from their life and impart advice. Some are somber, others lighthearted.

This new kind of video—sometimes called legacy or end-of-life videos—is becoming so popular that some funeral homes are being outfitted with video projection systems and churches that used to frown on them are embracing them.

Once you've seen one of the videos, advocates say, you'll understand why.

"The emotional impact of these is so powerful," said Ken Kurita, owner of Videon Productions in Excelsior, who made a memorial video for his father's recent funeral. "Which memory would you rather take with you [from a funeral]: the lifeless body lying in a casket, or the living, breathing person you loved, complete with all their mannerisms, their smile, their sense of humor?"

Kurita's father, who died in January at age 83, used his video to recall boyhood anecdotes and even worked in a little humor. "That was my dad," Kurita said, tearing up slightly as he watched the video in his editing booth. "This is all about life's treasured moments."

Sometimes, even the videographers are moved by the end result. Mike Madden from Moviescreen Films in St. Paul was recording a wedding when he coaxed the camera-shy father of the bride to sit down and give a 3-minute interview. The man died unexpectedly three weeks later.

The daughter told him the interview "is one of the most precious things she has," he said.

While the number of videos being shown at funerals is on the rise, just wait a decade, Naumann said. A lot of the work he does now involves people who want to get their stories on record while they're still sharp in their minds.

"We're shooting stuff that we'll have on file for years" before it's needed for memorials, he said.

A Pioneer

Naumann, who is credited with making one of the earliest memorial videos in 1988, said it came out of his dual background. In addition to being a minister, he's the owner of Minneapolis-based Memory Vision. In the late '80s, he was serving as the chaplain at Hillside Cemetery in northeast Minneapolis. He bought a video camera and started experimenting with it. One of those experiments was a video biography, and when he showed part of it at the subject's funeral, he knew immediately that he was onto something special.

"It was overwhelming," he said.

Still, memorial videos didn't catch on right away. For one thing, editing video was a laborious task because the tapes couldn't be cut and spliced like film. It wasn't until the digital revolution enabled editors to use a computer to mimic film editing that the memorials started to gain popularity.

It also took persuading to get some churches to allow them. Naumann made a video about a Roman Catholic nun, only to have her parish priest reject the idea as conflicting with the solemnity of the funeral mass.

"I called him up, clergy to clergy, and explained how the video was going to show all the wonderful things this woman did to help people," he said. "He finally agreed to let us show it. He was so impressed by the video that after the funeral, he started showing it to other groups. He became its biggest supporter."

Wide Price Range

The cost of a memorial video varies tremendously. Prices start as low as $200 for an electronic photo album to as much as $20,000 for one with exclusive music and interviews with relatives and friends. But a typical video consisting of an interview with the subject costs $1,000 to $2,000.

Memorial videographers take great pride in their interviews. Their goal is to have the subject reveal something that will surprise everyone. Kurita even managed to do that when he did the video with his father, Dr. Kenji Kurita.

Being of Japanese-American descent, he was sent to a so-called relocation camp at the start of World War II. He eventually enlisted in the Army and was assigned to one of the Japanese-American battalions. The younger Kurita always assumed that his patriotic father was bitter about having been sent to a pseudo-prison. When he did his interview, his father set him straight, and, in the process, drove home the video's potential to influence future generations.

"Many subjects see this as their last chance to tell people what's important to them," Kurita said. "He wanted to tell us not to waste time being angry and bitter over what happened in the past. He said to use that energy to follow your dreams."

Just Do It

While professional videographers would like you to hire them, many of them believe so strongly in the medium that they encourage people to do their own memorial video.

"If you can't afford to hire me, at least get a video camera, put it in front of Grandma and Grandpa and record them," Kurita insisted. "Everyone has a story, and we need to get those stories now."

Naumann is gathering material for a class on do-it-yourself memorial videos. But don't wait for that, he said.

"I got a call the other day from a woman who said, 'My mother just turned 90. When do you think I should start recording her story?'" he recalled. "And I said, 'How about yesterday?'"

Critical Thinking

1. How can memorial videos lead to a improved funeral service?
2. Do you think it is appropriate to include a memorial in a funeral service?
3. What is the role of memorial videos in the future of funeral service? Will it have increased popularity or will it be a dying augmentation?

Internet References

National Funeral Directors Association | Trends in Funeral Service
   http://www.nfda.org/news/trends-in-funeral-service
Operation Henry Tribute Pages
   https://www.operationhenry.org/tributepages/
Selfies at Funerals
   http://selfiesatfunerals.tumblr.com/

Article

Prepared by: George E. Dickinson, *College of Charleston*
Michael R. Leming, *St. Olaf College*

Speaking from Beyond the Grave; High-tech Headstones Use QR Codes to Link to Photos and Videos of the Dearly Departed

JEFF STRICKLER

Learning Outcomes

After reading this article, you will be able to:

- Come to understand that tombstone videos can provide another viable option for grievers and for family memories.

- Come to appreciate the social benefits of the high-tech headstones that allow the dead to speak from beyond the grave.

- Come to understand that video tombstones can create a link between the living and the dead for many generations.

Karen Shragg didn't go with traditional granite for her grandmother's headstone.

She went high-tech.

The marker features a QR code that allows visitors to a Richfield cemetery to read her grandmother's biography and view photographs of her, as well.

"This is just fantastic," Shragg said. "It's revolutionary."

The idea of sticking a QR code onto a headstone is the brainchild of a Twin Cities–based outfit determined to drag the industry into the 21st century.

More than just a marketing gambit aimed at a techno-obsessed society, it's an opportunity to document family stories before they fade away, said Norm Taple, president of Katzman Monument Co., which launched the QR codes in 2011. His company is believed to be one of four in the nation offering the QR code service.

"It's a chance for future generations to make a connection with a loved one," Taple said. "There's no emotional connection when all you can look at is a headstone, probably a dirty headstone, at that. We've got people telling their own stories, speaking directly to future generations."

The QR code allows people with smartphones to access a website paying tribute to the dearly departed. Cemetery visitors can read the deceased's biography, study their family tree, look at pictures or even watch videos of them talking about their lives.

The practice grew out of the surging popularity of memorial videos—sometimes called legacy or end-of-life-videos—in which people tape messages to be played at their funerals. Taple wondered why videos should be limited to funerals.

Thus was born the "interactive memorial." It's accessed via the QR code, which is on a 1-1/2-inch-square sticker similar to the renewal tabs used on license plates that can be attached anywhere on the tombstone. It's free with the purchase of a headstone from Katzman Monument, or you can add it to an existing tombstone for $150.

"As long as a cemetery is in an area with cellphone coverage—which these days is just about everywhere—it will work," he said.

Taple's company has been around for a little more than a year. Or a little over 77 years, depending on how you count.

It was started by Taple's grandfather, Jack Katzman, who opened shop at the corner of 19th Street and Nicollet Avenue in 1935. In 1981, with no one in the family interested in taking over the business, he closed it. Taple, his brother, Loren, and a longtime family friend, Michael Gregerson, decided to "reconstitute" the company, but in a technology-centric mode.

Instead of a brick-and-mortar showroom—which none of them could staff because they all have full-time jobs—they set up shop as an online business. Customers who log on to their website, katzmanmonument.com, can do everything electronically, including uploading photographs or other artwork to be etched into the granite.

"There are still companies where, when you walk in, there's a guy with a pencil and pad of sketch paper," he said. "This is an industry that has been missing the boat as far as the rest of the world goes."

Depending on how computer-savvy you are or how complex you want to make the memorial, you can do it yourself or arrange for the monument company to do it for you, either piecemeal or in its entirety. There are forms in which you can type biographies and fill in family trees. If you need help, prices range from $1 a piece to scan nondigital photos, to $45 to convert a VHS tape to digital format, to $215 to produce a 30-photo montage or $550 to shoot a simple video.

You can change the memorial at any time. "Anybody with a smartphone can access it and see it," Taple said, "but only one person has the log-in code that enables them to edit it."

Shragg, who is director of Wood Lake Nature Center and author of the book "Grieving Outside the Box" in which she interviewed people who dealt with grief in unusual ways, said it was insightful to work on her grandmother's QR memorial.

"I wish I had known about them [QR memorials] before I wrote the book," she said. "Any memorial—like the benches we dedicate [at Wood Lake]—is a way of calling attention to a person who was important in your life but is no longer here. But the QR code took it to a new level. It was a way to show people who my grandmother was."

The Rev. Alan Naumann, who also is a videographer, often helps people in hospice record a farewell message. He was doing that with a man in Rochester recently when he mentioned the QR code memorial.

"As we were getting done, I asked him one last question: If you could say something to the people who come to look at your headstone, what would you tell them?" Naumann said. The man said he'd advise his heirs to focus on the things that are important in life. "So then I told him that we can make that happen, and he got so excited about the fact that his life could still have an impact after he was gone.

"Legacy isn't just about money," Naumann continued. "The most important legacy we can leave behind are the lessons we learned and the values that steered our life. And to be able to do that in your own voice is very powerful."

Most cemeteries have embraced the idea. The only resistance Taple has encountered has come from Fort Snelling National Cemetery, which is subject to policies set on a national level. The Department of Veterans Affairs maintains a list of emblems that have been approved for inclusion on grave markers; QR codes aren't on it.

"It's all about uniformity," Taple said. "They don't want a marker to be unique. Well, these were your loved ones, and they were unique in many ways."

He's hoping that the VA will change its policies once it realizes the codes' potential, which he's convinced is almost limitless. His company is working with the creators of a veterans' memorial where visitors will be able to access the personal stories of 600 war dead.

"We're going to reach out to all 600 families," he said. "It's a wonderful opportunity. It's so much better than just a name etched into a monument."

Critical Thinking

1. What is the social benefit of the high-tech headstones that allow the dead to speak beyond the grave?
2. Do you think it is appropriate to have high-tech headstones that allow the dead to speak beyond the grave?
3. What is the role of high-tech headstones that allow the dead to speak beyond the grave? Will it have increased popularity or will it be a dying augmentation to cemeteries?

Internet References

Funeral Resources.com
https://funeralresources.com/memorial.../gravestone-technology/

Monuments.com | Living Headstones®
www.monuments.com/living-headstones

NBC News—Memorial videos played right on the tombstone
http://www.nbcnews.com/id/9257776/ns/technology_and_science-tech_and_gadgets/t/memorial-videos-played-right-tombstone/#.V0cpSpjrtaQ

Video Enhanced Gravemarker—Barrows
www.barrows.com/invention.html

VideoUniversity.com
https://www.videouniversity.com/.../video-tribute-plays-in-solar-powered...

Unit 6

UNIT

Prepared by: George E. Dickinson, *College of Charleston*
Michael R. Leming, *St. Olaf College*

Bereavement

In American society, many act as if the process of bereavement is completed with the culmination of public mourning related to the funeral or memorial service and the final disposition of the dead. For those in the process of grieving, the end of public mourning only serves to make the bereavement process a more individualized, subjective, and private experience. Private mourning of loss for most people, while more intense at its beginning, continues throughout their lifetime. The nature and intensity of this experience is influenced by the relationship of the mourner to the deceased, the age of the mourner, and the social context in which bereavement takes place.

This unit on bereavement begins with two general articles on the bereavement process. The first article, by Michael Leming and George Dickinson, describes and discusses the active coping strategies related to the bereavement process and the four tasks of bereavement. The rest of the articles focus on alternative perspectives on the understanding of the bereavement process, a discussion on the misinformation most people assume about grieving, and coping strategies employed by various grievers.

Key Points to Consider

Discuss how the seven stages of grieving over death can also be applied to losses through divorce, moving from one place to another, or the amputation of a limb (arm or leg). What is the relationship between time and the feelings of grief experienced within the bereavement process?

Describe the four necessary tasks of mourning. What are some of the practical steps one can take in accomplishing each of these tasks? How can one assist friends in bereavement?

What are the special problems encountered in the death of a child and in a perinatal death? How can one assist friends in this special type of bereavement?

How can one know if one is experiencing "normal" bereavement or "abnormal" bereavement? What are some of the signs of aberrant bereavement? What could you do to assist people experiencing abnormal grief symptoms?

Provide a list of "do's" and "don'ts" for dealing with children who have experienced a death.

How are bereavement needs of children and young adults different than those of adults?

Article

Prepared by: George E. Dickinson, *College of Charleston*
Michael R. Leming, *St. Olaf College*

The Grieving Process

MICHAEL R. LEMING AND GEORGE E. DICKINSON

Learning Outcomes

After reading this article, you will be able to:

- Better understand the process and stages of grieving.

- Identify the four tasks related to adjusting to the death of a loved one.

- Identify behaviors and attitudes one goes through as they adapt to a transition in the status of a relationship caused by death.

G rief is a very powerful emotion that is often triggered or stimulated by death. Thomas Attig makes an important distinction between grief and the grieving process. Although grief is an emotion that engenders feelings of helplessness and passivity, the process of grieving is a more complex coping process that presents challenges and opportunities for the griever and requires energy to be invested, tasks to be undertaken, and choices to be made (Attig, 1991).

Most people believe that grieving is a disease-like and debilitating process that renders the individual passive and helpless. According to Attig:

> It is misleading and dangerous to mistake grief for the whole of the experience of the bereaved. It is misleading because the experience is far more complex, entailing diverse emotional, physical, intellectual, spiritual, and social impacts. It is dangerous because it is precisely this aspect of the experience of the bereaved that is potentially the most frustrating and debilitating. (1991, p. 389)

Death ascribes to the griever a passive social position in the bereavement role. Grief is an emotion over which the individual has no control. However, understanding that grieving is an active coping process can restore to the griever a sense of autonomy in which the process is permeated with choice and there are many areas over which the griever does have some control.

Coping with Grief

The grieving process, like the dying process, is essentially a series of behaviors and attitudes related to coping with the stressful situation of a change in the status of a relationship. Many individuals have attempted to understand coping with dying as a series of universal, mutually exclusive, and linear stages. Not all people, however, will progress through the stages in the same manner.

Seven behaviors and feelings that are part of the coping process were identified by Robert Kavanaugh (1972): shock and denial, disorganization, volatile reactions, guilt, loss and loneliness, relief, and reestablishment. It is not difficult to see similarities between these behaviors and Kübler-Ross's five stages (denial, anger, bargaining, depression, and acceptance) of the dying process. According to Kavanaugh (1972, p. 23), "these seven stages do not subscribe to the logic of the head as much as to the irrational tugs of the heart—the logic of need and permission."

Shock and Denial

Even when a significant other is expected to die, at the time of death there is often a sense in which the death is not real. For most of us our first response is, "No, this can't be true." With time, our experience of shock diminishes, but we find new ways to deny the reality of death.

Some believe that denial is dysfunctional behavior for those in bereavement. However, denial not only is a common experience among the newly bereaved but also serves positive functions in the process of adaptation. The main function of denial is to provide the bereaved with a "temporary safe place" from the ugly realities of a social world that offers only loneliness and pain.

With time, the meaning of loss tends to expand, and it may be impossible for one to deal with all of the social meanings of death at once. For example, if a man's wife dies, not only does he lose his spouse, but also his best friend, his sexual partner, the mother of his children, a source of income, and so on. Denial can protect an individual from some of the magnitude of this social loss, which may seem unbearable at times. With denial, one can work through different aspects of loss over time.

Disorganization

Disorganization is the stage in the bereavement process in which one may feel totally out of touch with the reality of everyday life. Some go through the two- to three-day time period just before the funeral as if on "automatic pilot" or "in a daze." Nothing normal "makes sense," and they may feel that life has no inherent meaning. For some, death is perceived as preferable to life, which appears to be devoid of meaning.

This emotional response is also a normal experience for the newly bereaved. Confusion is normal for those whose social world has been disorganized through death. When Michael Leming's father died, his mother lost not only all of those things that one loses with a death of a spouse, but also her caregiving role—a social role and master status that had defined her identity in the five years that her husband lived with cancer. It is only natural to experience confusion and social disorganization when one's social identity has been destroyed.

Volatile Reactions

Whenever one's identity and social order face the possibility of destruction, there is a natural tendency to feel angry, frustrated, helpless, and/or hurt. The volatile reactions of terror, hatred, resentment, and jealousy are often experienced as emotional manifestations of these feelings. Grieving humans are sometimes more successful at masking their feelings in socially acceptable behaviors than other animals, whose instincts cause them to go into a fit of rage when their order is threatened by external forces. However apparently dissimilar, the internal emotional experience is similar.

In working with bereaved persons over the past 30 years, Michael Leming has observed that the following become objects of volatile grief reactions: God, medical personnel, funeral directors, other family members, in-laws, friends who have not experienced death in their families, and/or even the person who has died. Mildmannered individuals may become raging and resentful persons when grieving. Some of these people have experienced physical symptoms such as migraine headaches, ulcers, neuropathy, and colitis as a result of living with these intense emotions.

The expression of anger seems more natural for men than expressing other feelings (Golden, 2000). Expressing anger requires taking a stand. This is quite different from the mechanics

of sadness, where an open and vulnerable stance is more common. Men may find their grief through anger. Rage may suddenly become tears, as deep feelings trigger other deep feelings. This process is reversed with women, notes Tom Golden. Many times a woman will be in tears, crying and crying, and state that she is angry.

As noted earlier, a person's anger during grief can range from being angry with the person who died to being angry with God, and all points in between. Golden's mentor, Father William Wendt, shared the story of his visits with a widow and his working with her on her grief. He noticed that many times when he arrived she was driving her car up and down the driveway. One day he asked her what she was doing. She proceeded to tell him that she had a ritual she used in dealing with her grief. She would come home, go to the living room, and get her recently deceased husband's ashes out of the urn on the mantle. She would take a very small amount and place them on the driveway. She then said, "It helps me to run over the son of a bitch every day." He concluded the story by saying, "Now that is good grief." It was "good" grief because it was this woman's way of connecting to and expressing the anger component of her grief.

Guilt

Feelings of guilt are similar to the emotional reactions discussed earlier. Guilt is anger and resentment turned in on one's self and often results in selfdeprecation and depression. It typically manifests itself in statements like "If only I had . . . ," "I should have . . . ," "I could have done it differently," and "Maybe I did the wrong thing." Guilt is a normal part of the bereavement process.

From a sociological perspective, guilt can become a social mechanism to resolve the dissonance that people feel when unable to explain why someone else's loved one has died. Rather than viewing death as something that can happen at any time to anyone, people can blame the victim of bereavement and believe that the victim of bereavement was in some way responsible for the death—"If the individual had been a better parent, the child might not have been hit by the car," or "If I had been married to that person, I might also have committed suicide," or "No wonder that individual died of a heart attack, the spouse's cooking would give anyone high cholesterol." Therefore, bereaved persons are sometimes encouraged to feel guilt because they are subtly sanctioned by others' reactions.

Loss and Loneliness

Feelings of loss and loneliness creep in as denial subsides. The full experience of the loss does not hit all at once. It becomes more evident as bereaved individuals resume a social life without their loved one. They realize how much they needed and depended upon their significant other. Social situations in which we expected them always to be present seem different now that they are gone. Holiday celebrations are also diminished by their absence. In fact, for some, most of life takes on a "something's missing" feeling. This feeling was captured in the 1960s love song "End of the World":

Why does the world go on turning?

Why must the sea rush to shore?

Don't they know it's the end of the world

Cause you don't love me anymore?

("End of The World," written by Arthur Keat and Sylvia Dee. Used with permission of the Keat Estate.)

Loss and loneliness are often transformed into depression and sadness, fed by feelings of self-pity. According to Kavanaugh (1972, p. 118), this effect is magnified by the fact that the dead loved one grows out of focus in memory—"an elf becomes a giant, a sinner becomes a saint because the grieving heart needs giants and saints to fill an expanding void." Even a formerly undesirable spouse, such as an alcoholic, is missed in a way that few can understand unless their own hearts are involved. This is a time in the grieving process when anybody is better than nobody, and being alone only adds to the curse of loss and loneliness (Kavanaugh, 1972).

Those who try to escape this experience will either turn to denial in an attempt to reject their feelings of loss or try to find surrogates—new friends at a bar, a quick remarriage, or a new pet. This escape can never be permanent, however, because loss and loneliness are a necessary part of the bereavement experience. According to Kavanaugh (1972, p. 119), the "ultimate goal in conquering loneliness" is to build a new independence or to find a new and equally viable relationship.

Relief

The experience of relief in the midst of the bereavement process may seem odd for some and add to their feelings of guilt. Michael Leming observed a friend's relief six months after her husband died. This older friend was the wife of a minister, and her whole life before he died was his ministry. With time, as she built a new world of social involvements and relationships of which he was not a part, she discovered a new independent person in herself whom she perceived was a better person than she had ever before been.

Relief can give rise to feelings of guilt. However, according to Kavanaugh (1972, p. 121): "The feeling of relief does not imply any criticism for the love we lost. Instead, it is a reflection of our need for ever deeper love, our quest for someone or something always better, our search for the infinite, that best and perfect love religious people name as God."

Reestablishment

As one moves toward reestablishment of a life without the deceased, it is obvious that the process involves extensive adjustment and time, especially if the relationship was meaningful. It is likely that one may have feelings of loneliness, guilt, and disorganization at the same time, and that just when one may experience a sense of relief, something will happen to trigger a denial of the death.

What facilitates bereavement and adjustment is fully experiencing each of these feelings as normal and realizing that it is hope (holding the grieving person together in fantasy at first) that will provide the promise of a new life filled with order, purpose, and meaning.

Reestablishment occurs gradually, and often we realize it has been achieved long after it has occurred. In some ways it is similar to Dorothy's realization at the end of *The Wizard of Oz*—she had always possessed the magic that could return her to Kansas. And, like Dorothy, we have to experience our loss before we really appreciate the joy of investing our lives again in new relationships.

Four Tasks of Mourning

In 1982 J. William Worden published *Grief Counseling and Grief Therapy*, which summarized the research conclusions of a National Institutes of Health study called the Omega Project (occasionally referred to as the Harvard Bereavement Study). Two of the more significant findings of this research—displaying the active nature of the grieving process—are that mourning is necessary for all persons who have experienced a loss through death and that four tasks of mourning must be accomplished before mourning can be completed and reestablishment can take place.

According to Worden (1982), unfinished grief tasks can impair further growth and development of the individual. Furthermore, the necessity of these tasks suggests that those in bereavement must attend to "grief work" because successful grief resolution is not automatic, as Kavanaugh's (1972) stages might imply. Each bereaved person must accomplish four necessary tasks: (1) accept the reality of the loss, (2) experience the pain of grief, (3) adjust to an environment in which the deceased person is missing, and (4) withdraw emotional energy and reinvest it in another relationship (Worden, 1982).

Accept the Reality of the Loss

Especially in situations when death is unexpected and/or the deceased lived far away, it is difficult to conceptualize the reality of the loss. The first task of mourning is to overcome the natural denial response and realize that the person is dead and will not return.

Bereaved persons can facilitate the actualization of death in many ways. The traditional ways are to view the body, attend the funeral and committal services, and visit the place of final disposition. The following is a partial list of additional activities that can assist in making death real for grieving persons.

- View the body at the place of death before preparation by the funeral director.
- Talk about the deceased person and the circumstances surrounding the death.
- View photographs and personal effects of the deceased person.
- Distribute the possessions of the deceased person among relatives and friends.

Experience the Pain of Grief

Part of coming to grips with the reality of death is experiencing the emotional and physical pain caused by the loss. Many people in the denial stage of grieving attempt to avoid pain by choosing to reject the emotions and feelings that they are experiencing. As discussed by Erich Lindemann (1944), some do this by avoiding places and circumstances that remind them of the deceased. Michael Leming knows one widow who quit playing golf and quit eating at a particular restaurant because these were activities that she had enjoyed with her husband. Another widow found it extremely painful to be with her dead husband's twin, even though he and her sister-in-law were her most supportive friends.

Worden cites the following case study to illustrate the performance of this task of mourning:

> One young woman minimized her loss by believing her brother was out of his dark place and into a better place after his suicide. This might not have been true, but it kept her from feeling her intense anger at him for leaving her. In treatment, when she first allowed herself to feel anger, she said, "I'm angry with his behavior and not him!" Finally she was able to acknowledge this anger directly. (1982, pp. 13–14)

The problem with the avoidance strategy is that people cannot escape the pain associated with mourning. According to Bowlby (cited by Worden, 1982, p. 14), "Sooner or later, some of those who avoid all conscious grieving, break down—usually with some form of depression." Tears can afford cleansing for wounds created by loss, and fully experiencing the pain ultimately provides wonderful relief to those who suffer while eliminating long-term chronic grief.

Assume New Social Roles

The third task, practical in nature, requires the griever to take on some of the social roles performed by the deceased person or to find others who will. According to Worden (1982), to abort this task is to become helpless by refusing to develop the skills necessary in daily living and by ultimately withdrawing from life.

An acquaintance of Michael Leming's refused to adjust to the social environment in which she found herself after the death of her husband. He was her business partner, as well as her best and only friend. After 30 years of marriage, they had no children, and she had no close relatives. She had never learned to drive a car. Her entire social world had been controlled by her former husband. Three weeks after his funeral she went into the basement and committed suicide.

The alternative to withdrawing is assuming new social roles by taking on additional responsibilities. Extended families who always gathered at Grandma's house for Thanksgiving will be tempted to have a number of small Thanksgiving dinners at different places after her death. The members of this family may believe that "no one can take Grandma's place." Although this may be true, members of the extended family will grieve better if someone else is willing to do Grandma's work, enabling the entire family to come together for Thanksgiving. Not to do so will cause double pain—the family will not gather, and Grandma will still be missed.

Reinvest in New Relationships

The final task of mourning is a difficult one for many because they feel disloyal or unfaithful in withdrawing emotional energy from their dead loved one. One of Michael Leming's family members once said that she could never love another man after her husband died. His twice-widowed aunt responded, "I once felt like that, but I now consider myself to be fortunate to have been married to two of the best men in the world."

Other people find themselves unable to reinvest in new relationships because they are unwilling to experience again the pain caused by loss. The quotation from John Brantner provides perspective on this problem: "Only people who avoid love can avoid grief. The point is to learn from it and remain vulnerable to love."

Those who are able to withdraw emotional energy and reinvest it in other relationships find the possibility of a newly established social life. Kavanaugh depicts this situation well with the following description:

> At this point fantasies fade into constructive efforts to reach out and build anew.

> The phone is answered more quickly, the door as well, and meetings seem important, invitations are treasured and any social gathering becomes an opportunity rather than a curse. Mementos of the past are put away for occasional family gatherings. New clothes and new places promise dreams instead of only fears. Old friends are important for encouragement and permission to rebuild one's life.

New friends can offer realistic opportunities for coming out from under the grieving mantle. With newly acquired friends, one is not a widow, widower, or survivor—just a person. Life begins again at the point of new friendships. All the rest is of yesterday, buried, unimportant to the now and tomorrow. (1972, pp. 122–123)

Critical Thinking

1. Describe the seven behaviors and feelings that are part of coping with grief and loss.

2. What are the four tasks of mourning and how can the loss of closure relative to these tasks lead to impaired grieving?

3. How can relief and reinvestment in new relationships be important in normal grieving?

Internet References

Helpguide.org | Coping with Grief and Loss
www.helpguide.org/articles/grief-loss/coping-with-grief-and-loss.htm

WebMD | Grief & Depression
www.webmd.com/depression/guide/depression-grief and www.webmd.com/balance/tc/grief-and-grieving-topic-overview

Article

Prepared by: George E. Dickinson, *College of Charleston*
Michael R. Leming, *St. Olaf College*

Disenfranchised Grief

KENNETH J. DOKA

Learning Outcomes

After reading this article, you will be able to:

- Understand the concept of disenfranchised grief and how grieving can become disenfranchised.

- Come to be more understanding of people whose experience of loss is neither socially valuated nor supported?

- Come to be a more sympathetic friend and more valuable in supporting the grieving of others.

Introduction

Ever since the publication of Lindemann's classic article, "Symptomatology and Management of Acute Grief," the literature on the nature of grief and bereavement has been growing. In the few decades following this seminal study, there have been comprehensive studies of grief reactions, detailed descriptions of atypical manifestations of grief, theoretical and clinical treatments of grief reactions, and considerable research considering the myriad variables that affect grief. But most of this literature has concentrated on grief reactions in socially recognized and sanctioned roles: those of the parent, spouse, or child.

There are circumstances, however, in which a person experiences a sense of loss but does not have a socially recognized right, role, or capacity to grieve. In these cases, the grief is disenfranchised. The person suffers a loss but has little or no opportunity to mourn publicly.

Up until now, there has been little research touching directly on the phenomenon of disenfranchised grief. In her comprehensive review of grief reactions, Raphael notes the phenomenon:

> There may be other dyadic partnership relationships in adult life that show patterns similar to the conjugal ones, among them, the young couple intensely, even secretly, in love; the defacto relationships; the extramarital relationship; and the homosexual couple. . . . Less intimate partnerships of

close friends, working mates, and business associates, may have similar patterns of grief and mourning.

Focusing on the issues, reactions, and problems in particular populations, a number of studies have noted special difficulties that these populations have in grieving. For example, Kelly and Kimmel, in studies of aging homosexuals, have discussed the unique problems of grief in such relationships. Similarly, studies of the reactions of significant others of AIDS victims have considered bereavement. Other studies have considered the special problems of unacknowledged grief in prenatal death, [the death of] ex-spouses, therapists' reactions to a client's suicide, and pet loss. Finally, studies of families of Alzheimer's victims and mentally retarded adults also have noted distinct difficulties of these populations in encountering varied losses which are often unrecognized by others.

Others have tried to draw parallels between related unacknowledged losses. For example, in a personal account, Horn compared her loss of a heterosexual lover with a friend's loss of a homosexual partner. Doka discussed the particular problems of loss in nontraditional relationships, such as extramarital affairs, homosexual relationships, and cohabiting couples.

This article attempts to integrate the literature on such losses in order to explore the phenomenon of disenfranchised grief. It will consider both the nature of disenfranchised grief and its central paradoxical problem: the very nature of this type of grief exacerbates the problems of grief, but the usual sources of support may not be available or helpful.

The Nature of Disenfranchised Grief

Disenfranchised grief can be defined as the grief that persons experience when they incur a loss that is not or cannot be openly acknowledged, publicly mourned, or socially supported. The concept of disenfranchised grief recognizes that societies have sets of norms—in effect, "grieving rules"—that attempt to specify who, when, where, how, how long, and for whom people should grieve. These grieving rules may be codified in personnel policies. For example, a worker may be allowed a week off for the death of a spouse or child, three days for the loss of a parent or sibling. Such policies reflect the fact that each society defines who has a legitimate right to grieve, and these definitions of right correspond to relationships, primarily familial, that are socially recognized and sanctioned. In any given society these grieving rules may not correspond to the nature of attachments, the sense of loss, or the feelings of survivors. Hence the grief of these survivors is disenfranchised. In our society, this may occur for three reasons.

1. The Relationship Is Not Recognized

In our society, most attention is placed on kin-based relationships and roles. Grief may be disenfranchised in those situations in which the relationship between the bereaved and deceased is not based on recognizable kin ties. Here the closeness of other non-kin relationships may simply not be understood or appreciated. For example, Folta and Deck noted, "While all of these studies tell us that grief is a normal phenomenon, the intensity of which corresponds to the closeness of the relationship, they fail to take this (i.e., friendship) into account. The underlying assumption is that closeness of relationship exists only among spouses and/or immediate kin." The roles of lovers, friends, neighbors, foster parents, colleagues, in-laws, stepparents and stepchildren, caregivers, counselors, co-workers, and roommates (for example, in nursing homes) may be long-lasting and intensely interactive, but even though these relationships are recognized, mourners may not have full opportunity to publicly grieve a loss. At most, they might be expected to support and assist family members.

Then there are relationships that may not be publicly recognized or socially sanctioned. For example, nontraditional relationships, such as extramarital affairs, cohabitation, and homosexual relationships have tenuous public acceptance and limited legal standing, and they face negative sanctions within the larger community. Those involved in such relationships are touched by grief when the relationship is terminated by the death of the partner, but others in their world, such as children, may also experience grief that cannot be acknowledged or socially supported.

Even those whose relationships existed primarily in the past may experience grief. Ex-spouses, past lovers, or former friends may have limited contact, or they may not even engage in interaction in the present. Yet the death of that significant other can still cause a grief reaction because it brings finality to that earlier loss, ending any remaining contact or fantasy of reconciliation or reinvolvement. And again these grief feelings

may be shared by others in their world such as parents and children. They too may mourn the loss of "what once was" and "what might have been." For example, in one case a twelve-year-old child of an unwed mother, never even acknowledged or seen by the father, still mourned the death of his father since it ended any possibility of a future liaison. But though loss is experienced, society as a whole may not perceive that the loss of a past relationship could or should cause any reaction.

2. The Loss Is Not Recognized

In other cases, the loss itself is not socially defined as significant. Perinatal deaths lead to strong grief reactions, yet research indicates that many significant others still perceive the loss to be relatively minor. Abortions too can constitute a serious loss, but the abortion can take place without the knowledge or sanctions of others, or even the recognition that a loss has occurred. It may very well be that the very ideologies of the abortion controversy can put the bereaved in a difficult position. Many who affirm a loss may not sanction the act of abortion, while some who sanction the act may minimize any sense of loss. Similarly, we are just becoming aware of the sense of loss that people experience in giving children up for adoption or foster care, and we have yet to be aware of the grief-related implications of surrogate motherhood.

Another loss that may not be perceived as significant is the loss of a pet. Nevertheless, the research shows strong ties between pets and humans, and profound reactions to loss.

Then there are cases in which the reality of the loss itself is not socially validated. Thanatologists have long recognized that significant losses can occur even when the object of the loss remains physically alive. Sudnow for example, discusses "social death," in which the person is alive but is treated as if dead. Examples may include those who are institutionalized or comatose. Similarly, "psychological death" has been defined as conditions in which the person lacks a consciousness of existence, such as someone who is "brain dead." One can also speak of "psychosocial death" in which the persona of someone has changed so significantly, through mental illness, organic brain syndromes, or even significant personal transformation (such as through addiction, conversion, and so forth), that significant others perceive the person as he or she previously existed as dead. In all of these cases, spouses and others may experience a profound sense of loss but that loss cannot be publicly acknowledged for the person is still biologically alive.

3. The Griever Is Not Recognized

Finally, there are situations in which the characteristics of the bereaved in effect disenfranchise their grief. Here the person is not socially defined as capable of grief; therefore, there is little or no social recognition of his or her sense of loss or need to mourn. Despite evidence to the contrary, both the very old and the very young are typically perceived by others as having little comprehension of or reaction to the death of a significant other. Often, then, both young children and aged adults are excluded from both discussions and rituals.

Similarly, mentally disabled persons may also be disenfranchised in grief. Although studies affirm that the mentally retarded are able to understand the concept of death and, in fact, experience grief, these reactions may not be perceived by others. Because the person is retarded or otherwise mentally disabled, others in the family may ignore his or her need to grieve. Here a teacher of the mentally disabled describes two illustrative incidences:

> In the first situation, Susie was 17 years old and away at summer camp when her father died. The family felt she wouldn't understand and that it would be better for her not to come home for the funeral. In the other situation, Francine was with her mother when she got sick. The mother was taken away by ambulance. Nobody answered her questions or told her what happened. "After all," they responded, "she's retarded."

The Special Problems of Disenfranchised Grief

Though each of the types of grief mentioned earlier may create particular difficulties and different reactions, one can legitimately speak of the special problem shared in disenfranchised grief.

The problem of disenfranchised grief can be expressed in a paradox. The very nature of disenfranchised grief creates additional problems for grief, while removing or minimizing sources of support.

Disenfranchising grief may exacerbate the problem of bereavement in a number of ways. First, the situations mentioned tend to intensify emotional reactions. Many emotions are associated with normal grief. Bereaved persons frequently experience feelings of anger, guilt, sadness and depression, loneliness, hopelessness, and numbness. These emotional reactions can be complicated when grief is disenfranchised. Although each of the situations described is in its own way unique, the literature uniformly reports how each of these disenfranchising circumstances can intensify feelings of anger, guilt, or powerlessness.

Second, both ambivalent relationships and concurrent crises have been identified in the literature as conditions that complicate grief. These conditions can often exist in many types of disenfranchised grief. For example, studies have indicated the ambivalence that can exist in cases of abortion, among ex-spouses, significant others in nontraditional roles, and among

families of Alzheimer's disease victims. Similarly, the literature documents the many kinds of concurrent crises that can trouble the disenfranchised griever. For example, in cases of cohabiting couples, either heterosexual or homosexual, studies have often found that survivors experience legal and financial problems regarding inheritance, ownership, credit, or leases. Likewise, the death of a parent may leave a mentally disabled person not only bereaved but also bereft of a viable support system.

Although grief is complicated, many of the factors that facilitate mourning are not present. The bereaved may be excluded from an active role in caring for the dying. Funeral rituals, normally helpful in resolving grief, may not help here. In some cases, the bereaved may be excluded from attendance. In other cases, they may have no role in planning those rituals or in deciding whether even to have them. Or in cases of divorce, separation, or psychosocial death, rituals may be lacking altogether.

In addition, the very nature of the disenfranchised grief precludes social support. Often there is no recognized role in which mourners can assert the right to mourn and thus receive such support. Grief may have to remain private. Though they may have experienced an intense loss, they may not be given time off from work, have the opportunity to verbalize the loss, or receive the expressions of sympathy and support characteristic in a death. Even traditional sources of solace, such as religion, are unavailable to those whose relationships (for example, extramarital, cohabiting, homosexual, divorced) or acts (such as abortion) are condemned within that tradition.

Naturally, there are many variables that will affect both the intensity of the reaction and the availability of support. All the variables—interpersonal, psychological, social, physiological—that normally influence grief will have an impact here as well. And while there are problems common to cases of disenfranchised grief, each relationship has to be individually considered in light of the unique combinations of factors that may facilitate or impair grief resolution.

Implications

Despite the shortage of research on and attention given to the issue of disenfranchised grief, it remains a significant issue. Millions of Americans are involved in losses in which grief is effectively disenfranchised. For example, there are more than 1 million couples presently cohabiting. There are estimates that 3 percent of males and 2–3 percent of females are exclusively homosexual, with similar percentages having mixed homosexual and heterosexual encounters. There are about a million abortions a year; even though many of the women involved may not experience grief reactions, some are clearly "at risk."

Disenfranchised grief is also a growing issue. There are higher percentages of divorced people in the cohorts now aging. The AIDS crisis means that more homosexuals will experience losses in significant relationships. Even as the disease spreads within the population of intravenous drug users, it is likely to create a new class of both potential victims and disenfranchised grievers among the victims' informal liaisons and nontraditional relationships. And as Americans continue to live longer, more will suffer from severe forms of chronic brain dysfunctions. As the developmentally disabled live longer, they too will experience the grief of parental and sibling loss. In short, the proportion of disenfranchised grievers in the general population will rise rapidly in the future.

It is likely that bereavement counselors will have increased exposure to cases of disenfranchised grief. In fact, the very nature of disenfranchised grief and the unavailability of informal support make it likely that those who experience such losses will seek formal supports. Thus, there is a pressing need for research that will describe the particular and unique reactions of each of the different types of losses; compare reactions and problems associated with these losses; describe the important variables affecting disenfranchised grief reactions; assess possible interventions; and discover the atypical grief reactions, such as masked or delayed grief, that might be manifested in such cases. Also needed is education sensitizing students to the many kinds of relationships and subsequent losses that people can experience and affirming that where there is loss there is grief.

Critical Thinking

1. What is the meaning of disenfranchised grief?
2. How can grief be enfranchised?
3. Why does Dr. Doka believe that the proportion of disenfranchised grievers in the general population will rapidly increase in the future?

Internet References

Expressive Counseling & Coaching | Disenfranchised Grief
   www.expressivegriefcounseling.com/disenfranchised-grief-alone-ashamed/

Disenfranchised Grief: Recognizing Hidden Sorrow
   http://www.cruse.org.uk/sites/default/files/default_images/pdf/Events/KDDisenfranchisedgrief.pdf

Disenfranchised grief—Wikipedia, the free encyclopedia
   https://en.wikipedia.org/wiki/Disenfranchised_grief

KEN DOKA, PHD, is a professor of gerontology at the College of New Rochelle in New York. He became interested in the study of death and dying quite inadvertently. Scheduled to do a practicum in a facility that housed juvenile delinquents, he discovered that his supervisor had changed the assignment. Instead, Doka found himself counseling dying children and their families at Sloan-Kettering, a major cancer hospital in New York. This experience became the basis of two graduate theses, one in sociology entitled "The Social Organization of Terminal Care in Two Pediatric Hospitals," and the other in religious studies entitled "Pastoral Counseling to Dying Children and Their Families." (Both were later published.) His doctoral program pursued another longstanding interest: the sociology of aging. In 1983, Dr. Doka accepted his present position at the College of New Rochelle where he specializes in thanatology and gerontology.

Active in the Association for Death Education and Counseling since its beginnings, Dr. Doka was elected its president in 1993. In addition to articles in scholarly journals, he is the author of Death and Spirituality (with John Morgan, 1993), *Living with Life-Threatening Illness* (1993) and *Disenfranchised Grief: Recognizing Hidden Sorrow* (1989), from which the following selection is excerpted. His work on disenfranchised grief began in the classroom when a graduate student commented, "If you think widows have it rough, you ought to see what happens when your ex-spouse dies."

Article

Prepared by: George E. Dickinson, *College of Charleston*
Michael R. Leming, *St. Olaf College*

Challenging the Paradigm: New Understandings of Grief

Kenneth J. Doka, PhD

Learning Outcomes

After reading this article, you will be able to:

- Understand the concept of disenfranchised grief and how grieving can become disenfranchised.

- Understand the physical essentials in preparing yourself for grief work.

- Identify meaningful ways to commemorate the life of the loved one after the funeral.

Introduction

In 1989, Wortman and Silver published a controversial yet influential article entitled "The Myths of Coping With Loss," in which they identified five "myths" that were widely accepted by professionals treating bereavement:

- Depression and distress are inevitable in grief.
- Distress is necessary, and its absence is problematic.
- Survivors must "work through" a loss.
- Survivors can expect to recover from a loss.
- Survivors can reach a state of resolution.

The research, in Wortman and Silver's evaluation, did not support the widespread acceptance of these propositions.

Wortman and Silver's article crystallized a challenge to what might be called the *grief work hypothesis*. This hypothesis was really a conceptual belief that one must work through powerful feelings in order to detach from the deceased, reinvest in life, and recover from and resolve the loss. Originally derived from Freud's seminal 1917 article "Mourning and Melancholia,"

(Freud, 1957) the concept is pervasive in self-help books. Staudacher (1991), for example, expresses this notion:

> Simply put, *there is only one way to grieve* [emphasis in original]. That way is to go through the core of grief. Only by experiencing the necessary emotional effects of your loved one's death is it possible for you to eventually resolve the loss. (p. 3)

Although the grief work hypothesis was evident in much work in the field, especially in trade and self-help literature, it was not universally accepted. In the professional literature, the hypothesis was continually challenged in one way or another and coexisted with other ideas and approaches. In many ways, Wortman and Silver had oversimplified some very subtle and nuanced approaches to the understanding of grief and loss, but their article had great heuristic value, bringing forth many modifications and challenges to these early and popular understandings of grief.

The past 15 years have seen an increasing number of challenges to the early paradigms. In this chapter, I will describe five significant ways in which earlier understandings or paradigms of grief have been challenged. I will also discuss three current challenges to the field and two others that are likely to occur in the not-too-distant future.

Five New Understandings of Grief

1. Extending the Definition of Grief

One of the basic questions in the field relates to the definition of grief. Is grief a reaction to the death of a significant person, or can it be more broadly understood as a reaction to loss?

Freud's illustration of grief in "Mourning and Melancholia" is a bride left standing at the altar. Most contemporary work emphasizes grief as a reaction to death. Yet confusion over the issue still remains. The major death-related professional organization founded in the United States (though international in membership) was called the Association for Death Education and Counseling (ADEC). The Australian counterpart is called NALAG, the National Association for Loss and Grief. Yet, it remains unclear if the differences between these organizations, in terms of focus or mission, are, in fact, significant.

However, recent work has begun to emphasize grief as a more widespread reaction to loss. Some of this loss is certainly related to dying or death. For example, there has been long-standing recognition that people grieve *secondary losses;* that is, losses that follow a primary loss and engender additional grief. For example, a parent who has experienced the death of a child may mourn not only the loss of the child but also the absence of the child's friends, who were often present in the home. Rando's (1986, 2000) work on anticipatory mourning further develops the idea that losses other than death can generate grief. The original concept of anticipatory grief was that at the onset of a life-limiting disease, a person anticipated a future death and mourned that expected loss. Rando considerably expanded the concept to include anticipatory mourning, which she defined as a response to all the losses encountered—past, present, and future—in the course of an illness. For example, both patient and family may mourn the progressive disabilities and role losses that accompany the disease, as well as the loss of dreams, such as for an idyllic retirement, that now seem unlikely to be fulfilled. Rando's sensitivity to the myriad forms of loss is illustrated in *The Treatment of Complicated Mourning* (1993), in which she discusses tangible losses, such as an object that is stolen or a fire that destroys one's home, and intangible or symbolic losses, such as a divorce.

My work on disenfranchised grief (Doka, 1989, 2002) also addresses the wide range of losses that engender grief, stressing that the very lack of recognition of the grief experienced in such losses complicates grief. Some of these losses involved deaths that were unacknowledged by others—such as the deaths of former spouses, lovers, friends, and even animal companions. The work also emphasized the effects of other types of losses—such as incarceration, divorce, or infertility—that can generate significant grief. The concept of disenfranchised grief emphasizes that every society has "grieving rules" that determine a socially conferred "right to grieve." Generally, for example, these rules give family members the right to grieve the deaths of other family members. But in many situations—including non-death-related losses—a person might experience a significant loss but be deprived of the opportunity to publicly acknowledge the loss, openly mourn, and receive social support. This is disenfranchised grieving.

Harvey (1998) also notes the pervasiveness of loss and suggests the need for a larger psychology of loss that would complement and move beyond the study of dying and death. This shift is a critical one, as it allows the application of the study of grief to areas such as divorce and job loss, and allows the study to draw from the considerable literature around stress, coping, and adaptation (i.e., seeing grief as a type of stress reaction and mourning as a form of coping or adaptation).

However, the danger exists that grief will be trivialized. If every loss evokes "grief," the word becomes less important and signifies little. The antidote is to support research that clarifies the grief reactions and outcomes in a wide array of losses, allowing comparisons between grief reactions and outcomes from a death with those from other losses.

2. The Application of New Models

Most of the early models of grief were drawn from the work of Kubler-Ross (1969) and emphasized that people were likely to experience grief by going through a series of predictable reactions, or stages. Kubler-Ross originally studied the ways adults with life-threatening illness coped with impending death, but her work quickly was applied to the process of grief, in which a person was expected to experience a relatively linear movement through denial, bargaining, anger, and depression to reach a state of acceptance. This understanding of grief has become widespread.

Despite the popular embrace of these stages, most of the newer models have avoided the language and assumptions of stage theories. Worden (1982) broke new ground in his book *Grief Counseling and Grief Therapy* by conceptualizing mourning as a series of four tasks:

1. To accept the reality of the loss
2. To work through the pain of grief
3. To adjust to an environment where the deceased is missing.
4. To withdraw emotional energy and invest it in another relationship (In the second and third editions (1991, 2002), this task was revised to read "To emotionally relocate the deceased and move on with life," a modification that is discussed later in this chapter.)

While Worden's tasks clearly identified grief and mourning with death, they represented a significant paradigm shift from the predominant stage theories. Worden's task model was not linear; people worked on whatever issues arose in the process of mourning. The model stressed individuality (different survivors completed the tasks differently) and autonomy (survivors could choose when they were ready to tackle any task).

I recognized the value of Worden's approach and suggested a fifth task: to rebuild spiritual systems challenged by the loss

(Doka, 1993). This task recognizes that some losses challenge personal spiritual belief systems, causing individuals to question and possibly redefine their faith.

After Worden, other models appeared. Rando (1993), for example, proposed the "R" processes of mourning: recognizing the loss; reacting to the separation; recollecting and reexperiencing the deceased and the relationship; relinquishing the old attachments to the deceased and the old assumptive world; readjusting to move adaptively into the new world without forgetting the old; and reinvesting. Stroebe and Schut (1999) offered a dual-process model, suggesting that successful coping in bereavement means oscillating between loss-oriented and restoration-oriented processes.

Both these models, along with Worden's task model, reaffirmed that mourning was more than simply a series of affective responses to loss. In addition, the new models asserted that mourning involved not only a response to the loss of another but also an effort to manage life in a world altered by significant loss.

All these new models offer value to counselors in assisting bereaved persons. Stage models suggested a limited role for counselors: interpreting the reactions of bereaved persons and helping them move through the stages. The newer models allow a more significant role, in which the counselor helps the bereaved person understand what factors are complicating the completion of certain tasks or processes and develops interventions that can help the person adapt to loss.

The models also have implications for group programs. One way to evaluate a program is to determine the underlying model. Programs based on newer models should do more than simply allow participants to express affect. They should reflect the variety of tasks and processes that are part of the experience of grief and mourning.

3. Beyond Affect

While research from Lindemann (1944) has emphasized that grief is manifested in many ways—including cognitive, physical, emotional, behavioral, and spiritual reactions—much attention has been placed on affect, to the exclusion of other responses. This focus reflects a general Western preoccupation with affect in counseling and therapy (see Sue & Sue, 1999). A number of writers have stressed reactions to loss other than affect; two will serve as examples.

Neimeyer (2001) emphasizes that the reconstruction of meaning is a critical issue—if not *the* critical issue—in grief, adding strong cognitive and spiritual components to the study of grief. Neimeyer's "narrative" approach to therapy helps people "reweave" the narrative of their lives, which has been torn apart by significant loss.

Martin and Doka (2000) suggest a continuum of grieving styles ranging from the intuitive to the instrumental. Intuitive grievers experience, express, and adapt to grief in strongly affective ways. Instrumental grievers, on the other hand, are likely to experience muted affective reactions. Their experience is more likely to be cognitive and behavioral, and they will favor such strategies for expression and adaptation to loss. Martin and Doka's work strongly challenges the notion that expressing feelings is the most effective way to adapt to loss. The work began as an attempt to understand the grieving patterns of males; the authors now see these patterns as related to, but not determined by, gender.

Other researchers have strongly challenged the idea that expression of feelings and emotions in grief should be encouraged and that a lack of open affect suggests difficulty. In his social-functioning approach, Bonanno (2004) suggests that adaptation to loss is facilitated when grief-related distress is minimized and positive affect is accentuated. Similarly, Nolen-Hoeksema, McBride, and Larson (1997) suggest that excessive rumination might not be helpful and, in fact, is associated with poor outcomes. The excessive processing of loss can exacerbate distress. Resilient individuals minimize rumination by distraction—shifting their attention in a positive direction. However, Nolen-Hoeksema and her associates also found that deliberate avoidance and suppression of grief were maladaptive.

These insights have important implications for grief counselors, grief groups, and grief curricula. The ideas reflected in the newer models reaffirm that grief is more than emotion. They suggest that leaders should try to move their groups beyond shared anguish to discussions of effective ways to cope with grief and should encourage the recognition of positive memories and experiences, even within a state of grief. These concepts reaffirm the individuality of the grief experience and discourage dogmatic, one-size-fits-all strategies.

4. Beyond Coping

Early work in the field tended to emphasize the difficulty of coping with loss and focused on restoring a sense of equilibrium while slowly and painfully withdrawing emotional energy from the deceased. The perception of the survivor was primarily passive, besieged to cope with changes out of his or her control.

This concept was strongly challenged in the work of Catherine Sanders (1989). In her phase model of grief, Sanders suggested that the process of grieving involves a series of phases, and most people follow a common sequence. The first phase is *shock,* as the person begins to feel the impact of the death. In each phase, Sanders related the psychological, cognitive, and physical sequelae of grief. For example, in the shock phase, physical symptoms may include weeping, tremors, and loss of appetite. Bereaved persons may experience psychological distancing, egocentric phenomena, or preoccupation with thoughts of the deceased. Cognitive manifestations at this phase may include disbelief, restlessness, and a heightened state of alarm or a sense of unreality or helplessness. In each of the phases, Sanders recognized both the individuality and the multiplicity of grief reactions—a significant advance over the stage theory (Kubler-Ross, 1969).

The second phase, Sanders said, is *awareness of loss.* Here the funeral rituals are over and support has ebbed. Until now, shock and support have acted as a buffer. Now, as the shock recedes and family and friends withdraw, the primary grievers experience the full force of their loss. This is a period of high emotional and cognitive arousal; separation anxiety is intense and stress is prolonged. Grief is both raw and deeply painful. The bereaved person becomes exhausted and needs to withdraw from others to conserve limited energy.

Sanders proposed *conservation-withdrawal* as the third phase of bereavement. This is a long (possibly endless) phase of grief. The grieving person seems to be functioning, and pain is more chronic than acute. But the person feels physically weak and helpless—going through the motions rather than actively living life. Bereaved persons in this phase often express a belief that they are in state of hibernation, a sort of holding pattern as they struggle to adapt to the loss.

Sanders said that in the first and second phases, people are motivated largely by unconscious or biological factors. In this phase, she suggested that people have three choices. In the face of extreme physical and psychological stress, some may consciously or unconsciously seek their own death rather than live without the person who died. Others may assume that the necessary major life adjustments require more strength and power than they possess. They may choose the status quo, living the rest of their lives in a diminished state of chronic grief. Still others may decide to move forward and adjust to their loss.

According to Sanders, bereaved persons who choose to move forward often experience a fourth phase: *healing/the turning point.* In her research, many persons could point to a moment when they consciously decided that their lives needed to change. In one vignette, a widow recalled hearing her young granddaughter ask her mother, "Why does Grandma always cry?" The widow resolved then and there that she would not be remembered as "the grandma who always cried." In this phase, people reconstruct their identities and lives, and enjoy restored physical health, increased energy, and psychological vigor.

Finally, those who experience the turning point move to a fifth phase that Sanders called *renewal.* While they still experience occasional bad days and episodic moments of grief, they experience a new level of functioning characterized by enhanced self-awareness, increased levels of energy, personal

revitalization, and the renewal of social ties. At this phase, the bereaved person has learned to live without the physical presence of the loved one, while retaining an internal sense of the deceased person's presence. Sanders noted that in this phase, people could often process and even enjoy memories of the deceased without the high emotional arousal experienced earlier in the grieving process.

Later, Sanders began to develop the notion of a sixth phase: *fulfillment.* In this phase, the grieving person can look back on his or her own life in a way that integrates the loss into the fabric of that life. While the loss was neither expected nor welcomed, the person can no longer imagine what life would be like without the loss (Doka, 2006).

Sanders was one of the first theorists to affirm that people had choices in the mourning process. Her writing emphasized that bereaved persons were active participants in the mourning process rather than passive copers with little control. Her renewal phase presaged such trends in contemporary bereavement theory as grief as a transformative experience (Neimeyer, 2001; Prend, 1997; Schneider, 1994), in which loss can lead to significant personal growth as the bereaved person struggles to adapt to life without the deceased. These concepts are supported in the research of Calhoun and Tedeschi (2004), which emphasizes the human capacity for reliance and notes that loss may trigger growth and change.

This work emphasizes that the point of therapy is not to "recover" from the loss. Rather, it suggests that therapists can pose a larger question: "How will this loss change you?" The question implies an active response. Grieving persons are not passive: While they might have no choice about grief, they do have choices about what they will do with their loss.

5. Continuing Bonds

The Freudian notion that the work of grief is to detach from the deceased and reinvest in other relationships has been strongly challenged. In 1987, Attig compared "letting go" in grief to letting go of an adult child. By that Attig meant that even though there may be less physical presence, the connective bonds and sense of presence remain strong. Synthesizing other work, I suggested in the *Encyclopedia of Death* (Doka, 1984) that rather than emotionally withdraw, survivors might find ways to creatively retain their attachments to the loss object. Using his own research, Worden (1991) revised the wording of his fourth task from the Freudian concept of withdrawing emotional energy from the deceased to relocating the deceased, emphasizing that the bond between the deceased and the survivor continues, albeit in a different form.

In other work, LaGrand (1999) described a connection he labeled "extraordinary experiences," in which bereaved persons recounted dreams, sense experiences, and other phenomena after the death of someone they loved. Often these experiences were therapeutic—reaffirming a bond and offering comfort. Such experiences are so common that I suggest counselors routinely ask bereaved persons about them—they may be comforted by the experiences but reluctant to bring them up.

The challenge to the idea of withdrawal received its fullest treatment in the groundbreaking book *Continuing Bonds: New Understandings of Grief,* edited by Klass, Silverman, and Nickman (1996). The editors emphasize that throughout history and across cultures, bereaved persons have maintained bonds with their deceased. The research in this book deeply challenges the idea that emotional withdrawal is essential or even desirable.

Counselors should assure clients that the goal of grief therapy is not to abolish memories of the deceased. The amelioration of grief means that over time the intensity of the grief experience lessens and the bereaved person functions as well as (or perhaps even better than) before the loss, although surges of grief may occur even years later, brought on by significant transitions or other experiences. The point is that relationships continue even beyond death, and the grief process has no final end point.

However, not all bonds with the deceased are helpful. Some persons may retain connections to a loved one who has died that impair relationships with others or adaptation to the loss. Recent research described by Stroebe (2006) suggests that bonds may be supportive for some persons but maladaptive for others. The therapeutic challenge is to recognize that not all attachments are positive.

Current Challenges

These new understandings have received considerable attention and widespread acceptance. Three current challenges may further modify the way we understand grief.

1. Increasing Diversity: The Challenge of Culture

The United States and many other nations are becoming increasingly racially and ethnically diverse. Much of the research has been based on white, middle-class samples, so it may not be possible to generalize our understanding of grief. A more diverse society will cause us to rethink basic questions. For example, what does loss actually mean? Different societies, with different patterns of attachment and different expectations about life and death, may respond to a loss quite differently. What, for example, is the impact of a child's death in a society with high levels of infant and child mortality?

A more diverse society may challenge what we believe we know about grief. Different cultures may have distinct ways of describing the experience of grief, as well as their own modes of expressing grief and adapting to loss. It may be that the only thing all cultures share is that each one responds and adapts to loss. We may be able to learn from other cultures—their rituals and methods of expression and adaptation may teach us effective strategies and offer insights on different approaches to dealing with loss.

The issue of diversity also has programmatic implications for hospices and bereavement programs. How sensitive are programs to ethnic and cultural differences? Are there significant differences in participation or withdrawal from grief programs or bereavement groups? Do other programs reflect sensitivity to diversity? Do "interfaith services" truly reflect religious and cultural diversity? As Islam and other nonwestern faiths grow in the United States and many other western nations, is this growth reflected in the religious affiliations of chaplains and the nature of spiritual care? Are resources on grief—such as books or brochures—available in all the languages spoken in our communities?

Social class is another aspect of diversity, and strategies and programs need to acknowledge the differences. Are fees for services based on a sliding scale? Social class also encompasses differences in life style. For example, for many lower income families, photographs are a luxury. A common activity in children's groups involves creating photographic montages and picture boxes. Such exercises may isolate lower income children or expend a precious and not easily replaced resource.

Sexual orientation is yet another source of diversity. How inclusive are groups and materials? Are bereavement groups solely for widows and widowers or also for partners? Would bereaved unmarried partners—either gay or straight—be comfortable in the grief groups offered or is it clear that the groups are meant to serve heterosexual widowed spouses?

Sue and Sue (2003) remind us that counseling is a culture itself, with its own distinct values. How well do these values match the values and approaches of the cultures being served?

2. The Challenge of Research and Evidence-Based Practice

As Neimeyer (2000) notes, little research has been done on the actual methods of grief counseling and grief therapy. In the past, we simply assumed that these methods worked. Grief counseling requires the integration of theory, practice, and research. Interventions need to be theoretically grounded and empirically assessed. Evidence-based practice is becoming the standard.

This standard has implications for practitioners, including the need for constant evaluation of grief programs. How can we be sure that the programs we offer are effective? On what evidence do we base programs? More integration is needed between clinical practice and research. This integration is facilitated when researchers and theoreticians explore the practice applications of their work and when clinicians take an empirical approach to therapy—constantly assessing how well their therapy is helping the client adapt to loss. Research on the link between theory and practice will likely cause us to reassess and reevaluate the concepts and models that underlie the study of grief.

3. The Challenge of Technology
The challenge to research and evaluate is especially clear with regard to the many resources offered through the Internet. Online resources include grief information, grief groups, chat rooms, counseling, and opportunities for memorialization. Yet there has been little evaluation of these resources and little study of their efficacy.

The Internet may offer support for bereaved persons, but it may itself be a source of grief. The exponential increase in cyberspace relationships raises questions for the study of attachment and loss. If close relationships can form online, will these people constitute a future class of disenfranchised grievers? Will these relationships raise new questions regarding the processes of death notification?

On the Horizon
Two additional issues are likely to affect future understanding of grief. The first one is the move to add a "grief" category to the forthcoming *DSM-V*. One of the proposals before the American Psychiatric Association is on *complicated grief* (formerly called *traumatic grief*). Jacobs and Prigerson and others (see Jacobs & Prigerson, 2000; Prigerson & Maciejewski, 2006) suggest that certain symptoms evident early in the process of grieving predict problematic outcomes, and they recommend early intervention. For years, the field has eschewed a medical model of grief and avoided using terms like "symptoms." Grief, it is argued, is a normal part of the life cycle, not an illness. These proposals challenge that notion, asserting that at least some experiences of grief show evidence of psychiatric illness. The proposals are a sign of increasing recognition that there is a need for correction, that the emphasis on the normalcy of loss and grief has led to the neglect of problematic variants. Receptiveness to these proposals is probably also fueled by the growth of managed care in the United States and the need to have a clear grief-related diagnostic code. Regardless of the motivation, adding a diagnostic category for grief will constitute a paradigm shift.

The second issue is the demographic change as the baby boomers age. Many of them are experiencing the loss of their parents; in a few decades, they will face their own deaths. Also, each generation develops unique forms of attachment; many boomers have developed extremely close attachments to their children, so their deaths may create different problems for their offspring than in previous generations. This is a generation that has challenged and changed every institution it has experienced in its collective journey through the life cycle. Boomers demand choices in programs and avoid programs that ignore individual differences. They tend to trust individuals rather than institutions. They want to be active participants in programs rather than passive recipients. The baby boomers will surely change the ways we encounter loss, death, and grief.

Over the past 15 years, our understanding of grief has experienced major modifications. Changes and challenges are likely to continue to affect how we think about and respond to loss. As a popular Baby Boom song, Dylan's *"The World it Is a Changin"* put it "the wheel is still in spin."

References
Attig, T. (1987). Grief, love and separation. In C. Corr and R. Pacholski (Eds.), *Death: Completion and discovery.* Lakewood, OH: Association for Death Education and Counseling.

Bonnano, G. (2004). Loss, trauma and human resilience: Have we underestimated the human capacity to thrive after extremely aversive events? *American Psychologist, 59,* 20–28.

Calhoun, L. G., & Tedeschi, R. G. (2004). The foundations of posttraumatic growth: New considerations. *Psychological Inquiry, 15,* 93–102.

Doka, K. J. (1984). Grief. In R. Kastenbaum and B. Kastenbaum (Eds.), *Encyclopedia of death.* Phoenix, AZ: Oryx Press.

Doka, K. J. (1989). *Disenfranchised grief: Recognizing hidden sorrow.* Lexington, MA: Lexington Press.

Doka, K. J. (1993). The spiritual crises of bereavement. In K. J. Doka (with J. Morgan) (Ed.), *Death and spirituality* (pp. 185–195). Amityville, NY: Baywood Publishing Co.

Doka, K. J. (2002). *Disenfranchised grief: New directions, challenges, and strategies for practice.* Champaign, IL: Research Press.

Doka, K. (2006). Fulfillment as Sanders' sixth phase of bereavement: The unfinished work of Catherine Sanders. *Omega: The Journal of Death and Dying, 52,* 141–149.

Freud, S. (1957). *Mourning and melancholia.* London: Hogarth.

Harvey, J. (1998). *Perspectives on loss: A sourcebook.* Philadelphia: Brunner/Mazel.

Jacobs, S., & Prigerson, H. (2000). Psychotherapy of traumatic grief: A review of evidence for psychotherapeutic treatments. *Death Studies, 21,* 471–498.

Klass, D., Silverman, P., & Nickman, S. (Eds.). (1996). *Continuing bonds: New understandings of grief.* Washington, DC: Taylor & Frances.

Kubler-Ross, E. (1969). *On death and dying.* New York: Macmillan.

LaGrand, L. (1999). *Messages and miracles: Extraordinary experiences of the bereaved.* St. Paul, MN: Llewellyn Publications.

Lindemann, E. (1944). Symptomatology and management of acute grief. *American Journal of Psychiatry, 101,* 141–148.

Martin, T., & Doka, K. J. (2000). *Men don't cry, women do: Transcending gender stereotypes of grief.* Philadelphia: Brunner/Mazel.

Neimeyer, R. A. (2000). Grief therapy and research as essential tensions: Prescriptions for a progressive partnership. *Death Studies, 24,* 603–610.

Neimeyer, R. A. (2001). *Meaning reconstruction and the meaning of loss.* Washington, DC: American Psychological Association.

Nolen-Hoeksema, S., McBride, A., & Larson, J. (1997) Rumination and psychological distress among bereaved partners. *Journal of Personality and Social Psychology, 72,* 855–862.

Prend, A. (1997). *Transcending loss.* New York: Berkley Books.

Prigerson, H., & Maciejewski, P. (2006). A call for sound empirical testing and evaluation for complicated grief proposed for *DSM-V. Omega, The Journal of Death and Dying, 52,* 9–20.

Rando, T. A. (1986). *Loss and anticipatory grief.* Lexington, MA: Lexington Books.

Rando, T. A. (1993). *The treatment of complicated mourning.* Champaign, IL: Research Press.

Rando, T. A. (2000). *Clinical dimensions of anticipatory mourning: Theory and practice in working with the dying, their loved ones, and their caregivers.* Champaign, IL: Research Press.

Sanders, C. (1989). *Grief: The mourning after – Dealing with adult bereavement.* New York: Wiley.

Staudacher, C. (1991). *Men and grief.* Oakland, CA: New Harbinger Publications.

Stroebe, M., & Schut, H. (1999). The dual process model of coping with bereavement: Rationale and description. *Death Studies, 23,* 197–224.

Stroebe, M. (2006, April). *Continuing bonds in bereavement: Toward theoretical understanding.* Keynote presentation to the Association of Death Education and Counseling, Albuquerque, NM.

Sue, D.W., & Sue, D. (2003). *Counseling the culturally diverse: Theory and practice.* New York: John Wiley and Sons.

Worden, J. W. (1982, 1991, 2002). *Grief counseling and grief therapy: A handbook for the mental health practitioner* (eds.1–3). New York: Springer.

Wortman, C., & Silver, R. C. (1989). The myths of coping with loss. *Journal of Clinical Counseling, 57,* 349–357.

Critical Thinking

1. According to Dr. Doka, what are the five significant ways in which earlier understandings or paradigms of grief have been challenged?
2. Describe the three current challenges that may further modify the way we understand grief.
3. How will demographic changes change the way in which Americans grieve?

Internet References

10 Types of Disenfranchised Grief
www.calebwilde.com/2014/12/10-types-of-disenfranchised-grief/

Ambiguous Loss and Disenfranchised Grief
www.indiana.edu/~famlygrf/units/ambiguous.html

Life and Health: Disenfranchised Grief—Vision
https://www.vision.org/visionmedia/grief-and-loss/disenfranchised-grief/2202.aspx

Article

Prepared by: George E. Dickinson, *College of Charleston*
Michael R. Leming, *St. Olaf College*

Educators Tend to Overlook Student Grief, Experts Say

Evie Blad

Learning Outcomes

After reading this article, you will be able to:

- Assist and support children when they attend funerals.

- Understand ways in which one can assist others who are experiencing trauma in grieving.

- Understand high-risk factors which can predispose an individual to complicated grieving.

A teenage boy who survived a high-profile shooting was frequently missing school in the weeks after the incident.

School counselors had worked with him to address the trauma associated with the shooting, in which two people standing near him died, said David J. Schonfeld, the director of the National Center for School Crisis and Bereavement, who later counseled the boy.

But the school hadn't addressed the student's grief. One victim was a longtime friend, and he didn't want to go to school without her.

Many schools fail to properly assist grieving students, according to the Coalition to Support Grieving Students, a group of education organizations. The group recently launched a website of free materials to help schools address grief, which can be a barrier to engagement.

"For some reason with bereavement, it's not a mental illness and it's not something you diagnose, so it's not something that you treat," said Dr. Schonfeld, a pediatrician who specializes in developmental and behavioral issues.

While schools have increased their focus in recent years on nonacademic factors—like trauma, bullying, and mental-health issues—that affect a student's ability to engage with classroom content, many still lag behind in efforts to help students as they deal with death and loss, child-bereavement experts say.

Resources for Educators

For the teenage boy dealing with the aftermath of the shooting, that meant his school focused on the more unusual experience of trauma rather than the more common experience of grief, said Dr. Schonfeld.

Grief is seen as a normal part of life, so it often isn't addressed, he said.

And that's problematic, the Coalition to Support Grieving Students said, because many students struggle with the loss of a friend or family member at some point in their K-12 experience. And the fallout from grief can make it difficult to focus in the classroom and connect with their peers, the group said.

To help remedy the problem, the coalition launched a website, grievingstudents.org, earlier this month. It's the culmination of several years of work to develop resources to help educators understand and address student bereavement.

The website includes online professional-development modules—crafted in consultation with Dr. Schonfeld and the Philadelphia-based National Center for School Crisis and Bereavement—that address subjects like classroom discussions, consultation among educators to plan for students' re-entry to school, funeral attendance, and the psychology of child grief.

The coalition, convened in 2013 by the New York Life Foundation, quickly identified a lack of educator training as a barrier to helping students dealing with death.

The coalition estimates that one in 20 American children will lose a parent by the time they reach 16, and "the vast

HOW TO TALK TO GRIEVING STUDENTS

Because many educators fear saying the wrong thing to a grieving student, they don't say anything at all, the Coalition to Support Grieving Students says. Here are examples of what not to say, pulled from the coalition's new online training resources.

DON'T SAY THIS

"I know just what you're going through."

You cannot know this. Everyone's experience of grief is unique.

"You must be incredibly angry."

It is not helpful to tell people how they are feeling or ought to feel. It is better to ask. People in grief often feel many different things at different times.

"At least he's no longer in pain."

Efforts to "focus on the good things" are more likely to minimize the student or family's experience (see above). Any statement that begins with the words "at least" should probably be reconsidered.

"I lost both my parents when I was your age."

Avoid comparing your losses with those of students or their families. These types of statements may leave children feeling that their loss is not as profound or important.

SOURCE: Coalition to Support Grieving Students

SAY THIS INSTEAD

"Can you tell me more about what this has been like for you?"

"Most people have strong feelings when something like this happens to them. What has this been like for you?"

"What sorts of things have you been thinking about since your loved one died?"

"Tell me more about what this has been like for you."

---

majority of children will experience the loss of a family member or friend by the time they complete high school."

In a national survey administered in 2012 by the New York Life Foundation and the American Federation of Teachers, 69 percent of responding teachers reported having at least one grieving student in their classroom, but only 7 percent said they had received any training on how to support grieving children.

That may be because dealing with death is seen as a common experience, Dr. Schonfeld said.

But an experience doesn't have to be unusual to affect student learning, he said.

Dealing with Death

Students trying to cope with the death of a parent, for example, may have lost the person who drove them to school every day. Students adjusting to the loss of a sibling may be facing the dual challenge of dealing with their own emotions while trying to support their grieving parents, and the loss of a beloved family pet can cause a student to read words over and over again without understanding the concept of the text.

The death of a friend or loved one may also make students more aware of their own mortality, researchers say.

That can lead teenagers, especially those with repeated experiences of loss, to engage in risk-taking behaviors like drug use and violence just to prove to themselves that they will survive, Dr. Schonfeld said.

At an event held in Washington last week to announce the coalition and release its materials, Randi Weingarten, the president of the AFT and a former teacher in New York City, described her experience working with a student whose father had been killed.

"The fact that she came to school said something about her feeling safe in my classroom, which made me feel responsible," Ms. Weingarten said.

Teachers and administrators, afraid of saying the wrong thing to a hurting student, sometimes don't say anything at all, Dr. Schonfeld said.

"They don't know what to do, but also, it's painful to watch a kid grieve," he said. "They're afraid to get too close or to start something they don't think they can finish."

So the new guidance includes a module on "what not to say" that addresses some common conversational missteps and suggests alternatives.

Coordination and Support

The guidance also recommends that teachers coordinate with one another to ensure that a student returning to school isn't greeted by a pile of homework and tests in every class. Schools should also establish a point of contact with families to help monitor a child's progress, it says.

Moreover, the guidance includes materials on how to foster positive peer support for classmates of those who are grieving.

"Children who are uninformed or unprepared may unintentionally isolate or even tease a grieving classmate," the guidance says.

Organizers in the coalition also are working to complete materials on special circumstances, including grief after a suicide.

In addition, a module on "cumulative loss" may be helpful for students in high-crime areas, who may experience several deaths of family or community members in a short span of time.

The coalition will continue to develop and add new documents and videos to the website, members said.

David Esquith, the director of the office of safe and healthy students at the U.S. Department of Education, said it's important for schools to address issues like grief through ongoing training so that teachers and administrators can be ready to meet the needs of all students.

Grief and mental-health issues are too often overlooked until there is a large-scale crisis or tragedy, such as shootings and natural disasters, he said.

"The bad news is that we tend to be very reactive as a nation to the nonacademic needs of our students," Mr. Esquith said.

Busra Aydin, a 4th grade teacher at Noyes Education Campus in the District of Columbia, said she sees the need for more resources to address student bereavement.

"It can be really uncomfortable to talk about this," she said. "It can be really difficult to determine how your audience is going to react."

Ms. Aydin recalled teaching a boy who struggled emotionally and behaviorally after his father died. The experience was confusing for the student, who hadn't known his father well, she said.

A group of teachers and school staff members met to figure out a plan for how to support him. They found a mentor, a male physical education teacher with whom the student could relate.

The group also gave the student a journal to document his thoughts and a pass to take a daily 15-minute break from class when he was feeling emotional.

"Teachers should be equipped [to discuss death]," Ms. Aydin said. "How else are they going to support their students and meet their needs so they can actually focus on instruction?"

Members of the Coalition to Support Grieving Students include the AASA, the School Superintendents Association; the AFT; the National Association of School Psychologists; and the National Education Association Health Information Network.

Critical Thinking

1. Why do educators tend to overlook student grief?
2. What can educators do to help students who grieve?
3. What are some of the resources for educators who wish to attend to the needs of student grievers?

Internet References

6 Ways That Adolescent Grief Is Different—Huffington Post
http://www.huffingtonpost.com/kenneth-j-doka/six-ways-that-adolescent-_b_5148211.html

Helping a Teenager Deal with Grief—What's Your Grief?
www.whatsyourgrief.com/helping-a-teenager-deal-with-grief

Helping Teens Work Through Grief—Toolkits by K4Health
https://www.k4health.org/toolkits/alhiv/helping-teens-work-through-grief

How to Help a Grieving Teen | The Dougy Center
http://www.dougy.org/grief-resources/how-to-help-a-grieving-teen/

Article   Prepared by: George E. Dickinson, *College of Charleston*
Michael R. Leming, *St. Olaf College*

Children at the Grave

Melissa Florer-Bixler

Learning Outcomes

After reading this article, you will be able to:

- Assist and support children when they attend funerals.

- Understand ways in which one can assist others who are experiencing trauma in grieving.

- Understand high-risk factors which can predispose a child to complicated grieving.

Last spring the principal of my daughter's elementary school invited me to attend career day. I showed up in the lobby, alb on hanger, and sat with a pizza shop owner, filmmaker, and cardiologist before being ushered into the classroom to share about my job as a pastor. I'd brought pictures with me of some of the things I do—Sunday school, hospital visits, committee meetings, and funerals.

The children were mostly interested in the funerals. "Have you ever seen a dead person?" one asked. "Do you have to dig the hole to bury them?" "What happens when you die?" "Someone told me that dead people go to heaven. Is that true?"

Eventually the teacher announced that it was time for the next parent to take my place, but the children wouldn't let me go. Robed in white and crouched on a blue plastic chair, I watched as a small line formed in front of me. I felt like a priest hearing confession as each child came forward and whispered in my ear a story of death.

"My cousin, he got killed selling drugs," one boy said in a hushed tone, looking around to make sure that no one was watching him. "He owed a gang money. They threatened to kill his mother."

A girl came up next. She looked me in the eye and said, quietly, "My baby brother died last year. We had a funeral. I was so sad. I am still sad."

They talked to me about what they'd seen, what had happened to their lives. They shared with me their grief and bewilderment. I realized that this might be the first time they had told anyone these stories. We often shield our children from death. We hide the news, tuck it away, hoping that we can avoid a collision of sorrow and childhood. We want to guard these precious years. But children know. They are seers, reading our bodies and anxiety and energy. They know much more than sometimes we hope they do.

Recently I preached at the funeral of a 99-year-old member of my congregation. As I sat in a back room behind the sanctuary, preparing the family for the service, I noticed two of Doreen's great-grandchildren, a little boy and a little girl, sitting in a couple of the chairs. The girl was crying. I went over to them. "Is this your first funeral?" I asked. The girl nodded her head yes. I talked her through the service. We talked about cremation, about the box with her grandma's ashes. I told her we would sing, and pray, and tell stories. I let her know that if she had any questions she could talk to me after the service.

Many children, including my own, are fascinated with death— fascinated by talking about it, acting it out, and making light of it. I recently sat next to a little boy who introduced himself to me by sharing his name and age. The next fact he offered was that his grandmother was dead. This event was significant; it marked him. Why wouldn't he share it with a new person who was getting to know him?

Death is a strange land for all of us. But for children it is another mystery to be explored, another in a long series of human events to be worked out through investigation, questions, testing, and play.

Funerals make space within the church, among God's people, for children to explore the strangeness of life's end. It is here that they see adults vulnerable to grief, that they sense the magnitude of what we face. Here children also learn that we carry this grief together. It is at funerals that we discover that, even in the end, there is nowhere we can go from God's love—because we see it in the people gathered around us.

This is why I am always concerned when a parishioner talks about wanting a memorial service, void of tears and wailing, a "celebration of life" that drives out any possibility of public grief. Getting the sadness out of the service may spare children our pain. But it doesn't protect them from death. Instead it changes grief from a communal act to something experienced alone, without others to bear it, without sharing in death's sorrow.

A funeral, on the other hand, offers a structure for the work of grief—the tools and words and actions that allow children to give shape to death's mystery. And it offers evidence that no matter how great the mystery, no matter how devastating the pain and sadness that follow, even when facing death we are never alone. The people of God who bear witness to the saints of God will one day hold us in their care.

At the graveside, I gathered Doreen's great-grandchildren around me. The little ones were toddlers; the oldest was 11. I bent down and told them that we were here to bury their granny, to say our final good-bye in this life. But in God's love, I said, we never have to say good-bye for good. One day we will have new bodies, and we will be together forever. In the meantime we may find that we get scared or sad when we think about death. Death is a bad thing. It's a sad thing. But we also believe that God is always with us. There's no place we can go to get away from God, not even when we die.

When it was time, we buried Doreen—ashes to ashes, dust to dust. Many of her family members took a shovel in hand and scooped dirt into the grave. The last to take up the shovel was Margaret, the little girl I'd talked with before the funeral. She joined the saints in the drama of worship, returning her beloved great-grandmother to the One who breathes life into our bodies of dust and who will love us into resurrected life in a communion of love.

Critical Thinking

1. How can you prepare children for a funeral experience?
2. Why are adults reluctant to help student grievers? How can we be trained to better equip children in supporting their grief?
3. What are some of the signs that a child griever may be in need of help? What can adults do to support children grievers?

Internet References

Counseling Adolescents Dealing with Grief and Loss
   http://c.ymcdn.com/sites/www.myprevention.org/resource/collection/246ADC1F-6ACD-403B-A496-9A0D7045E1C3/AdolescentsGriefAndLoss.pdf
Helping a Teenager Deal with Grief—What's your grief?
   www.whatsyourgrief.com/helping-a-teenager-deal-with-grief-2/
Teen Grief—Grief Speaks
   www.griefspeaks.com/id33.html

MELISSA FLORER-BIXLER is minister of nurture at Duke Memorial United Methodist Church in Durham, North Carolina.

Prepared by: George E. Dickinson, *College of Charleston*
Michael R. Leming, *St. Olaf College*

Article

Programs Help Chaplains Handle Their Grief

Adelle M. Banks

Learning Outcomes

After reading this article, you will be able to:

- Understand that chaplains also need to grieve after conducting so many funerals for the men and women they have served.

- Understand ways in which one can assist others who are experiencing trauma in grieving.

- Understand the many ways in which chaplains can promote self-care.

Seated at a table with other chaplains who have comforted grieving military families, retired army chaplain John Schumacher held the red rose in his hands before he passed it along, pausing to remember those who had died on the battlefield.

Schumacher then took the rose and added it to a memorial wreath. Two days later, he and another chaplain placed the wreath at the Tomb of the Unknowns in Arlington National Cemetery.

"I've been in combat. I've been with a lot of wounded men. I've been with dead men who were my friends," said Schumacher, a two-tour Vietnam veteran. "Chaplains give so much and carry all that pain with them for so long. It was such a tremendous honor to feel some of that pain kind of ooze out a little bit."

The memorial ceremony in January, organized for the first time by the National Association of Evangelicals Chaplains Commission, gave chaplains, who often help others grieve, a chance to grieve themselves.

This often unspoken need is now being addressed across the country with new training and a greater emphasis on mentoring. As these initiatives take hold, chaplains working in hospitals, hospice, and the military are finding ways to cope.

Valerie Storms, president of the Association of Professional Chaplains, said many chaplains' organizations, including Catholic and Jewish groups, tell chaplains to take care of themselves as well as others.

Self-care ranges from knowing a chaplain they can contact on the spur of the moment to developing hobbies—from running to making jewelry—to maintain their spiritual and emotional equilibrium.

Storms, who is affiliated with the Alliance of Baptists, tends her garden to help her through tough days as the manager of chaplaincy care at Moffitt Cancer Center in Tampa, Florida.

"I can go mow my lawn and edge my lawn and trim my bushes, and I see what's done," she said. "When you deal with people, you don't often see the results of your work."

Kristin Lindholm Gumminger, who teaches communication at Trinity International University in Illinois, said hospice chaplains "debrief" with similar personal rituals or by talking with a professional counselor. In her 2008 dissertation on hospice chaplains, one told her that personal grief was a "constant companion."

Gumminger is developing a workshop to help hospice chaplains. Others are working to help chaplains recognize and improve the ways they deal with grief.

Later this year, the U.S. Army Chaplain Center and School in South Carolina will introduce a new training session developed by the University of Georgia that includes secondary traumatic stress among chaplains and grief counselors.

The army's chief of chaplains has encouraged a "Care to Caregiver" initiative that matches retired chaplains to serve as mentors to younger chaplains.

Chaplain Milton Johnson, a soldier and family minister at Fort Sam Houston in San Antonio, said he relies on fellow chaplains, his wife, and pastors of his Seventh-day Adventist denomination to help him channel his grief—including when he lost his running buddy to suicide.

But he said the new initiatives put a sharper focus on the need for chaplains to get help as they suffer along with their comrades. Chaplains need to heed the lesson taught by flight attendants who warn airline passengers to put a flotation device on themselves before others, he said.

"With chaplains and other professionals, sometimes it's just the opposite; we have a tendency to put the float device on everybody else first and then put the float device on self and that's really not the most healthy way to take care of self," he said. "I think we are turning the corner on that. I think the paradigm is shifting."

Steven Spidell has measured some of the toll on chaplains. In a 2009 survey, he found that one-fifth of health-care chaplains reported "disenfranchised grief," or grief that was not supported in the workplace.

"Clergy are trained to be caregivers—that's what we're hired to do," said Spidell, a staff chaplain at Houston Methodist West Hospital in Texas. "That we would need care is a foreign concept, I think, to most faith groups."

Spidell said the hardest part of his job is when he cares for a family that has suddenly and unexpectedly lost a relative at the hospital—"their pain is so intense."

Such an episode leaves him "physically and emotionally exhausted," and sometimes it takes days for him to admit how tough it was. But he said he is grateful for the time he spends with a family, which moves on to the funeral without him. "I'm on to the next code blue," he said. "My job continues."

Critical Thinking

1. Why is it difficult for chaplains in caring for grievers?
2. What advice would you give chaplains who serve grievers?
3. Why might it be difficult for chaplains who serve grievers to see the results of their work? What difference does this make?

Internet References

Easy Living Inc. | Professional Caregiver Grief: The Hidden Loss for Senior Caregivers
> www.easylivingfl.com/professional-caregiver-grief-the-hidden-loss-for-s.

For Professionals—What's Your Grief?
> www.whatsyourgrief.com/for-professionals/

Grief and Loss Training for Healthcare Professionals | LifeNet Health
> https://www.lifenethealth.org/transplant-services-opo/healthcare-professionals/grief-and-loss-training-healthcare-professionals

Prepared by: George E. Dickinson, *College of Charleston*
Michael R. Leming, *St. Olaf College*

Article

Memorial Hashtags and Selfies at Funerals: How We Mourn in the Digital Age

Laurie Penny

Learning Outcomes

After reading this article, you will be able to:

- Appreciate that contemporary Internet opportunities can cut both ways in promoting grieving and adding to the pain carried by grievers.

- Understand how digital resources affect funeral planning and ways to support the bereaved.

- Begin to understand the pros and cons related to Internet grieving.

How do we deal with death in the digital age? In recent weeks and months, social media has been unremittingly macabre, reacting to the passing of public figures and political heroes. Lou Reed. Sue Townsend. Nelson Mandela. Philip Seymour Hoffman. Bob Crow. Tony Benn. Most recently, the 25-year-old Peaches Geldof was found dead in her home and after everyone from Boy George to Phillip Schofield tweeted their condolences, the commentariat queued up to ask: had the "frenzy" of digital mourning gone too far? Was the hand-wringing just unscrupulous new media "cashing in" on tragedy? Was it all—and what a peculiarly Anglo-American complaint this is—just a bit too emotional?

Memorial hashtags, selfies at funerals, maudlin Facebook memorial pages, orchestrated mobs of mourners for the latest celebrity to die young: the consensus among the self-designated guardians of cultural standards is that internet grief has become monstrously inappropriate, an insult to propriety. But what is monstrous is not the awkward intersection of modern media and public mourning. What is monstrous is that 25-year-olds die before their time. What is inappropriate is that brave activists and beloved writers continue to age, sicken and die when we need their wisdom and courage more than ever.

It is not social media that makes these deaths shocking. Death is shocking and remains so in every medium. As Judith Butler wrote in *Violence, Mourning, Politics:* "What grief displays is the thrall in which our relations with others holds us, in ways that we cannot always recount or explain . . . Let's face it. We're undone by each other. And if we're not, we're missing something."

There is nothing particularly new about "excessive public mourning." As the age of mass media dawned, melodramatic mourning for public figures, from Marilyn Monroe and John F. Kennedy to Elvis Presley, became a stock part of the sales plan. And if you think Twitter is macabre, consider that the obituaries for most old famous people have already been written. I was recently contacted by a television studio with a request to record a tribute to a member of the royal family who is still in good health.

One morning last September, I got the call that every child dreads: our dad had had a heart attack and was in a coma. On the way to the hospital, I tweeted that my father was seriously ill and I was rushing to see him. Several internet denizens replied that I should be ashamed of "capitalising" on what had happened. Rage ran through me like a knife. What gave these people the right to tell me how to express grief and shock? What gave anyone that right? I was so caught up that I neglected to change out of the T-shirt I was wearing, which happened to have a giant grinning skull on it—which actually was inappropriate attire for an intensive care unit.

When Dad's life support was withdrawn several days later, my sisters and I sat down to decide what to say on social media, eventually settling on a short, sad message that all of us could use. It was one of the most difficult parts of the most difficult week of our lives. For everything else, there was a set way of doing things: relatives to call, forms to fill in, decisions to be made to a schedule. But with this, we were on our own.

There are no rules for what to do online when someone dies and we had to come to the best compromise we could. A few weeks later, the singer Lou Reed passed away. Amid the tidal wave of popular sentiment, the Twitter storms and tributes, I found myself irrationally cross that the internet was not mourning my lovely but objectively unfamous father with the same zeal.

Grief is an ersatz maze of emotions in the digital age. The dead, however, are beyond caring whether somebody makes a gaffe on Twitter. Public mourning is for those left behind. When it comes to the rightness and fitness of the rituals, there is only one question that matters and it is this—is enough being done to support the family and friends of the person who has died? If the answer is yes, you are probably OK. What was disgraceful in the days after Peaches Geldof's death was not the hundreds of thousands of strangers who had never met the young journalist and socialite tweeting what some called "shallow grief" but the snooty comment pieces opining that she really wasn't worth all the fuss.

Brendan O'Neill, the *Spiked* editor and professional heartless contrarian, asked his readers, "Just what were the achievements of this young woman everyone was suddenly weeping for? She wore clothes, that's one thing." O'Neill deemed this a "pressing question." It was not a pressing question. It was a cruel and degrading question, next to which the reported 370,000 tweets about Geldof in the hours after her death was announced seem positively respectful.

We live in interesting times—times of weird technology and easy outrage—but death is still the weirdest and most outrageous thing of all. There is nothing we can do to make normal or "appropriate" the death of a dear friend, or a beloved public figure, or a young person who should have had years of fun and growing up still to live.

Death itself is deeply inappropriate. It is crass and comes too soon. When it does, leaving the rest of us at our most awkwardly, awfully human, all we can do is be as kind to each other as possible.

Critical Thinking

1. How does the Internet make grieving more problematic?
2. How are Internet postings relating to death similar to old forms of public grieving?
3. Explain the following quotation by the author of this article: "We live in interesting times—times of weird technology and easy outrage—but death is still the weirdest and most outrageous thing of all. There is nothing we can do to make normal or "appropriate" the death of a dear friend, or a beloved public figure, or a young person who should have had years of fun and growing up still to live."

Internet References

A New Mourning: Grief in the Digital Age—The Irish Times
http://www.irishtimes.com/life-and-style/people/a-new-mourning-grief-in -the-digital-age-1.1941728

Grieving in the Digital Age: A Short Film Explores How We Live on Through Facebook
http://www.huffingtonpost.com/2015/04/02/grieve-digital-age_n_6991698 .html

How the Digital Age has Changed Our Approach to Death and Grief
http://theconversation.com/how-the-digital-age-has-changed-our-approach -to-death-and-grief-38207

LAURIE PENNY is the contributing editor of the *New Statesman*

Prepared by: George E. Dickinson, *College of Charleston*
Michael R. Leming, *St. Olaf College*

Article

Parting Is Such Tweet Sorrow

SABRINA BACHAI AND ELIJAH WOLFSON

Learning Outcomes

After reading this article, you will be able to:

- Understand how digital resources affect funeral planning and ways to support the bereaved.

- Come to appreciate the possibility of the opportunity of grievers to have an active role at funerals leading to better mourning.

- Come to understand that most people grieving through social media are using it to reach out more than they are to withdraw. Whether it is sharing in someone's joy or sadness, feeling connected is a part of the human experience, technology is making that easier.

For years, Lisa Bonchek Adams has been documenting her experience living with incurable, stage 4 breast cancer. She shared very publicly, first on Facebook, then on her personal blog, and ultimately, on Twitter, always receiving wholehearted support, until recently, when editorials appeared in both *The Guardian* and *The New York Times* criticizing Adams for her use of social media as a "kind of self-medication." What followed was a full-throttled media frenzy, with every publication rushing to take sides.

The hysteria is indicative of how social media has begun to make visible many of those troubling things long kept hidden: Cancer, terminal illness, and death itself are being reframed by the new modes of communication.

Nowhere is this more obvious than in the mourning process, which has, for many, moved out of the quiet shadows of the bedroom and hushed congregation of nearest and dearest, to the explosively large world of social media. Twitter streams are the new eulogy; Facebook profiles are the memorial sites. When Nora Ephron passed away in 2012, her Facebook page became a meeting place for people she had touched with her work

and life. It's still active to this day: Fans post quotes on Ephron's wall, and messages are sent out by "Ephron" (her publisher).

It's a weird new world, where an afterlife is eternal and in the present. But since everything else happens on Facebook, why *wouldn't* it be the place where people go to mourn?

Almost everyone is familiar with the five-step grieving process described by Elisabeth Kübler-Ross in her 1969 book, On Death and Dying: denial and isolation, anger, bargaining, depression and, finally, acceptance. The first four steps, quite clearly, are not much fun—they are the things you have to go through in order to reach a point where you can live with your loss. And in the old days, it was easy to become mired in step one; it required your initiative to reach out to others. But now, with Twitter, Facebook, and Tumblr always at hand, it's nearly impossible to isolate yourself.

Maybe that's a good thing. When the "Selfies at Funerals" Tumblr, with its images of apparently self-absorbed teens preening for their iPhones while at memorial services, went viral this past year it seemed to validate the claims made by University of Michigan study that our inability to tear ourselves away from social media reflects and amplifies the growing narcissistic quality of contemporary culture. But maybe that criticism reflects more a generational divide than a character flaw. Adults who have experienced loss may see teens taking photos of themselves on their way to a funeral and tagging them #sadday and think, Disrespectful twits! But what teen knows how to deal with death? It's not such a stretch to imagine that this was the best way they knew to reach out and share with their friends. (Although it might be a little harder to cut President Barack Obama the same slack.)

"People want to feel like they are part of something," Tamara McClintock Greenberg, a professor of psychiatry at the University of California, San Francisco, told *Newsweek*. "Facebook allows people to find their network of people who are going to be really supportive."

Ben Nunnery, a 34-year-old Kentucky native whose wife Ali passed away in 2011 from lung cancer, learned that oversharing can sometimes lead to healing. Before Ali died, the couple took pictures together in their first house; after she passed, Ben re-created the photographs with his 3-year-old daughter, Olivia, standing in for Ali. He shared the images online for his entire social network, and got back an avalanche of support. Nunnery never expected the photos to make such an impact, but he is grateful.

"I think that [social media] allows people to connect easier and . . . that it not only gives us a platform to share our grief, which I think helps other people, but . . . it helps other people support the grief," Nunnery told *Newsweek.*

There are some things to consider though, before you mourn on SnapChat. While it may feel like you're getting tons of support by exposing yourself on social media, you may face criticism from strangers and, worse, rejection from friends and family. The public display of grief and emotion comes with risks.

"People you might really want to hear from might get anxious and not contact you; maybe the distance [with your friends] in social media will make it harder to cope," said McClintock Greenberg. "It's complicated." Of course, that's not necessarily different from any other part of life, where some step up and provide excellent support in times of need, while others run from any mention of death and grieving. The world of social media just amplifies both: more support, but more disappointment, too."

There's also the danger that new technologies might foster denial and make it harder to let go. In 2009, after users complained of seeing "suggested friends" from people who had passed away, Facebook began memorializing users who had died, deactivating their profiles and creating "memorials" at the request of loved ones. Memorialized profiles don't go away—they live in perpetuity (or at least as long as Facebook lasts) and give friends and family members the opportunity to look back on old posts, Facebook messages and pictures.

That's the kind of thing that can facilitate healing, but it, too, can go too far. An app launched last year called LivesOn, for example, offers the promise that "when your heart stops beating, you'll keep tweeting." Here's how it works: You give it full access to read through everything you've ever said online, and it creates a "virtual continuation" of your personality after you die, mimicking you.

It's a weird thing, the Internet, both transient and permanent. It's a place where 140 characters (#RIP) can count for meaningful sentiment and where funeral selfies are posted by 14-year-olds who can't conceive of a year past 2015, but it's also a place where memorial services take on a tone of indefiniteness and death can extend both forward and backward. Ultimately, just like IRL, grieving online is often complicated, contradictory and very personal—but most people grieving through social media are using it to reach out more than they are to withdraw. Whether it is sharing in someone's joy or sadness, feeling connected is a part of the human experience. Technology is making that easier.

Critical Thinking

1. How can Facebook and Twitter facilitate grieving and bereavement?
2. What are some of the limitations and obstacles to adjustment of the death of a loved one caused by Internet strategies?
3. What precautions might one take as one depends on the Internet in the grieving process?

Internet References

Grieving in the Digital Age
   https://krex.k-state.edu/dspace/handle/2097/15668

Grieving My Mother in the Digital Age—Femsplain
   https://femsplain.com/grieving-my-mother-in-the-digital-age-1090924e228e#.5gm8vs91w

Redefining The Grieving Process in the Digital Age | NPR
   http://www.npr.org/2012/02/08/146585372/redefining-the-grieving-process-in-the-digital-age